The Press and the
Bush Presidency

Recent Titles in the Praeger Series in Presidential Studies
Robert E. Denton, Jr., *General Editor*

Leadership and the Bush Presidency: Prudence or Drift in an Era of Change?
Edited by Ryan J. Barilleaux

The Presidency and the Persian Gulf War
Edited by Marcia Lynn Whicker, James P. Pfiffner, and Raymond A. Moore

THE PRESS AND THE
BUSH PRESIDENCY

Mark J. Rozell

Praeger Series in Presidential Studies

Westport, Connecticut
London

Library of Congress Cataloging-in-Publication Data

Rozell, Mark J.
    The press and the Bush presidency / Mark J. Rozell.
       p.   cm. — (Praeger series in presidential studies, ISSN
1062–0931)
    Includes bibliographical references and index.
    ISBN 0–275–95653–9 (alk. paper)
    1. United States—Politics and government—1989–1993. 2. Bush,
George, 1924– —Relations with journalists. 3. Press and
politics—United States—History—20th century. I. Title.
II. Series.
E881.R69 1996
973.928'092—dc20   96–10429

British Library Cataloguing in Publication Data is available.

Library of Congress Catalog Card Number: 96–10429
ISBN: 0–275–95653–9
ISSN: 1062–0931

First published in 1996

Praeger Publishers, 88 Post Road West, Westport, CT 06881
An imprint of Greenwood Publishing Group, Inc.

Printed in the United States of America

The paper used in this book complies with the
Permanent Paper Standard issued by the National
Information Standards Organization (Z39.48–1984).

10 9 8 7 6 5 4 3 2 1

Contents

Preface

This book is the third that I have written on the elite press coverage of modern presidents. As with the earlier studies on the Ford and Carter years, this one examines the nature of the coverage of one presidency in comprehensive fashion. With the benefit of those earlier studies, this one offers a comparative analysis of the press coverage of modern presidents.

The study of George Bush's coverage is noteworthy because the president appeared to thoroughly reject the lessons of the Reagan years when most analysts had expected greater continuity in presentational style and press relations. Bush had the unenviable task of following the "Great Communicator" and journalists—who tend to take a short-term historical view of the presidency—evaluated his performance against the backdrop of the Reagan years. For example, when Bush adopted a relatively open, informal relationship with reporters—many of whom had earlier complained of Reagan's media manipulation—they were more likely to criticize him for not knowing how to control the message than to praise his departure from the use of mostly controlled public relations events.

In their reporting and commentary, those who covered Bush exhibited a strong preference for an activist, progressive-oriented presidency. Bush liked to say that he had difficulty with "the vision thing." That was a candid acknowledgment that, when planning an agenda, he did not operate with a grand, large-scale plan for the future. Bush was an incrementalist in domestic affairs, and consequently his coverage suffered at the hands of those who demanded visionary leadership.

This book shows that not only did the leading reporters who covered Bush subscribe to a different view of successful leadership, but that the elite press sources continued to be the trend setters in the media. Much has been written lately about the enormous transitions taking place in the media and the impact on the elite press. Yet it is undoubtedly clear that the leading press, despite predictions of its decline, has proven resilient. Not only are the Bush years testimony to that fact, but so too are the Clinton years. President Bill Clinton learned the hard way that trying to override the traditional White House press corps is both futile and destructive.

I am grateful to a number of individuals who helped to guide me through this project. My colleagues James Pfiffner (George Mason University) and Robert Denton (Virginia Polytechnical Institute) read early drafts of the manuscript and offered helpful comments. Karen Duffy and Jack Bales assisted with the searches for press commentary on the Bush presidency. Dora Minor and Victoria Meador assisted with the typing of the manuscript. I benefited from the opportunity to interview a number of Bush White House staffers whose observations provided the foundation for chapter 7.

1

Introduction

When George Bush assumed the presidency on January 20, 1989, he faced the unenviable task of following a man who had left office enormously popular and had succeeded at fully exploiting the public relations powers of the office. Ronald Reagan had conducted perhaps the most public relations–conscious presidency in U.S. history. Reagan's critics may have complained about his administration's P.R. gimmickry and media manipulation, but few doubted his success at using the public presidency to promote his policies.

For eight years Bush had toiled as Reagan's loyal vice president. During those years critics charged that he was too loyal to the president, had failed to establish an independent identity, and had made many compromises with his own generally moderate principles to appease conservative Reaganites. Some critics labeled Bush a "wimp"—a moniker that caught on with the press and hounded the vice president's image. In a widely repeated term, influential columnist George F. Will called Bush a "lapdog" for President Reagan.

Vice presidents are easy targets for both partisan and press criticism. On the one hand, the vice president has a responsibility to be loyal to the chief executive; on the other, political observers demand that the vice president establish a separate identity.

In an interview for this book, Bush press secretary Marlin Fitzwater said that he helped set up a number of one-on-one media interviews with the vice president in 1985 and 1986. Fitzwater saw the interviews as a good opportunity for Bush to get to know the reporters who might later cover a

Bush presidency. The reporters nonetheless came to the interviews "to see if they could get the vice president to have an opinion different from the president. . . . The result was that the interviewers were always disappointed when they left." Bush presented the president's views when asked about issues and the administration's actions.

Bush's best opportunity to establish an independent identity was the 1988 presidential campaign. Without a doubt, he lost that opportunity by running a low-road campaign that perhaps refuted the charge that he was a wimp but helped to create the image of a politician who offered no positive program and would say or do almost anything to get elected.

From the standpoint of press relations, Bush consequently entered the presidency with a number of disadvantages. He lacked Reagan's gift of eloquence and suffered from the comparisons to his predecessor. Bush had to establish his own identity after eight years as vice president and a presidential campaign that failed to adequately communicate his positive qualities and policy objectives.

Bush nonetheless had available to him the knowledge of what his predecessor had done well and the opportunity to draw on the experiences of those who had worked in the Reagan White House. Despite all of the concern about the cynical age in which we live and the role of the media in fueling public anger toward the government, the Reagan years demonstrated that presidents need not be mere helpless victims of a critical media onslaught. Presidents have means of somewhat blunting outside criticism and getting their messages out to the public. It is up to the chief executive and his advisers to use the powers of the public relations presidency. The Reagan White House did so more effectively than any modern administration.

Bush did not employ the public and press relations strategies of his predecessor—to the surprise of many. Bush rejected the advice of some in the White House to run a more stage-managed presidency and to place greater emphasis than he did on focusing his message by making thematic addresses and creating a "line of the day" for each daily news cycle.

For nearly three years, with relatively high public approval and seeming political invincibility, Bush's approach appeared vindicated. But when Bush's fortunes began to change in late 1991, his failure to have cultivated a positive image of his own impressive background and accomplishments—and to have developed a coherent message of what his administration stood for—doomed his presidency when the public begged for a sense of direction to lead the country out of its problems. Lacking a coherent message, Bush was popular during good times, and then people blamed him for the perceived bad times. The public did not see any sense of direction from the White House and consequently blamed the president for what many perceived as an ailing economy.

In 1992, in a desperate last-ditch effort to save Bush's presidency, the White House and the reelection campaign floated a sequence of unconnected themes to try to undo the earlier lack of a message. In perhaps the least credible tack, the man who had run for president in 1988 as the candidate of continuity tried to present himself in 1992 as the candidate of change. The attempts fell flat and voters rejected a second Bush term, despite a clear lack of enthusiasm for the alternatives.

Bush's own press relations strategy was to differentiate his approach from Reagan's as much as possible. Bush made far more public speeches than Reagan, gave many more press conferences and fewer prime-time addresses. His press conferences usually were informal and relaxed. He generally avoided the more theatrical prime-time press conferences and national addresses. Bush was more open to reporters' questions than his predecessor and was informal and friendly in his dealings with the press. His rhetoric promising a "kinder, gentler" conservatism appeared to be a rebuke of Reagan-era policies.

Bush's openness toward the press did little to improve the nature of his coverage. Journalists still characterized the Bush presidency as lacking an agenda and the president himself as lacking a "vision" for the nation's future. Bush's inability to effectively use the "bully pulpit" contributed significantly to this problem. As presidential scholar James Pfiffner points out, in an era of fragmented political power, presidents who want to have a substantial influence on the policy process, to lead Congress, must use the bully pulpit effectively.[1]

White House staff interviewed for this book confirmed that Bush was acutely aware that he lacked Reagan's skills and that he refused advice to be more dramatic—more "Reaganesque"—in his presentations. According to several Bush speechwriters, the president would even delete rhetorical flourishes from speech drafts and explain that he did not want to sound too much like Reagan.

Bush speechwriter Tony Snow pointed out that the president paid attention to the basic needs of the press: making sure that announcements were made on time, answering media inquiries in a timely fashion, being open with reporters and meeting with them frequently. Bush delegated a great deal of responsibility to the respected press secretary Marlin Fitzwater to "tend to the caring and feeding of the White House press corps." Yet Snow observed that these details, although necessary to keep reporters contented, could not overcome the problems caused by presidential inattention to broader media strategy: establishing themes to match policy goals, using the bully pulpit to lead the national debate on issues.

Part of Bush's difficulties with press coverage came from the criteria that leading journalists employ when they analyze the president's leadership. Modern journalists are much more like public teachers, and much less like stenographers, than they used to be. They do not merely report the president's activities. They also evaluate his actions and even speculate about possible underlying motivations.

Political journalists employ two different categories of evaluation when assessing the president's actions: first, there are *general expectations of presidential leadership* that they apply to all modern presidents. In brief, the president must project the proper "aura" of strong leadership, define a vision for the nation's future, and articulate a broad-ranging policy agenda. These expectations do not suit very favorably a president who is cautious and believes, like Bush, that a good president is a strong steward abroad who does no harm at home. But as Charles O. Jones pointed out, such expectations persist nonetheless. After the Persian Gulf War, for example, journalists called on the president to exploit his personal popularity and potential new clout on Capitol Hill with an activist domestic agenda. Yet it remained unclear whether Bush could turn personal popularity into domestic policy clout—even if he were so inclined—in a Democrat-controlled legislature.[2]

Second, there are *specific expectations of the president*. That is, based on their knowledge of George Bush, journalists harbored certain beliefs about how he was likely to conduct his presidency. For example, although Bush had campaigned in 1988 as the candidate of continuity, journalists nonetheless expected him to chart his own policy direction. Bush ultimately disappointed these expectations. *New York Times* columnist James Reston had seen in Bush the potential for a highly qualified "gentleman president" capable of "calm thinking and honest talking." Reston concluded that his expectations of the president had been illusory.[3]

The overriding purpose of this book is to identify and assess the press perceptions of the Bush presidency. These perceptions illuminate journalists' evaluative criteria for the modern presidency. Although journalists work with short deadlines and information constraints and are generally atheoretical, they have implicit values about presidential leadership. Identifying these values can help us to understand the judgments that journalists make about our presidents. Whereas some critics of the media suggest that reporters are merely cynical or hypercritical of all public officials, some leaders undoubtedly fare much better than others in press coverage. What are the underlying values that lead journalists to define some leaders as successful and others as failures—when success and failure are not always self-evident?

PRESIDENTIAL–PRESS RELATIONS

The constitutional framers did not expect, nor did they want, the president to engage in direct popular leadership. They feared the consequences of a demagogic leader who enhanced his powers by flattering and ultimately misleading the public. Throughout the nation's first century, presidents generally did not lead in the modern sense of appealing to the people to pressure Congress to support an administration program.

In the twentieth century, a different view of presidential leadership emerged. The newer outlook ultimately embraced the concept of the president advancing his agenda through direct popular leadership. Theodore Roosevelt maintained that the president must be a "steward" of the people. That is, he must define for the public the national interest and advance programs to achieve that end. T.R. envisioned the presidency as a bully pulpit from which the chief executive leads the people.

Franklin D. Roosevelt's actions most influenced the development of the newer conception of presidential leadership. Perhaps no president has ever been—or ever will be—as adept at news management and direct popular leadership as FDR. In part, the willingness of reporters to slant coverage in favor of the administration reflected the nature of the times—economic calamity at home and then foreign aggression.

But FDR also captivated reporters and used them with great effect to promote the White House slant on events. For press conferences, he established firm rules regarding what information could be put on the record. Newspapers strictly abided by the rule that FDR not be photographed in a wheelchair. The administration established a government bureau to promote the White House slant. When FDR met resistance to his policies from conservative editorial writers, he promoted his agenda through friendly and more liberal-leaning reporters.

That reporters admired FDR and the people supported him redounded to the benefit of his programs. No chief executive since has so succeeded at turning the working press into virtual presidential sycophants. And none—with the possible exception of Ronald Reagan—has had FDR's gift of eloquence and ability to lead the people.

Perhaps the only president nearly as adored by the press as FDR was John F. Kennedy. In part because of that popularity, and in part because of the nature of the times, journalists did not report information about JFK that would have destroyed his finely honed image as a vigorous athlete and good family man. They were well aware of his poor health—his chronic bad back and adrenal insufficiency—as well as his many marital infidelities, yet they did not consider such matters of import to the public.

Many refer to JFK as the nation's first "television president." Indeed, the visually appealing, charismatic president and television were a perfect match. With the growing influence of television as a news medium, some speculated that the traditional print media would decline in importance to setting coverage patterns and establishing a presidential image.

To be sure, newspapers and magazines could not match the immediacy of television reporting, just as they could not compete with the immediacy of radio. Bernard Roscho shows that print journalism in the 1960s began to distinguish itself from television by offering more in-depth news analysis articles by political reporters. As the ethic of objective reporting changed, political interpretation expanded beyond the realms of editorial writers and opinion columnists to include political reporters who covered events.[4] Interpretive reporting consequently had a profound impact on establishing the general tone of the news media.

Yet interpretive reporting fell into the same trap as objective coverage. During the FDR era, print journalists reported the news with a presidential slant. During JFK's short tenure in office, news reporting and interpretation lacked a critical edge, as many reporters—most conspicuously Ben Bradlee—even became a part of the president's close circle of "friends."

Journalists who had allowed themselves to get close to FDR or JFK undoubtedly believed that such access was good for their careers. Yet in so doing, many reporters had become conduits for presenting the presidential slant on events. Any reporter today who allowed himself to so lose his professional objectivity would rightfully be derided by his colleagues. In the 1960s and 1970s, journalists had learned the hard way the downside of being so easily seduced by their political leaders: sometimes those leaders concealed information and lied. And nothing so angered the reporters as being turned into unwitting agents of official deception.

The events of the Vietnam War and Watergate resulted in a measure of media cynicism toward official Washington that is still being felt today. Much of that cynicism has focused on the presidency and the occupants of that office, as reporters, who had for a long time trusted official White House sources, discovered that they had been lied to and deceived. Relations between reporters and the White House broke down during the Lyndon B. Johnson and, especially, Richard M. Nixon administrations.

The White House press corps responded by treating Nixon's immediate successors, Gerald R. Ford and Jimmy Carter, with the skepticism that the reporters wished that they had exhibited toward Nixon. The press coverage of Presidents Ford and Carter was debilitating to their administrations. By the end of Carter's term, many began to wonder whether comity ever would be restored to presidential press relations.

Ronald Reagan proved that it is still possible for the modern president to win the battle of imagery with the media. The former movie actor had a unique set of skills conducive to image crafting, and his administration placed a high priority on the public presidency. The Reagan White House more importantly linked imagery with policy substance in a strategic way. The White House worked hard to stay "on message" by generating a "line of the day" and "theme of the week" and by ensuring that administration officials reinforced one another in their public pronouncements. The Reagan White House understood well the relationship between positive coverage and moving forward a policy agenda.

President Bush did not follow in these footsteps. Bush failed to strategically link a press relations plan with a policy agenda. Consequently, the image of his White House was one of inertia. By the end of his term, voters had no reason to return Bush to the White House other than their fear of the alternatives. That fear did not override the public judgment that the president had lost touch with his people and had no plan to deal with the domestic economy.

Bush had also failed to live up to the very stable and consistent journalistic measures of presidential success defined in this study. Bert Rockman has aptly described Bush as an "old-fashioned Tory" with a preference for incremental rather than bold action.[5] As the following makes clear, presidential journalists show a strong preference for "visionary" leaders with bold policy agendas. Bush's leadership approach may have suited his own personality and policy goals, but not the expectations of journalists whose evaluations help to frame a presidential image.

METHOD OF ANALYSIS

The following five chapters provide a comprehensive review of the press assessments of the Bush presidency. Chapter 7 examines the perspectives of White House communications advisers on Bush's press relations and strategies. The concluding chapter analyzes press evaluations of the modern presidency, drawing on the findings of this study and my two earlier books on the press–presidency relationship.

The review of press assessments is based on the judgmental commentary about the Bush presidency from three leading news dailies (*New York Times, Washington Post, Wall Street Journal*) and three leading news weeklies (*U.S. News and World Report, Time, Newsweek*). I selected these sources from Stephen Hess's description of the news media hierarchy in *The Washington Reporters*.[6] Hess argues correctly that the major news dailies establish a rhythm for news that comes out of Washington, D.C. This news "travels a circuitous route back into the political government and out again to the rest of the country via the electronic media."[7] Print journalism is thus the focal point of national opinion development, and journalists are the molders of public perceptions of presidential leadership and performance. Television has a "secondary impact" on the political government.

In collecting data I read every news article, news analysis, editorial, and opposite-editorial page column (by the regularly featured syndicated columnists) from the six sources during the Bush years. I transcribed all of the judgmental commentary about Bush's leadership and the performance of his administration. I then organized these commentaries both chronologically and thematically—chronologically to give insight into the development of press perceptions of the president over time and thematically to provide an understanding of the leading portrayals of the president and the underlying values of presidential leadership among prominent journalists.

The chronological narrative of Bush's coverage conveys how certain journalistic assessments developed and became reinforced, molding Bush's press image. The Bush image as an overly cautious leader who lacked leadership vision and resisted change was difficult to change once firmly established in press evaluations of his actions. The early image of Bush endured in part because journalists "frame the news in themes" as a way to simplify complex events and then reinforce these themes through constant repetition. Thus, journalists create images or stereotypes that others perceive as "reality."[8] Indeed, numerous studies confirm the crucial role that the media play in establishing what Richard Neustadt calls "a dominant tone, a central tendency, in Washington appraisals of a president."[9] Samuel Kernell writes that "prominent journalists serve as important opinion leaders in establishing a president's reputation."[10] William L. Rivers reports that Washington's leading journalists have been elevated "to a kind of academy of national sages and prognosticators."[11] Leading studies establish the link between journalistic opinion and public perceptions of political leaders and institutions.[12] As George C. Edwards writes,

It is the press that provides citizens with most of what they know about the chief executive, his policies, and their consequences. . . . The press is thus the principal intermediary between the president and the public, and relations with the press are an important aspect of the president's efforts to lead public opinion. If the press portrays the president in a favorable light, he will have fewer obstacles in obtaining public support. If, on the other hand, the press is hostile toward his administration, the president's task will be more difficult.[13]

This study employs a qualitative content analysis approach to develop an understanding of the context of press evaluations. The purpose is to identify the major themes in press assessments of the president in order to understand journalists' underlying leadership values. My purpose, therefore, is quite different from those of leading quantitative studies of press coverage of presidents. I want to identify and assess the broadly thematic and judgmental press commentary on the presidency to develop a theoretical understanding of journalistic values about presidential leadership.

In constructing the chronological narrative of the press coverage of the Bush presidency, I organize the data into five different categories of analysis:

Timing. This category has two facets: the period of time in which Bush served (the leadership context) and the different stages of his term in office. For the former, Bush came to the presidency after the Reagan era and during a period of time in which dramatic changes in the world often dictated his presidential priorities. For the latter, journalists base many of their expectations of how the president should behave on the stages of the four-year term. For example, press assessments during the so-called honeymoon period evidence a strong bias in favor of early presidential activism and bold leadership. Press assessments during a reelection campaign tend to place presidential actions in the context of their political ramifications.

Symbolism/Rhetoric. These evaluations concern the president's role as a public leader. Journalists place a heavy emphasis on the symbolic and rhetorical aspects of the modern presidency. It is through symbolic gestures and public speaking that presidents try to lead public opinion and create the conditions for the favorable enactment of administration programs. Although constitutionally there is no expectation that the president play such a leadership role—and indeed the constitutional framers feared the consequences of presidents so doing—modern political observers demand that all presidents spend much of their time on the public presidency.

Agenda. Journalists evaluate the quality of a president's programs. Their evaluations evidence a strong preference for an activist agenda, and journalists seem to have little regard for a cautious, status-quo program, especially in the domestic realm.

Policy Development. Journalists' preference for activism entails the expectation that the president will set the national agenda, build public support for it, and get the Congress to act according to his priorities. The press consequently assesses the president's strategies and tactics to move forward the administration's programs.

Staff. Journalists' perceptions of the people surrounding the president have an impact on how they view his leadership. In addition to press assessments of the quality of the White House staff, for this study I also include the coverage of Bush's vice presidential selection and discuss how that decision influenced journalists' views of the president's leadership.[14]

Following the narrative of press evaluations of the Bush presidency, I turn in chapter 7 to the perceptions of the president's communications advisers on the administration's press strategies and the nature of its press coverage. For that chapter I interviewed the following persons: Marlin Fitzwater (press secretary); David Demarest (communications director); Dan McGroarty (deputy director of speechwriting); Andrew Furgeson (speechwriter); Curt Smith (speechwriter); Mary Kate Cary (speechwriter); Tony Snow (director of speechwriting).

The concluding chapter reviews the major findings of this study. It summarizes the major themes in the press coverage of the Bush presidency and identifies the elements of the press's implicit theories of presidential leadership. Drawing on the findings of my three books on the press coverage of individual presidencies, I conclude with a comparative analysis of the nature of modern presidential journalism and a critique.

The comparative analysis makes it clear that although there have been substantial changes in the media in the past two decades—led most recently by the rise of talk radio and legitimization of tabloid coverage—the underlying values that drive presidential interpretation have remained consistent. The reigning journalistic paradigm is little changed during the post-Watergate era. And despite the rise of alternative news media, the inner-circle sources identified by Hess in the 1980s remain the leaders in establishing coverage patterns and a presidential image.

NOTES

1. James Pfiffner, *The Modern Presidency* (New York: St. Martin's Press, 1994), p. 14.
2. Charles O. Jones, *The Presidency in a Separated System* (Washington, D.C.: Brookings Institution, 1994), pp. 113–114, 143–145.
3. James Reston, *Deadline: A Memoir* (New York: Random House, 1991), p. 447.
4. Bernard Roscho, "The Evolution of News Content in the American Press," in Doris Graber, ed., *Media Power in Politics* (Washington, D.C.: Congressional Quarterly Press, 1984), pp. 7–22.
5. Bert Rockman, "The Leadership Style of George Bush," in Colin Campbell, S. J., and Bert Rockman, eds., *The Bush Presidency: First Appraisals* (Chatham, N.J.: Chatham House, 1991), p. 15.
6. Stephen Hess, *The Washington Reporters* (Washington, D.C.: Brookings Institution, 1981).
7. Ibid., p. 96.
8. George C. Edwards, *The Public Presidency: The Pursuit of Popular Support* (New York: St. Martin's Press, 1983), pp. 159, 166.
9. Richard Neustadt, *Presidential Power and the Modern Presidents: The Politics of Leadership from Roosevelt to Reagan* (New York: Free Press, 1990), p. 53.
10. Samuel Kernell, *Going Public: New Strategies of Presidential Leadership*, 2d ed. (Washington, D.C.: Congressional Quarterly Press, 1993), p. 55.
11. William L. Rivers, *The Other Government: Power and the Washington Media* (New York: Universe Books, 1982), p. 9.
12. See Paul Brace and Barbara Hinckley, *Follow the Leader: Opinion Polls and the Modern Presidents* (New York: Basic Books, 1992); Douglass Cater, *The Fourth Branch of Government* (Boston: Houghton Mifflin, 1959); Bernard C. Cohen, *The Press and Foreign Policy* (Princeton, N.J.: Princeton University Press, 1963); Robert E. Denton, Jr., and Gary C. Woodward, *Political Communication in America*, 2d ed. (New York: Praeger, 1990); Doris A. Graber, *Mass Media and American Politics*, 4th ed. (Washington, D.C.: Congressional Quarterly Press, 1993); Thomas Mann and Norman Ornstein, eds., *Congress, the Press and the Public* (Washington, D.C.: American Enterprise Institute/Brookings Institution, 1994).
13. Edwards, *Public Presidency*, p. 104.
14. My earlier studies of the press coverage of the Ford and Carter presidencies did not merit any special attention to the role of the vice president in influencing a presidential press image.

2

The 1988 Presidential Election and the Reagan–Bush Transition

George Bush entered the 1988 campaign an enigma to much of the press. Despite a record of public service spanning more than two decades, journalists lacked a clear definition of the man and his beliefs. One reason for such confusion was Bush's apparent transformation from the moderately conservative presidential candidate of 1980 to the staunch conservative vice president in Ronald Reagan's administration. Many observers wondered whether the "real George Bush" would emerge in the 1988 campaign once nominated for president by the Republican Party. An examination of press coverage and analysis of the final week of the 1988 campaign, the election results, and the presidential transition provides telling evidence of the development of Bush's presidential press image.

   Timing. This nearly three-month period—November 1, 1988, to January 20, 1989—constitutes the initial stage in the development of Bush's presidential press image. Journalists perceived this period as the first real opportunity for Bush to define himself to the American people independent of Ronald Reagan. According to the journalists, during the presidential campaign Bush had failed to define either himself or his philosophy of governance. He merely ran a negative campaign and did not focus on the issues of import to the country. Journalists nonetheless praised Bush's transition as smoothly run and properly calculated to distance himself from his predecessor. Consequently, he had failed to use the campaign period to establish an agenda and a leadership mandate, but he used the transition period to somewhat recover from that failing.

Rhetoric/Symbolism. During the 1988 campaign journalists characterized Bush's political rhetoric as "mean spirited," "demagogic," "divisive," "distorted," "dishonest," and so forth. They lampooned his legendary muddled syntax and highlighted the unflattering contrasts between Bush's and Reagan's communications abilities. Although this perception of Bush as a poor communicator and an attack-oriented politician did not change, during the transition period journalists applauded the president-elect's symbolic gestures and efforts to present himself as a conciliatory leader of moderate views and temperament.

Agenda. Throughout this three-month period, journalists described Bush as a man with no agenda, no "vision" for the nation's future. According to this view, Bush merely wanted to be president, but he had no idea what he wanted to do with the office, how he wanted to lead. This perception of the man as lacking a leadership vision became a constant theme in the press coverage of the Bush presidency.

Policy Development. Many press commentaries predicted that Bush would experience great difficulty moving his policies through Congress. Journalists attributed this prediction to several factors: Bush ran a divisive, mean-spirited campaign, leaving many Democrats eager to embarrass him; Bush lacked Reagan's ability to persuade and cajole; Bush lacked a governing mandate because he had conducted a content-free campaign. Nonetheless, during the transition period, press commentaries noted that Bush's efforts to heal the scars of the 1988 campaign, as well as his selection of many highly professional staffers, had created the hope that the president-elect would be positioned to enact some far-reaching domestic and foreign policies.

Staff. Bush received almost uniformly positive reviews in the press for his selection of a White House political staff and cabinet. According to the journalists, Bush distinguished himself by appointing highly experienced, professional people to key White House and cabinet posts. Nonetheless, early critical reports of Bush's choices for chief of staff (John Sununu) and secretary of defense (John Tower) portended bad news for the Bush presidency.

No analysis of Bush's press image is complete without some consideration of his curious vice presidential selection of Indiana Senator J. Danforth (Dan) Quayle. The issue of the wisdom of that selection cannot adequately be assessed here. What is unarguable is the severity of the negative press response to that selection and the widespread belief that such a selection reflected poorly on Bush.

During the 1988 campaign press reports and commentaries savaged Quayle as a vacuous-minded, lightweight legislator of no stature who had no business being in national politics. Journalists wondered whether Bush had demonstrated a serious flaw in judgment by choosing for vice president a man who seemed so poorly suited to be "one heartbeat away" from the presidency.

THE 1988 CAMPAIGN

From a public relations standpoint, George Bush entered the 1988 general election campaign with both substantial advantages and disadvantages. Considering his advantages, as a two-term vice president under the leadership of a popular president during a period of economic prosperity, Bush could claim to be the true heir to the Reagan legacy. Bush benefited from the Republican "stay-the-course" theme at a time when the public did not want fundamental policy change. Bush claimed some credit for the perceived economic accomplishments of the Reagan presidency while he defined his own governing style as a "kinder, gentler" Republicanism than that associated with the Reagan social and civil rights programs.

Nonetheless, an incumbent vice president seeking the nation's highest office suffered the disadvantage of convincing people that he truly was his own man. The public image of George Bush from the vice presidential years was unflattering. The most recognized label used to describe Vice President Bush was the "wimp." Somehow he lacked Reagan's commanding stature and the wimp label appeared apt to many people. The most memorable line about George Bush was columnist George Will's description of the vice-president as Ronald Reagan's "lapdog."[1]

For a former war hero who could perhaps claim the most distinguished record of service for any man or woman who had sought the presidency, these characterizations certainly seemed unfair. Yet any vice president necessarily stands in the shadow of the chief executive and, given the nature of the office of vice president, ultimately is portrayed as a player of slight significance on the national political scene.

Furthermore, the vice president must conform to two contrasting expectations: one, that he be completely loyal to his chief executive—the responsibility that might earn him the label "lapdog"; and two, that he show himself to be his own man—a role that, if not played carefully, can make him look disloyal to the president. Whatever George Bush's faults, a shortage of personal loyalty to any man or office he had served certainly was not one of them.

The 1988 campaign provided George Bush the opportunity that he needed to define himself for the public. Who was this man, really? What did he stand for? What were his strongest convictions? Was he the George Bush of presidential campaign 1980—a moderate to conservative Republican: probusiness, pro–defense policy, advocate of progressive social and civil rights policies, abortion rights advocate? Or was he the George Bush of the Reagan era: staunchly conservative, prolife advocate, in the words of Republican Rep. Robert Dornan (Calif.) a "pit-bull" rightist?[2]

During the final week of the 1988 presidential campaign a number of press profiles of the candidates addressed similar questions. The answers given by the journalists reveal the widespread perception that Bush had failed to define himself—what he stood for, how he would lead the country—in the campaign.

Walter Shapiro of *Time* described Bush as a "political chameleon," a man who lacked a core governing philosophy.[3] Kenneth T. Walsh of *U.S. News and World Report* wrote that Bush had run "a content-free campaign." Walsh's report maintained that, even in likely victory, Bush would lack a governing mandate because the vice president had not defined "a governing strategy" and had failed to "lay out his plans."[4] Jonathan Alter and Mickey Kause of *Newsweek* reported that "Bush's ideological amorphousness is still troubling to anyone trying to predict how he will govern."[5] Their report agreed that Bush had provided no insight in the campaign into how he would govern and that Bush adopted any position that he believed would get him elected.[6]

Consequently, all three news weeklies presented the same portrait of Bush's campaign as ideologically vacuous, content-free. Columnists both liberal and conservative agreed. The liberal-leaning Richard Cohen described Bush as "a man of uncertain ideology and confused self-image."[7] Conservatives Rowland Evans and Robert Novak criticized Bush's "ideological flabbiness" and his lack of interest in policy issues during the campaign.[8] Fellow conservative George Will offered the most severe indictment of Bush, an "ominously empty" man, "a sailor without a compass."

He seems to have passed through the tumults of the 20th century unmarked by any of its great passions or arguments or aspirations. . . . He is moved entirely by an abstract duty to "serve," not by any idea he wants to be in the service of. In the absence of ideas, mere tactics are everything.[9]

In a preelection *Newsweek* column, Will declared that he had no more patience with the (not yet existent) Bush administration. Will further described Bush as "running on empty, intellectually," a man with "no ideas to utter." Consequently, "his honeymoon has ended before the transition has begun."[10] Lacking ideas to utter, with what did Bush fill the campaign vacuum? According to the press, mean-spirited, demagogic attacks on his opponent, Democrat Michael Dukakis. During the campaign, Bush characterized his opponent as a dangerously naive, liberal ideologue, a "card carrying member of the American Civil Liberties Union," who, as governor of Massachusetts, had coddled criminals and failed to defend the rights of law-abiding citizens. Bush campaign commercials decried a Massachusetts prisoner furlough program during Dukakis's governorship that resulted in one notorious criminal, Willie Horton, committing a gruesome crime in Maryland while on a weekend furlough. Dukakis had actually inherited the furlough program from his Republican predecessor. Nonetheless, he ended the controversial program too slowly for many critics. Bush campaign advertisements also blamed Dukakis for failing to enact programs to clean up environmental pollution in Boston Harbor. Bush had put his opponent on the defensive, and Dukakis never adequately responded to all of the negative characterizations.

Because of what most observers agreed was a poorly run campaign by both candidates, the reliably liberal *Washington Post* refused to endorse either one of them and described Bush and Dukakis as "deeply flawed." The *Post* declared that "Mr. Bush was really the major source and cause of the tawdriness of this campaign and that much of what he said was divisive, unworthy and unfair." Furthermore, "much of Mr. Bush's campaign has been reckless demagogic nonsense, which at once trivialized and distorted the issues."[11]

The *New York Times* lambasted the Bush campaign for failing to put an expeditious end to advertising "smears" against Dukakis by an independent political action committee that had spent over $7 million supporting Bush's election.[12] The offensive advertisements displayed a menacing-looking picture of Willie Horton, an all-the-more offensive tactic because Horton is black, and the television commercial not so subtly appealed to a vicious racial stereotype.

A *U.S. News and World Report* story declared the 1988 campaign "the most negative race in modern times" and placed the onus of negative campaigning on Bush.[13] A *Time* news report lamented the "trivial and nasty campaign" of 1988. "The ease with which Bush has skirted the boundaries of truth in the campaign remains troubling."[14]

Influential columnists joined the drumbeat of criticism of Bush's negative campaign. Colman McCarthy declared that "Bush has run a conniving and dirty campaign." Not content with either candidate, McCarthy advocated nonvoting as a means of political protest.[15] David Broder observed that "the level of distortion and demagoguery in the Bush campaign suggests that he is prone to let the end justify the means. He chose to seek victory by making his vaguely defined opponent seem radical and risky, rather than seeking a mandate for his own policies."[16] George Will lambasted Bush's "low, dishonest campaign."[17] According to Will, Bush ran a negative campaign because the vice president knew that "he cannot win an election on his own merits."[18] Richard Cohen criticized Bush for conducting "one of the nastiest and least honest campaigns on record." Cohen called Bush's campaign politically "effective" though "divisive and dishonest."[19]

Although journalists chastised Bush for lacking a positive, policy-oriented campaign theme, one Bush policy promise did stand out: "read my lips—no new taxes." Bush's pledge at the 1988 Republican National Convention to rule out a priori any tax increases played into the hands of critics who believed that he would say or do anything to get elected. David Broder characterized that pledge as "undoubtedly popular" yet "irresponsible."[20]

George Will, himself an advocate of higher taxes, assessed that Bush had failed the test of leadership by not summoning people to forgo some private consumption for the public good.[21]

During this final week of the 1988 campaign, Bush received little favorable press commentary. Some did express a favorable view of the man's public experience and potential for foreign policy acumen. An otherwise negative *Washington Post* editorial did admit that Bush had considerable knowledge of foreign and defense policy.[22] David Broder concluded that during the campaign, "for the most part, Bush has dealt responsibly with foreign policy and national security issues." Broder also noted that a Bush administration would be run by experienced, highly professional individuals—the kind of people with whom Bush preferred to work.[23] A *Time* report commented that Bush would bring to the presidency "firsthand knowledge of East-West relations and the concerns of European allies."[24]

Bush's selection of Indiana Senator J. Danforth (Dan) Quayle as a vice presidential running mate did much to undermine the vice president's reputation for preferring the company of professionally competent, highly experienced individuals. This is not the place to assess the merits and demerits of Bush's vice presidential selection. It is the place to consider how that selection affected Bush's reputation among leading journalists.

After Bush had announced his surprise vice presidential nomination at the Republican National Convention, the media pilloried the forty-one-year-old conservative senator as an intellectual lightweight, a mediocre legislator who had possibly used family influence to avoid military service in the Vietnam War. Quayle's frequent misstatements in campaign appearances and embarrassing performance in a vice presidential debate against Democratic candidate Senator Lloyd Bentsen (Texas) reinforced the press image of the Indiana senator as a disastrous vice presidential choice.

By the end of the 1988 campaign, Quayle had been temporarily exiled to campaign in out-of-the-limelight, small Republican-leaning towns where he could do little damage to Bush's electoral chances. Press commentaries nonetheless raised the issue of whether the Quayle selection reflected poorly on Bush's leadership ability and judgment. A *Time* news story called Bush's VP selection "nearly indefensible" and an example of how Bush behaves under pressure from movement conservatives.[25] David Broder made the devastating charge that "Quayle sends a disturbing signal about George Bush." By selecting Quayle, Bush had displayed "disdain . . . for the nation's future."[26] The *Washington Post* agreed.

His choice of Dan Quayle, who, under scrutiny turns out to be a very weak read, even by past lowly standards, was wrong—and if Bush wins, the prospect of Dan Quayle suddenly having to succeed him in office will remain a legitimate anxiety.[27]

THE 1988 ELECTION

George Bush defeated Michael Dukakis in the November 8, 1988, election in a popular vote (54%–46%) and electoral vote (426–112) landslide. Despite Bush's overwhelming victory as the nation's incoming forty-first president, almost every press analysis of the election stated that the newly elected candidate had failed to achieve a governing mandate. *Newsweek* reported that "the outcome gave Bush no sweeping mandate." Bush's "low-road campaign . . . had set no agenda for the voters to endorse."[28] Walter Shapiro wrote in *Time* that "for Bush it was a victory without drum rolls, a majority without a meaningful mandate."[29] David Beckwith wrote in *Time* that "the new President enters office with no clear mandate for imposing the tough solutions that will be necessary to tackle the nation's festering budget crisis."[30] Kenneth T. Walsh of *U.S. News and World Report* declared that the voters elected Bush "without a mandate for specific programs."[31] James M. Perry and Gerald F. Seib reported for the *Wall Street Journal* that Bush would "take office without a mandate or a strong signal that voters are enamored of Republican policies."[32]

Editorial writers and columnists agreed. The *New York Times* said of Bush's victory that "it cannot fairly be called a mandate. His agenda is unformed, and Congress remains ever more firmly . . . in Democratic hands."[33] Richard Cohen wrote that Bush entered the presidency "lacking a clear mandate."[34] Tom Wicker added that a forty-state electoral victory provided a "pretty strong mandate—but for what, besides Bush over Dukakis. The victor put forward virtually no program except 'more of the same, more or less.' "[35] William Safire summed up the meaning of the 1988 electoral outcome as voters saying, " 'O.K. I agree it shouldn't be [Dukakis], but I'm not so sure about you.' "[36] The *Wall Street Journal* described the "drumbeat" of postelection analyses as "no mandate, raise taxes, no mandate, raise taxes, no mandate, raise taxes." Differing with the conventional wisdom, the *Journal* decried the "ubiquitous talk about the lack of a mandate" and concluded that "a mandate is what you make it."[37] Charles Krauthammer also complained that "the 'mandate' nonsense has been going on nonstop since election night" and observed that "Bush's only promise was more of the same."[38]

Most journalists suggested that Bush lacked a governing mandate because he had conducted a content-free, negative campaign. Michael Kinsley intoned that Bush wouldn't know what to do once in office because "he won't have Willie Horton to kick around anymore." Rather than campaigning with a vision for the future, Bush characterized his opponents as people who "love the thought of murderers frolicking in the streets, oppose the Pledge of Allegiance. . . , want a weak America and are dying to pay more taxes." The *New York Times* blasted Bush's "brutally negative ads."[39] The *Times* questioned whether Bush could govern effectively with a Democratic-dominated Congress after the "harshness" and "mendacity" of his campaign attacks.[40] David Broder wrote that Bush had conducted "a campaign in which the vitriol drowned the vision."[41] A. M. Rosenthal described Bush's campaign as "one of the least kind and gentle" in memory. Bush had set "a mean example."[42] Tom Wicker characterized Bush's "derogation of his opponent" as "unpresidential." Therefore, "in the winning of his great office, he may have prejudiced at the outset his chances to succeed in it."[43]

Journalists attributed Bush's campaign style to a lack of a system of beliefs. Roger Rosenblatt described how his colleagues generally perceived Bush: "he is a cheerful but empty vessel, available to be filled with any dominant influence or ideology, loyal, frequently naive, overeager to please, tough and honorable."[44] Considering the following assessments, Rosenblatt was correct.

Walter Shapiro wrote that Bush "has always resisted definition. His career has been marked by ideological gyrations . . . [and] a lack of inner clarity."[45] David Beckwith added that "Bush does not have a deeply held personal agenda. He has few strong ideological or intellectual beliefs at all. . . . Nor does Bush have a keen intellect or a mind that is adept at placing events and challenges within a conceptual framework."[46] *Newsweek* assessed that after a long public life "Bush remains an opaque and elusive man, more question than answer." Furthermore, Bush lacked "bedrock beliefs" and seemed to be "an unreflective man, lacking much depth or ideological conviction."[47] Frequent Bush critic George Will described the president-elect as "all sail and no anchor." Consequently, "Bush must do two things that he showed no inclination to do during the campaign. He must think. And he must tell people things they do not want to hear."[48] Gerald M. Boyd reported that "despite hundreds of position papers and thousands of speeches since, what George Bush truly stands for remains an issue."[49]

A major cause of Bush's press image problem was the apparent contrast of his political style to that of Ronald Reagan. As Kenneth T. Walsh summed up the problem: "Yes, George Bush is no Ronald Reagan."

Bush's inclination is to consolidate rather than to innovate. . . . A tinkerer will succeed a visionary. A man of pliable commitments will replace a steadfast crusader. A man who joshes about his own lack of charisma will replace the most stunningly appealing leader of the post war era.[50]

Richard Cohen explained that "unlike the amiable Reagan, Bush's campaign points to no program, no policy changes."[51] *Newsweek* reported that "unlike Ronald Reagan who ran for president to lead a conservative revolution, Bush seemed only to want to be president."[52] Albert R. Hunt declared that "Bush may be the victim of circumstances. . . . Poor George Bush has the misfortune of being compared with a highly successful predecessor."[53]

The differences between Bush and his predecessor resulted in some favorable assessments of the president-elect. As David Broder pointed out, "everybody who knows him expects Bush to be a more personally engaged president than Reagan has been." Broder reported that Bush would staff the administration with competent, mainstream Republicans and avoid the Reagan preference for ideological "crusaders."[54] Kenneth T. Walsh believed that "Bush will be an active leader, far more engaged in the doings of his government than his predecessor ever was." Furthermore, Bush's personnel selections "were oriented toward pragmatism rather than ideology."[55] A *Newsweek* report added that Bush would probably exceed Reagan in giving attention to governing details, civil rights, and ethics.[56]

Despite their positive grades for Bush's personnel selections, journalists awarded the president-elect more low marks for Dan Quayle. David Beckwith wrote that the choice of Quayle confirmed that "Bush values loyalty more than brilliance."[57] Richard Cohen claimed that Bush had "lost the confidence of millions" by choosing Quayle.[58] Numerous reports iterated that theme of Quayle as not prepared for national office.[59]

THE TRANSITION

The traditional eleven-and-one-half-week presidential transition period, from the day after the election until the inauguration, provides a crucial opportunity for the president-elect to establish his press image. That opportunity was especially important to George Bush. His press image already suffered from the vague duties of the vice presidency as well as from the negative tone of the 1988 campaign.

Despite Bush's press image problem entering the transition, journalists had always suspected that for eight years as vice president he had obscured his own views from the public in order to remain loyal to President Reagan. Many suspected that Bush never felt completely comfortable with Reagan-style conservatism and, once elected, would show himself to be an establishment-oriented and moderate-to-conservative Republican.

Consequently, Bush used the transition period to differentiate himself from his predecessor and to establish a positive tone for his own administration. He effectively did so in both substantive and stylistic ways.

But the early transition press commentaries iterated the postelection themes of Bush as having no core beliefs and no mandate to govern. E. J. Dionne, Jr., for example, wrote that Bush had made the election "a referendum against liberalism" and had left no clear evidence of a governing philosophy. "It would not be a surprise if his administration proved to be stoutly conservative, in the Reagan mold, or only moderately so, on the model of Dwight D. Eisenhower."[60]

The press answered the mystery by favoring the moderate, pragmatist definition of Bush over the Reagan-retread one. As Richard Cohen concluded, "George Bush turns out to be a pragmatist who masqueraded as a conservative . . . The man elected as a conservative will turn out to be a moderate." Furthermore, "the campaign was a sham—and the choice of Dan Quayle a diversion to mollify conservatives."[61] Numerous journalists arrived at similar conclusions. To establish Bush's emergence as a moderate they cited evidence that he had started to put together an administration of moderate Republicans and pragmatists, including James Baker (Secretary of State), Brent Scowcroft (National Security Adviser), Richard Darman (Office of Management and Budget Director), Elizabeth Dole (Labor Secretary), and Louis W. Sullivan (Secretary of Health and Human Services). Bush had kept on some moderate Reagan appointees: Nicholas Brady (Treasury Secretary) and Richard Thornburgh (Attorney General). Bush chose a conservative hero, Jack Kemp, as Secretary of Housing and Urban Development. Kemp's philosophy of compassionate, tolerant conservatism had earned him the respect of liberals. Bush had clearly avoided ideological crusaders in his appointments and received substantial press praise in so doing.

George Hackett wrote in *Newsweek* that in choosing persons to staff the new administration Bush had favored "pragmatic problem solvers" and avoided "ideological cowboys." Hackett extolled Bush's choices as committed to public service, "a sense of duty to the greater good" rather than ideology. "The man who campaigned as Ronald Reagan's heir has signaled, in his appointments, that he will be a very different sort of president."[62] Donald Baer of *U.S. News and World Report* noted that, although Bush "has not produced a clear agenda," the president-elect "has defined his administration in terms of lives and experiences of people he has recruited." Baer described Bush's choices for key posts, especially in foreign affairs, as not "ideologically driven," not committed to "radical change." Some reflected Bush's "tweedy rectitude and disapproval of Reagan-era profligacy."[63] The *New York Times* approved of Bush's choices of moderate Republicans for cabinet posts. Those selections "convey a welcome message that he is more interested in solving problems than in flaunting ideology."[64] Bush had demonstrated "a healthy preference for non-ideological, practical people," including such "tough-minded pragmatists" as James Baker and Brent Scowcroft. Consequently, Bush had shown that "he'd rather govern than confront."[65] James Reston observed that "unlike Carter and Reagan, who ran against the Washington 'insiders,' Bush is hiring them . . . Bush scattered the plums around: the moderates got most of them, the conservatives got Sununu and Kemp and the golfers got Quayle."[66]

Not every Bush appointee received press approval. Journalists did not confer the seal of approval on either the choice of John Sununu for chief-of-staff or John Tower for secretary of defense. Regarding Sununu, although press reports acknowledged the man's intelligence, they described him as a deeply partisan, strident, arrogant person.[67] John Tower received exceptional press scrutiny because of unsubstantiated rumors of alcoholism and extramarital affairs. Some journalists questioned the man's fitness for defense secretary given his close financial ties to defense-related interests.[68] Press commentaries continued to question Bush's earlier choice of a vice president.[69]

Many press reports emphasized Bush's contrast with Reagan. R. W. Apple noted that Bush had signaled the intention to be "more energetic" as well as "more deeply involved" in governing than Reagan.[70] Eleanor Clift of *Newsweek* described Bush as "an insider who likes to work the levers of power—a welcome change after Reagan's sound-bite government in which the backstage players made many of the decisions."[71] Tom Morganthau, also of *Newsweek*, exclaimed "something startling has happened to the man who was once mocked as Ronald Reagan's lap dog. Poppy Bush is acting *presidential*." Morganthau focused on Bush's professional transition and experienced cabinet.[72]

Transition press commentaries also speculated about Bush's policy agenda. In domestic policy, much commentary not surprisingly focused on the budget debt and how Bush would handle that problem without raising taxes. Few journalists found Bush's no-new-tax pledge credible. A *Newsweek* report suggested that Bush promised Americans no pain in order to win the presidency, but that once in office, he would have to act like a president and consider all options.[73] The *New York Times* opined that Bush could not fight deficits without new taxes and that he would have to be "flexible" on that issue.[74] The *Washington Post* agreed. "Whether to raise taxes was a campaign question. The real questions are which taxes and when."[75]

In foreign policy, journalists praised Bush's efforts to establish a relationship with the Soviet leader Mikhail Gorbachev. A good many commentaries speculated that Bush would focus his efforts on foreign affairs, given the politically difficult deficit issue and Democratic dominance of Congress. Some credited Gorbachev with having created the conditions for a new era in world politics without traditional cold war struggles. The journalists called on Bush to meet the challenges of a new era with "visionary leadership" and "new thinking."[76]

CONCLUSION

The presidential transition provides the initial opportunity for journalists to assess how the president might govern. This period is characterized by a great deal of speculation about the president-elect's leadership style and policy priorities. The most substantive actions at this stage, presidential appointments to high offices, offer the first real look at how the president-elect makes decisions.

Journalists gave Bush good marks for appointing some experienced, nonideological people to the cabinet. Although not all of the appointees met with approval, journalists saw a favorable contrast with Bush's predecessor: a willingness to put pragmatic leadership above ideological crusading.

Nonetheless, by inauguration day, journalists agreed that Bush still had not adequately defined himself or his leadership style. Bush's 1988 campaign and the transition period had yet to offer a clear picture of his administration's goals and objectives.

NOTES

1. George F. Will, "George Bush: The Sound of a Lapdog," *Washington Post*, January 30, 1986, p. A25.

2. See *National Review* cover story, November 6, 1987.

3. Walter Shapiro, "The Differences That Really Matter," *Time*, November 7, 1988, p. 24.

4. Kenneth T. Walsh, "The Passive Mandate," *U.S. News and World Report*, October 31, 1988, p. 20. See also David R. Gergen, "The Perils of the President," *U.S. News and World Report*, November 14, 1988, p. 26.

5. Jonathan Alter and Mickey Kause, "The Big Questions," *Newsweek*, November 7, 1988, p. 55.

6. Ibid., pp. 54, 57.

7. Richard Cohen, "The 'Wimp' Becomes a Bully," *Washington Post*, November 1, 1988, p. A19. See also Anthony Lewis, "Who Is George Bush?" *New York Times*, November 6, 1988, sec. 4, p. 25.

8. Rowland Evans and Robert Novak, "Coasting, Bush Style," *Washington Post*, November 7, 1988, p. A23.

9. George F. Will, "A Case for George Bush," *Washington Post*, November 6, 1988, p. C7.

10. George F. Will, "Trickle-Down Tawdriness," *Newsweek*, November 7, 1988, p. 132.

11. "No Endorsement," *Washington Post*, November 2, 1988, p. A20.

12. "George Bush and Willie Horton," *New York Times*, November 4, 1988, p. A34.

13. Peter Ross Range, "The Lessons of Campaign '88," *U.S. News and World Report*, November 7, 1988, p. 18.

14. Shapiro, "The Differences That Really Matter," pp. 22, 24.

15. Colman McCarthy, "The Message in Staying Home on Election Day," *Washington Post*, November 5, 1988, p. A23.

16. David S. Broder, "Bush—The Good News and the Bad," *Washington Post*, November 2, 1988, p. A21.

17. Will, "A Case for George Bush."

18. Will, "Trickle-Down Tawdriness."

19. Richard Cohen, "The 'Wimp' Becomes a Bully."

20. Broder, "Bush—The Good News and the Bad."

21. George F. Will, "A Case for Dukakis," *Washington Post*, November 3, 1988, p. A27.

22. "No Endorsement."

23. Broder, "Bush—The Good News and the Bad."

24. Shapiro, "Differences," p. 26.

25. Ibid., pp. 24, 25.

26. Broder, "Bush—The Good News and the Bad."

27. "No Endorsement."

28. Larry Martz, "The Tough Tasks Ahead," *Newsweek*, November 21, 1988, p. 10.

29. Walter Shapiro, "The Election," *Time*, November 21, 1988, p. 25.

30. David Beckwith "What to Expect," *Time*, November 21, 1988, p. 26.

31. Kenneth T. Walsh, "How Bush Will Run The Country," *U.S. News and World Report*, November 21, 1988, p. 26.

32. James M. Perry and Gerald F. Seib, "Bush's Clear Victory, Less Than Resounding, Bodes Conflict Ahead," *Wall Street Journal*, November 9, 1988, p. A1.

33. "Ideology, Competence and Mr. Bush," *New York Times*, November 10, 1988, p. A30. See also "A Mandate to Make Sense," *New York Times*, November 11, 1988, p. A30; "The Great Mandate Hunt . . . " *Washington Post*, November 14, 1988, p. A10.

34. Richard Cohen, "Now for the Hard Part," *Washington Post*, November 10, 1988, p. A23.

35. Tom Wicker, "Bush at the Outset," *New York Times*, November 11, 1988, p. A31.

36. William Safire, "The Voters' Message," *New York Times*, November 10, 1988, p. A31.

37. "Where Was George?" *Wall Street Journal*, November 10, 1988, p. A22.

38. Charles Krauthammer, "But He Never Asked for a Mandate," *Washington Post*, November 11, 1988, p. A23.

39. Michael Kinsley, "Too Close to Call," *Washington Post*, November 13, 1988, p. C7; and "Ideology, Competence and Mr. Bush."

40. "What George Bush Won," *New York Times*, November 9, 1988, p. A34.

41. David S. Broder, "Voters Again Opt for a Divided Government," *Washington Post*, November 9, 1988, p. A1.

42. A. M. Rosenthal, "A Kinder, Gentler Nation," *New York Times*, November 11, 1988, p. A31.

43. Wicker, "Bush at the Outset."

44. Roger Rosenblatt, "At Long Last, Hail to the Chief," *U.S. News and World Report*, November 21, 1988, p. 23.

45. Shapiro, "The Election," p. 24.

46. Beckwith, "What to Expect," p. 27.

47. Martz, "The Tough Task Ahead," p. 10.

48. George F. Will, "Another Muddy Message," *Newsweek*, November 21, 1988, p. 30.

49. Gerald M. Boyd, "A Victor Free to Set His Own Course," *New York Times*, November 9, 1988, p. A1.

50. Walsh, "How Bush Will Run the Country," p. 24.

51. Cohen, "Now for the Hard Part," p. A23.

52. Martz, "The Tough Tasks Ahead," p. 10.

53. Albert R. Hunt, "Now Bush Needs a Mandate Campaign," *Wall Street Journal*, November 11, 1988, p. A14.

54. David S. Broder, "Bush Will Set His Own Agenda," *Washington Post*, November 10, 1988, p. A23.

55. Walsh, "How Bush Will Run the Country," pp. 25, 27.

56. Martz, "The Tough Tasks Ahead," p. 10. Profiles of Bush personnel choices iterated the view that the president-elect had started to put together a staff of highly competent, professional insiders. See Susan Dentzer, "The Man [James Baker] behind the Throne," *U.S. News and World Report*, November 21, 1988, pp. 33–35; "The Baker–Darman Axis: Rebirth of a Power Couple," *U.S. News and World Report*, November 21, 1988, p. 35; Kenneth T. Walsh, "Bush's Plan for John Sununu," *U.S. News and World Report*, November 28, 1988, p. 31.

57. Beckwith, "What to Expect," p. 28.

58. Cohen, "Now for the Hard Part."

59. See, for example, B. Drummond Ayres, Jr., "A Partner Seasoned by the Campaign," *New York Times*, November 9, 1988, p. A26; George Hackett, "The 'Phantom Candidate' Has to Keep on Running," *Newsweek*, November 21, 1988, p. 13; Andy Plattner, "Dan Quayle's Fast Fade," *U.S. News and World Report*, November 21, 1988, p. 26.

60. E. J. Dionne, Jr., "Coming Up: The Debate America Wanted," *New York Times*, November 13, 1988, sec. 4, p. 1.

61. Richard Cohen, "George Bush, Closet Moderate, Will Have to Speak Up," *Washington Post*, December 29, 1988, p. A23.

62. George Hackett, "The Bush Revolution," *Newsweek*, December 5, 1988, p. 21.

63. Donald Baer, "A White House of Many Mansions," *U.S. News and World Report*, January 23, 1989, pp. 15–17.

64. "Mr. Bush's Impracticality," *New York Times*, November 22, 1988, p. A26.

65. "Mr. Bush's Practical Choices," *New York Times*, December 7, 1988, p. A30. See also "Conservatives Likely to Conserve," *New York Times*, December 26, 1988, p. 30.

66. James Reston, "Rating Bush: So Far, Not Bad," *New York Times*, December 22, 1988, p. A23. See also David Ignatius, "Establishment Redux: New Jobs for the Old Guard," *Washington Post*, January 15, 1989, pp. C1, C2.

67. See, for example, "Mr. Bush's Practical Choices"; Allan R. Gold, "Sununu Is Called Smart, Decisive and Impatient," *New York Times*, November 20, 1988, p. 28; R. W. Apple, Jr., "Bush as His Own Man," *New York Times*, November 25, 1988, p. B13; Michael Duffy and Dan Goodgame, "The Markets Vote," *Time*, November 28, 1988, p. 21.

68. See, for example, "Mr. Bush's Practical Choices"; "Better Choices Than John Tower," *New York Times*, November 23, 1988, p. A22; Michael Duffy, "John Tower's Hesitation Blues," *Time*, December 12, 1988, p. 25.

69. See, for example, B. Drummond Ayres, Jr., "Quayle Says His Work Will Take Care of Image," *New York Times*, November 20, 1988, sec. 1, p. 30; Reston, "Rating Bush: So Far, Not Bad," *New York Times*, December 22, 1988, p. A23.

70. R. W. Apple, Jr., "Bush, Early On: Very Much Involved," *New York Times*, November 20, 1988, sec. 1, p. 1. See also Apple, "Bush as His Own Man," pp. A1, B13.

71. Eleanor Clift, "The Surprise Honeymoon," *Newsweek*, December 12, 1988, p. 26.

72. Tom Morganthau, "The 'Liberation' of George Bush," *Newsweek*, January 16, 1989, p. 28.

73. Duffy and Goodgame, "The Markets Vote," p. 22; see also Bill Powell, "Bush's No. 1 Challenge," *Newsweek*, November 28, 1988, pp. 28–31.

74. "Mr. Bush's Impracticality."

75. "Why Not Budget Surplus?" *Washington Post*, December 27, 1988, p. A14. A *Washington Post* poll found that only one in three voters expected Bush to fulfill the no-new-taxes pledge. See David S. Broder and Richard Morin, "Bush Will Increase Taxes, Most People in Survey Believe," *Washington Post*, November 12, 1988, p. A10.

76. "George Bush's New World," *New York Times*, January 15, 1989, sec. 4, p. 26; John Barry and Tom Morganthau, "The Defense Dilemma," *Newsweek*, January 23, 1989, pp. 12–18; Walter Isaacson, "The Gorbachev Challenge," *Time*, December 19, 1988, pp. 16–18; Steven V. Roberts, "In Foreign Policy, the Bush Era Is Here," *New York Times*, November 20, 1988, sec. 4, pp. 1, 4; Stephen S. Rosenfeld, "The Heroic Age Is Over," *Washington Post*, November 11, 1988, p. A23; Strobe Talbott, "Paint the Town Red," *Time*, December 12, 1988, pp. 20–22.

3

Status Quo–Plus or No Vision? (1989)

When George Bush took the presidential oath of office on January 20, 1989, leading journalists already had defined him as, at best, a competent, cautious, and pragmatic man with conservative views and a moderate temperament, and, at worst, an ambitious man who wanted power but lacked a philosophy of governance and any idea of the purposes for which he would exercise power. The early stage of Bush's presidency finally offered journalists the chance to observe the man's leadership and to define whether he was up to the job of being president. An examination of Bush's press coverage in 1989 reveals a mixed, though mostly negative review of his leadership acumen.

Timing. The early stage of an administration provides journalists with the most clues to how a president leads: his style of leadership and his ability to project power and attain his goals. In fact, a president's actions during his first several weeks in office have an enormous, perhaps exaggerated, impact on the man's press image.

In 1989, journalists criticized Bush for getting off to a slow start. From their vantage, Bush failed to take advantage of his "honeymoon" period in a way that would have enabled him to achieve substantial policy innovations in short order. The president's disavowal of any 100–days plan to enact his agenda perplexed journalists who believed that the first three months of the term constituted the prime opportunity for the chief executive to make his mark on the presidency.

Journalists portrayed Bush's early months as a lost opportunity in another way: the nature of the times, particularly in international affairs, presented the president a unique chance to achieve great things. Yet Bush did not appear to these journalists to be a man for extraordinary times.

Symbolism/Rhetoric. When it comes to the use of speech and symbolism, no modern president, except perhaps Harry S Truman, has had a more difficult act to follow than George Bush. How could any president, especially George Bush, look good after Ronald Reagan?

In judging a president, journalists place a great deal of emphasis on style. Bush did not excel in that area. Journalists made much of Bush's bland presentational style, boring speeches, and his inability to stir the public imagination with words. In 1989, press coverage emphasized these stylistic and rhetorical shortcomings. Some press commentaries described Bush's style as "Carteresque": folksy, bland, lacking in grandeur.

Bush received some positive press note for his convention promise of a "kinder, gentler nation"; a pledge perceived by many as a break from the Reagan era ethos. Journalists responded favorably to much of the substance of Bush's inaugural address—in particular to his call to the nation for more civic spirit and less materialism. Nonetheless, throughout 1989, Bush more often than not disappointed those who expected Reagan-like rhetoric or majesty from their chief executive.

Agenda. Bush initiated a number of policy proposals in 1989 in such areas as the economy, environment, drug abuse, and education. Despite these initiatives, journalists frequently chided the president for a lack of bold, visionary goals. When Bush presented an antidrug initiative, journalists reported that the president's proposal did not seek to spend enough money to solve the problem. Journalists criticized the president's deficit reduction plan as not bold enough to dramatically reduce the budget shortfall. They credited him with the renewal of the Clean Air Act and then criticized him for not proposing new environmental policies. Many journalists mocked Bush's emphasis on volunteerism and charity as a weak federal response to domestic problems.

In foreign policy, Bush described his program as an incremental adjustment to his predecessor's agenda. Many journalists again criticized Bush for a lack of "vision," a failure to define his own unique agenda. Although Bush fared better in press coverage of foreign policy than in domestic policy, he still disappointed expectations for far-reaching, innovative efforts.

Policy Development. Journalists reserved many of their harshest assessments for Bush's strategy of agenda development. According to the widely held view, Bush lacked a clear strategy for moving forward his policy objectives. Instead, he promoted incremental change to existing programs. Journalists criticized Bush's failure to open his presidency with a bold policy agenda. When Bush did not conform to a model of presidential leadership that demanded bold, early initiatives, journalists defined his leadership as lacking. They decried his failure to establish a 100–days plan of action and reported that he did not adequately use his honeymoon period to set the nation's agenda.

Although journalists emphasized Bush's apparent lack of a bold domestic policy agenda, they also criticized his responses to foreign affairs challenges. According to the journalists, Bush responded too cautiously to the challenges to East–West relations presented by Soviet leader Mikhail Gorbachev; the president did not respond strongly enough to Chinese government human rights abuses; and he responded with timidity to the leadership crisis in Panama. Nonetheless, some press commentaries did regard Bush's foreign policy initiatives as sometimes properly cautious, even "prudent."

Staff. During the transition period, Bush received high praise for putting together a White House team of competent insiders. In 1989, the emphasis on Bush's appointments changed. Press coverage focused heavily on allegations of professional and personal improprieties by several Bush appointees. None of the controversial appointees received so much press coverage as Bush's initial choice for secretary of defense, former Texas Senator John Tower. Because Bush had pledged to conduct an administration of high ethical standards, his selection of Tower became a major embarrassment. Although nobody had proved the scurrilous charges against Tower, that nomination appeared to conflict with Bush's own stated ethics code and resulted in serious criticism of the president for not being serious about fulfilling a key pledge.

Two other Bush appointments came under journalistic fire: those of Chief of Staff John Sununu and Budget Director Richard Darman. Both men had reputations for being standoffish toward the media, and many journalists perceived these appointments as evidence of Bush's indifference to appearances.

THE INAUGURATION

The presidential inaugural address plays an important role in establishing the tone and the themes of a new administration. Bush laid the groundwork with a relatively smooth transition during which the press highly praised his personnel choices. Nonetheless, by inauguration day, January 20, 1989, Robert L. Bartley explained that "the essential character of the Bush presidency remains to be seen. There is always the possibility, of course, that George Bush has an agenda he hasn't told us about."[1]

Despite the smooth transition, the journalists believed that Bush had yet to offer the country a policy direction. They identified some overriding themes in Bush's inaugural speech and further praised him for an address that contrasted with a negative aspect of the Reagan era image—the 1980s era of materialism.

In his address, Bush proclaimed a "new breeze" sweeping through the capital. In his words,

Use power to help people. . . . We are not the sum of our possessions. . . . We cannot hope only to leave our children a bigger car, a bigger bank account. We must hope to give them a sense of what it means to be a loyal friend, a loyal parent, a citizen who leaves his home, his neighborhood and town better than he found it . . . in all things, generosity.

Bush spoke of the needs for "duty, sacrifice, commitment and a patriotism that finds its expression in taking part and pitching in."[2]

Harrison Rainie of *U.S. News and World Report* exclaimed that with such rhetoric Bush "had repudiated the ethos of the Reagan era."[3] According to the *Washington Post*, the address had "distanced Mr. Bush, as politely as possible, from the worst part of the ethos of the administration in which he was vice president."[4] Michael Kramer of *Time* described Bush's theme as "a new altruism, a move away from the Reagan era's tacit approval of selfishness, an end to the glorification of greed." [5] Jonathan Alter of *Newsweek* called Bush's speech a rejection of "Reaganite paeans to the beauty of the market." Also, "by employing so momentous an occasion to strike a blow against materialism . . . Bush could help hasten the close of an ugly era of greed."[6]

Some journalists criticized Bush's speech for a lack of policy specifics and for an emphasis on the virtues of volunteerism and charity. Alter asked, "how can someone with Bush's experience in government seriously believe that private giving is a substitute for government services?" Alter identified "The Missing Link of the Bush Presidency": "It's clear from his desperate campaign tactics how much he wanted to *be* president. But not even his close advisers know exactly what he wants to *do* as president . . . [R]arely in recent history has a chief executive come to office revealing so little policy direction."[7]

The *New York Times* noted that "the President's ideas still lack tangibility and will require elaboration." Nonetheless, the *Times* took issue with "the laments from commentators that the new President failed to lay out stirring plans for his Hundred Days." The *Times* praised Bush's "measured" and "modest" inaugural address as appropriate to the moment.[8] The *Wall Street Journal* defended Bush's call for volunteerism against the "laments" of those who expected an elaboration of big government solutions to problems.[9]

EARLY EVALUATIONS

Despite these assertions that an inaugural address was not the place to develop policy specifics and bold plans, many of the earliest commentaries on Bush's presidency emphasized the "no mandate" and "no broad vision" themes. The *Washington Post* opined that Bush lacked a Reagan-style "mandate for change."[10] R. W. Apple, Jr., wrote that "there is no disposition toward sudden or radical change, as [Bush] made clear . . . in disavowing any interest in opening his administration with a 100–day burst of innovation."[11] David R. Gergen expressed concern that Bush had not yet established any clarity of purpose, had rejected the concept of an activist first hundred days, and had still not filled many government positions.

With his government slow in forming, Bush will advance few, if any, grand strategies and proposals. . . . There are no signs that he will launch a crusade against difficult, underlying problems such as poverty and the collapse of city schools. . . . Historically, America's strongest presidents have been those who began with clear goals and wrestled events to the ground. They have seized the country's imagination and drawn sustenance from its support. . . . Unless he takes special care, he could wind up closer to Jimmy Carter, who had no clear vision for his presidency, than to Ronald Reagan, who did.[12]

David Hoffman contrasted the leadership styles of Ronald Reagan the ideological crusader and George Bush "who has not defined the presidency in such broad strokes." Hoffman described Bush as a man without ideological tenets and also without a known strategy for enacting an agenda. Hoffman, like Gergen, identified the criteria by which to judge Bush's leadership: "He must find a way to persuade, cajole and stimulate the mighty instruments of government, the vast electorate and, perhaps most important, the rest of the world, to follow his lead."[13]

Journalists wasted no time after the Bush inauguration demanding an action-oriented agenda from the new president. When Bush did what many presidents do their first days in office—use symbolic gestures to build public support—journalists emphasized the need for substantive presidential actions.

George F. Will described the first days of Bush's presidency as heavily loaded with symbolism. Will cautioned that a "frenetic reliance on symbolism indicates uncertainty about what you want to do." By focusing on imagery, Bush had "hit the ground running in place. . . . Beyond 'serving,' is there something he wants to do?"[14] Charles Krauthammer expressed concern that Bush had entered the presidency merely with a desire to serve the country. "To serve is nice, but to what end? Bush's problem is that he does not know. . . . Ends—the vision thing—are not his forte. His will be a government of means."[15] Richard Cohen lambasted Bush's symbolic gestures as "no substitute for direction—for leadership." Eleven days after Bush's inauguration, Cohen wrote,

How is it that a man who has been vice president for eight years and president or president-elect since last November, has been unable to hit the ground running? Why is it that in matters of paramount importance . . . Bush does not seem to know where he is going? . . . What we are seeing is Jimmy Carter redux. . . . Bush has substituted a Carter-like atmosphere of good intentions for sound programs.[16]

A *Newsweek* story also reported a "lack of direction" early in the Bush administration. The story acknowledged that Bush appeared to be working hard, but "while Bush clearly *likes* being president, he hasn't completely thought through what he intends to *do*. In other words, while there was plenty of motion, the direction remained unclear."[17]

These early criticisms of Bush's leadership reveal not only the rapid pace by which journalists begin to define a presidency but also their strong bias in favor of immediate presidential policy activism. Even though Bush had sought the presidency promising policy continuity and only incremental change, journalists held him to a very different standard—one demanding bold policy action during the first one hundred days. David Gergen maintained that "the one great opportunity for leadership by a president comes at the early stages of an administration."[18] This assertion typifies much journalistic thinking about the presidency.

To be sure, journalists feel a great deal of competitive pressure to define a presidency very early in the term, during a period in which there may not be a great deal of substantive policy activity going on.[19] In retrospect, the intense press interest in many nonsubstantive stories about Bush—his affection for pork rinds, country music, and playing horseshoes—appears frivolous. Yet much of this press focus had serious consequences for Bush's presidency because, while the press was defining his administration, it also suggested similarities with the unfavorable image of Carter's presidency— too "folksy," "homespun," lacking grandeur.[20]

The Budget Plan and Address

On February 9, 1989, Bush made a nationally televised address on the federal budget before a joint session of Congress. As political imagery, the speech received unfavorable reviews. For example, *Washington Post* television critic Tom Shales noted Bush's boring presentational style and awkward speaking tendency to pause at certain intervals and wait for the audience to applaud.[21]

More substantively, the journalists criticized Bush's speech for not offering any bold or visionary plans to end the federal budget problem. Bush told Congress that "I don't propose to change direction. We are headed the right way." He proposed to modestly increase federal spending on some domestic programs (e.g., child care, education, attacking the drug problem), a one-year freeze on defense spending combined with budget process reform, and to cut spending on unspecified other programs.[22]

David S. Broder lambasted the proposal as "a 'Willie Horton' budget, a smart tactic for putting the opposition on the defensive." That is, rather than specify unpopular budget cuts, Bush had placed the onus on Congress to do so. Bush had presented a spare domestic agenda" and thereby had "squandered an opportunity to put his mark on the future." Broder maintained that a president's "most lasting domestic accomplishments generally occur early in the first year in office. Yet Bush chose incrementalism.

It confirms the suspicion that Bush has nothing very much he hopes to accomplish here at home. If he makes his mark in the history books, he intends to do it in foreign policy—not in domestic affairs. Those may seem sweeping conclusions to draw barely a month into the new administration. . . . There's not a hint that Bush or his associates have a real passion to do any one thing well or an idea that could lead to a breakthrough on any of the intractable problems facing the country's schools, cities, transportation system or trade practices. Most of all, the budget tacitly concedes that Bush will settle for tiny, marginal improvements in the federal deficit.[23]

David Gergen wrote that "a more visionary leader" would have used the budget address to outline a bold policy agenda because "the one great opportunity for leadership by a president comes at the early stages of an administration."

The President has clearly rejected the performance tests set by the 20th-century leaders Roosevelt and Reagan. He will not be bound to FDR's 100–days standard for decisive legislative victories and executive action. Nor will he be bound by the sense that a president must author sweeping proposals for change.[24]

Numerous other accounts criticized Bush's budget plan as inadequate to meet the nation's problems.[25] Even the *Wall Street Journal*'s editors, who were somewhat sympathetic to Bush's approach of "fine-tuning" Reagan's legacy, concluded that the president needed "to offer a more coherent philosophy about the limits of federal paternalism."[26]

Ethics and the Character Issue

Bush's early presidential image suffered a more serious setback when press commentaries focused on allegations of impropriety by various administration appointees. Bush had emphasized during his transition and early days as president the intention to uphold the highest ethical standards. To back up that intention, Bush appointed an ethics-in-government commission to study this complicated subject and to offer proposals for reform. Bush learned the hard way what Jimmy Carter earlier had learned during the 1977 controversy surrounding OMB Director Bert Lance: that a president who sets very high standards of conduct will be judged harshly any time that he, or anyone else in the administration, appears to fall short of those standards.[27]

In the abstract, reporters find ethics stories difficult to write. Federal policy regarding ethics in government is complicated and usually not very interesting. A presidential proposal to set up an ethics commission or to reform conflict-of-interest laws usually does not generate a great deal of press interest. When Bush adopted such actions he generated some favorable press commentary, but very little enthusiasm.[28]

The ethics issue becomes an appealing political story when it is associated with a prominent person's actual or alleged lapses in conduct. Bush's early press coverage suffered from high profile allegations of unethical conduct by several of his top appointees. The first such case, ironically, concerned Bush's counsel and often-dubbed "ethics czar," C. Boyden Gray. News stories revealed that Gray had served as chairman of the board of a large communications conglomerate while he had worked for Vice President Bush. To avoid the appearance of impropriety, Gray recused himself from policy-making decisions regarding communications issues. Nonetheless, Gray had acted in conflict with a White House policy that prohibited officials from serving on company boards. By earning outside income from this endeavor, Gray had violated another White House policy. Numerous press accounts noted these ethics lapses, and some criticized President Bush for not living up to his own standards of conduct.[29]

News accounts also noted that Secretary of State James Baker held substantial financial interests in a company whose fortunes would be influenced by U.S. policy on restructuring Third World debt. Again, the apparent disjuncture between Bush's high-minded goals and the activities of his appointee resulted in critical coverage.[30]

Two other cases drew some press attention. Secretary of Housing and Urban Development Jack Kemp had accepted speaking fees above the legal limit years earlier as a New York congressman. He returned the fees once he was nominated to the cabinet post. Secretary of Health and Human Services Louis Sullivan had requested that he be allowed to receive an income from his previous employer, a medical college, while serving in government. That request conflicted with Bush's ethics standards. Consequently, Sullivan withdrew that request.

None of these ethics controversies received nearly as much attention as that of Bush's nominee for secretary of defense, former U.S. Senator John Tower. Once nominated for that post, Tower encountered numerous critics who levied serious charges of personal and professional misconduct against him. Specifically, after leaving the Senate, Tower did consulting work for defense firms that had substantial business dealings with the Pentagon. In two and a half years of such work, Tower had earned over $750,000, leading critics to charge that he had unduly profited from his years of public service. Furthermore, some of Tower's critics maintained that he frequently drank heavily and had sexually harassed women on many occasions. *U.S. News and World Report* called Tower "the most embarrassing example" of the disjuncture between Bush's standards of rectitude and "Washington's peculiar ethical culture."[31]

An FBI investigation of the many rumors surrounding Tower's personal life held up the confirmation process for weeks. While the Senate considered Tower for the post of defense secretary, the nominee tried to overcome concerns about his drinking by pledging on national television not to drink any alcoholic beverages during his time in the public service. Despite Tower's unusual pledge and the fact that investigators could not confirm rumors about his behavior, on February 23, 1989, the Senate Armed Services Committee voted 11–9, on strict party lines, to reject his confirmation. Bush refused to accept the committee judgment as proof that Tower could not be confirmed and moved the nomination to the full Senate, where Tower's former colleagues voted on March 9, 1989, against confirmation, 53–47.

The battle for Tower's confirmation became a Bush presidency public image problem.[32] Press reports and commentaries maintained that, despite Bush's emphasis on ethics, the president cared more about personal loyalty than principles.[33] Richard Cohen wrote that "Bush's decision to nominate Tower (given all the accusations) is well nigh inexplicable." The columnist compared the Tower selection to Bush's earlier choice of Dan Quayle to become vice president.

Quayle and Tower were Bush's personal choices, chosen because he feels comfortable with them. He brushed aside objections, even though in both cases they were consequential. And having made his decisions, he stuck with them, confusing stubbornness with decisiveness.[34]

George C. Church added that "Bush's personal and political judgment has once again been called into question." Church also compared the Tower selection to that of Dan Quayle. The *Time* reporter observed that by defending Tower, Bush was "running a risk of subtly and unintentionally undermining his administration." Bush had diminished his own stature early in the term on a battle that he had little chance of winning. He had lost "not just a secretary of defense, but the all-important impression that he is in command of a government with sound judgment, creative ideas and lots of momentum."[35]

Church's conclusion reiterated a point raised by many press commentaries: that the early impressions of a president's leadership have a lasting impact. Some journalists compared Bush's early leadership problems to those experienced by Jimmy Carter in 1977.[36] This analogy anticipated the difficulties that Bush experienced overcoming negative early press perceptions of his leadership. Bush's critics bragged that the president had been "Carterized," and the label began to stick. The *New York Times* opined that "the Tower defeat will inevitably reinforce the notion, now popular in Washington, that Mr. Bush's young administration is already in terminal decline."[37]

For David Broder, the Tower case evidenced many weaknesses "in the political intelligence and operations of the Bush White House that make the fledgling president appear more vulnerable than supporters find comfortable to contemplate."[38] Gerald F. Seib and John J. Fialka reported that the controversy made it clear that Bush needed to repair "the flaws in his White House political machinery that helped doom" the Tower nomination.[39]

The Tower controversy coincided with some other stories (discussed later) that gave rise to press criticism of Bush's leadership. Lou Cannon's analysis of Bush's troubled "honeymoon" period led the columnist to conclude that "it is difficult to ascertain whether [Bush] is unwilling to stand up for his principles or is simply befuddled. . . . Bush seems to have few clues about where he wants to take his presidency."[40] *Washington Post* editorial writer Peter Milius summarized the leading press criticism of Bush's leadership during the early days of the term.

The wimp thing may have been right after all, that the Bush administration sadly lacks both a compass and an engine, can't get off the ground, is floundering, drifting, aimless, forfeiting good-will, wasting its honeymoon and—well, not to put too fine a point on it—that the Bush administration seven weeks after inauguration is just about over.

Milius argued that the journalists who had demanded charisma and "great policy shifts" from George Bush had misread the president. Furthermore, "forty-nine days of age is a little early for the obit page."[41]

Several days after Milius's article appeared, the Senate rejected Tower, and President Bush nominated Representative Dick Cheney (R–Wyo.) for defense secretary. The choice of the highly respected and popular Representative Cheney received nearly uniform press plaudits. According to the *New York Times*, although the Tower controversy had raised "questions about the quality of [Bush's] judgment and his White House staff . . . the choice of Mr. Cheney begins to revive the expectation that George Bush knows how to run a government."[42] David S. Broder wrote that "the Cheney nomination demonstrates . . . that George Bush has quick recuperative powers and the ability to do well with his second efforts."[43] *U.S. News and World Report* concluded that "in subbing Dick Cheney for John Tower, George Bush showed he can bounce back after a big loss."[44]

The First Hundred Days

Ever since Franklin D. Roosevelt's famed first 100 days as president in 1933, journalists have used the hundred–days stage of each administration as a benchmark for evaluating the president's record. To be sure, such a time frame is a premature, even arbitrary benchmark for evaluating any presidency.

President Bush dismissed the concept of a hundred-days evaluation of his administration. He came to the presidency promising policy continuity, not radical change. When asked to evaluate his first 100 days' performance, Bush said "about the same as Martin Van Buren's. . . . He was not radically trying to change things, but then that's about where the parallel ends, because I don't know what he did in his first one hundred days."[45]

Journalists nonetheless looked at Bush's hundred days and found his leadership lacking Rooseveltian political acumen. Columnist Philip Geyelin summarized his colleagues' reviews of Bush's 100 days as follows: "He has no agenda, conveys no mission, reveals no core philosophy. . . . He is too ready to compromise, it is said, as if he is in a position to overwhelm a Congress controlled by Democrats."[46]

Kenneth T. Walsh wrote that "the capital culture, having adjusted to the bold certainties and predictable course of the Reagan era, seems mystified with Bush's goals and performance." Walsh referred to the president as "a work in progress"—that is, a man who, after three decades in public service, had not yet defined himself, his philosophy, or goals.

Bush's inclination in almost all matters of foreign affairs, and many domestic issues as well, is to deliberate. . . . Bush is somewhat unpredictable. So broad and eclectic are his contacts and so malleable is his belief system that no one can say for sure what will sway the president, which person will most galvanize his sentiments, what time of day is best to make an argument to him and when the magic moment of decision will arrive.[47]

David Gergen also offered an unflattering portrait of Bush's first 100 days:

the administration is mopping up old problems where they exist, gingerly reacting to new ones as they pop up but rarely looking over the horizon. At a time of enormous ferment, observers here and abroad can't figure out what kind of world Bush wants and how he plans to get there. The administration is complacent where it should be urgent, shortsighted where it should be long-headed.[48]

R. W. Apple, Jr., assessed that Bush had adopted a "less dramatic" leadership approach than that associated with FDR's famed 100 days. Furthermore, by "lowering partisan temperatures, and finding ways around vexatious issues" Bush had surrendered "at least some political momentum to the Democrats on Capitol Hill."[49]

During the first weeks of the Bush presidency, journalists had developed generally negative perceptions of the man's leadership acumen. According to the prevailing journalistic profile, Bush lacked a leadership vision, did not aspire to activist government, and had not made a substantial enough break from the Reagan years, except symbolically. On a number of policy issues, journalists portrayed Bush's leadership as overly cautious, lacking innovation or inspiration. Let's turn to press assessments of Bush's leadership on some leading domestic and foreign policy issues.

DOMESTIC POLICY

On the home front, in 1989 the issues of drug abuse, air quality, and the state of the economy/budget crisis dominated the government's agenda. Bush identified the first two issues as among his domestic priorities. Economic conditions and public concern over the budget deficit required him to focus on those problems as well.

The War on Drugs

During the 1988 presidential campaign, Bush had given a great deal of emphasis to his pledge to solve the nation's drug problem. In a campaign context, such rhetoric is understandable. No candidate for public office can afford to ignore that issue or not sound tough enough in offering solutions. As a candidate, Bush frequently boasted that if he were elected, drug dealers would be captured and dealt with harshly. "Drug dealers," he intoned, "you're history."

Bush surprised many political observers by continuing to emphasize this issue once elected because the drug crisis appears to be intractable, and there is no national consensus on how to deal with the problem. Nonetheless, Bush appointed the controversial William Bennett to the newly created post of "drug czar" and devoted his first nationally televised presidential address to the drug problem. Bush also proposed to Congress a program of law enforcement, prison building, drug abuse treatment, increased border patrols, and international aid.

Despite these actions, journalists characterized Bush's efforts as too incremental and even "cheap." One week after the presidential inauguration, A. M. Rosenthal criticized Bush for failing to immediately commit large sums of federal monies to fight drug abuse through education programs and increased border patrols.[50] In June, Rosenthal complained that Bush had done "nothing" to fight the national drug scourge.[51]

On September 5, the president made his nationally televised address on the drug problem. Bush offered stern rhetoric about the extent of the problem and the need for action. In a memorable moment, he displayed a small envelope of "crack" cocaine and said, "it's as innocent looking as candy, but it is turning our cities into battle zones, and it is murdering our children."

Press commentaries focused on Bush's proposal to commit $7.9 billion of federal aid to fight the drug problem. According to the journalists, Bush had proposed to fight the war on drugs on the cheap. From that perspective,

Bush had failed to show true vision by not proposing a more massive spending program.

Robert M. Morgenthau analyzed Bush's budgetary proposal and concluded that the president could not win the drug war without a larger commitment of federal funds.[52] Tom Morganthau wrote that "they are trying to fight the war against drugs on the cheap." Morganthau noted that Bush's plan called for the use of federal matching dollars at a time when states and localities had their own budgetary problems. "Even worse, the total amount of federal aid under the Bush-Bennett plan is nowhere close to the amount the cities need to clean up the crack trade."[53]

Newsweek also called Bush's plan "a war on the cheap" and compared that plan to other federal budgetary priorities. For example, Bush proposed $1.6 billion for border patrols. The Stealth bomber program alone cost $1.8 billion. Bush proposed $1.6 billion for federal prisons, $300 million less than what California spent on its prisons. *Newsweek* made similarly unflattering comparisons regarding Bush's proposals for law enforcement, treatment, and international aid.[54] A *Time* report agreed that Bush's "much trumpeted war against drugs was more an underfinanced skirmish."[55]

The *New York Times* agreed that "the price tag is all-important." The editorial placed responsibility for what the *Times* considered inadequate spending on the drug problem on Bush's no-new-taxes pledge.

Lamentably, having pointed in the right direction, Mr. Bush offers a program that would bring progress measured in inches. . . . His words say nothing is more important. His actions say that in fact, he considers something else more important: his stubborn promise not to raise taxes. . . . Until he puts fighting illegal drugs ahead of reading his lips, his call to arms sounds more like a whisper.[56]

Congress added $900 million to Bush's proposal. Consequently, the program nearly doubled federal spending on drug programs. Journalists nonetheless did not credit the Bush program as visionary or even far-reaching. Bush's efforts on this issue reinforced, rather than called into question, the press image of him as a president lacking leadership vision.

Clean Air

During the 1988 campaign, Bush promised that, if elected, he would be the "environmental president." Critics lambasted Bush for making such a pleasing pledge without offering enough specifics on how to improve the environment.

Bush's critics had some cause to question the sincerity of his pledge. During the Reagan–Bush administration, environmentalists criticized the federal government for failing to take action to resolve pollution problems. The administration's lack of vigorous enforcement of environmental regulations especially angered many critics. The nation's leading environmental law, the Clean Air Act of 1970, was due for renewal in 1981. The administration and Congress failed to renew the act and instead kept it in effect through the use of continuing resolutions.

Bush broke the political logjam on clean air policy in 1989 by working to renew the Clean Air Act. In June he offered what a *Time* report called a "political tour de force"—an environmental plan that had substantial support from both environmental and business groups. Bush's plan called for federal regulations to reduce urban smog, toxic air pollution, and acid rain. *Time* lauded Bush's proposal for a fleet of alternative fuel cars as his "most visionary" proposal. The article criticized the Bush plan for not going far enough to control automobile emissions through gas tax increases and tough emissions controls. Nonetheless, the article concluded that "Bush has given another reason to hope that what appeared to be the administration's early drift and indecision was really only a matter of a new president taking his time."[57]

Editorials in the *New York Times* and the *Washington Post* reflected similar viewpoints. The *Times* characterized Bush's plan as not far-reaching enough, yet a positive departure from the environmental indifference of the Reagan administration.[58] The *Post*, too, emphasized some of the plan's "shortcomings" but praised Bush for taking the initiative to renew the Clean Air Act.[59] *Time* magazine, despite the praise its earlier story gave to Bush's plan, cited his efforts as an example of "government by symbolism." This story criticized the automobile emissions proposal as nothing new, "adapted from California's strict limits for the 1990's."[60]

After months of legislative gridlock on the Bush proposals, Congress approved the renewal of the Clean Air Act in the fall of 1989. This program constituted Bush's major legislative achievement during his first year in office. For a significant change, Bush received some press plaudits for his leadership on the issue, though much of that praise was qualified with "but he didn't do enough" assessments. Overall, this policy accomplishment did little to change the basic press assessments of Bush's leadership.

Economy/Budget Deficit

Journalists gave Bush low marks for economic policy during his first year. Earlier I discussed the very negative responses to Bush's first address to Congress in February. As Walter Shapiro summarized the problem, "governance requires agonizing choices, and Bush, like his mentor Ronald Reagan, stoutly declined to confront them publicly. The president's program . . . is all gain and no pain, with scant need to explain the inherent contradictions." Furthermore, "instead of clear priorities, the president offered a clutter of programs, almost all marginal adjustments in the status quo."[61]

On April 14, Bush and the Democratic Congress achieved a budget compromise that offered little hope for federal deficit reduction. The *Washington Post* blasted the agreement for not controlling inflationary forces.[62] The *Post* also criticized the plan for not offering tax increases and real deficit reduction.[63] Hobart Rowen called the compromise a "fraud" because of its failure to seriously attack the deficit.[64]

In October, the president and Congress concluded a bipartisan final budget package that, again, offered no income tax increases and very weak budget deficit reduction. David S. Broder lamented this failure to get serious about the deficit. He largely blamed Bush's no-new-taxes pledge for the government's inability to enact serious deficit reduction.[65] George J. Church attributed the apparent lack of economic policy leadership to "now-nowism," the desire to gratify short-term needs.[66] Stanley W. Cloud wrote that "leadership is generally left to the president. Yet George Bush seems to have as much trouble as ever with 'the vision thing.' Handcuffed by his simplistic 'read my lips' campaign rhetoric against a tax increase as well as by his cautious personality, Bush too often appears self-satisfied and reactive."[67] Robert J. Samuelson offered the following evaluation:

Bush's proposals have often been motivated by the crudest sort of short-term political calculus: the desire to look good or appeal to selected constituencies. It's this triumph of showmanship over substance that leads me to give the administration's economic policies only a mediocre grade of "C."[68]

Other Issues

Several other policy issues received press attention in 1989. Most prominently, the president held an education summit with the nation's governors in the fall in Charlottesville, Virginia. During the 1988 campaign, Bush promised that he would be the "education president," focusing attention on the need to improve national educational standards and performance. The education summit highlighted Bush's commitment to his campaign promise.

Bush received a good deal of press criticism for not following up on his campaign promise with a proposal for vastly expanded, expensive federal education programs. A *Time* story called Bush's budgetary proposal for education a "paltry" sum, evidence that he really was not serious about being an "education president."[69] Stanley W. Cloud noted that "the president's recent 'education summit' with the nation's governors produced some interesting ideas about national standards but little about how to pay the costs of helping public schools meet them."[70] George F. Will wrote that "the 'education president' proposes an education initiative costing 1/800th of the cost of the manned flight to Mars that he blithely endorses. No one bats an eye, because no one really believes that anyone means much of anything said about anything."[71]

Because Bush did not project a strong ideological commitment to certain ideas and policies, journalists often questioned the genuineness of his convictions. On a number of issues, journalists suggested that Bush adopted positions out of political convenience. In Will's sarcastic phrase, "the symbol of this administration should be a wetted finger held up to the breezes."[72] To cite just a few examples, Bush favored a constitutional amendment to prohibit flag burning as a way to overturn a Supreme Court decision giving free speech protection to such a form of protest. The *Washington Post* suggested that Bush had adopted this controversial position to mollify conservatives, so that he wouldn't have to yield to them on "more substantive issues." The *Post* opined, "the tragedy is that George Bush knows better, or so we continue to think."[73] Bush opposed abortion rights, even in cases of rape and incest. He also opposed policies to restrict the sale of automatic assault rifles over the counter. A. M. Rosenthal argued that Bush really didn't believe such things. According to Rosenthal, the president adopted these positions merely for political, not policy, reasons.[74]

Journalists frequently criticized Bush's emphases on volunteerism and charity as means to solve public problems. Although many journalists acknowledged that Bush's call for a more public-spirited citizenry moved him away from the worst image of the Reagan years—the so-called era of greed—they maintained that solving problems required activist government. Mary McGrory wrote that "all the individual good will and energy cannot lay the foundations and raise the roofs to bring the homeless in from the cold. Only massive spending is called for there."[75]

A frustrated White House press secretary, Marlin Fitzwater, complained about the press criticism of Bush for not proposing massive spending programs. "You liberal writers are just like the Democrats in Congress. You think government isn't doing anything unless it's taxing and spending and creating new bureaucracies."[76]

Time reporter Stanley W. Cloud responded somewhat defensively to this argument. He called Bush's leadership approach "fundamentally flawed" and retorted that government must be the vehicle for solving national problems.

Of course, the government must do something. That is why it exists: to act in ways that improve the lives of its citizens and their security in the world. The list of missed opportunities and ignored challenges is already much too long. The sooner government sets about doing its job again, the better.[77]

FOREIGN POLICY

During his presidency, Bush received the most press plaudits for his foreign policy leadership. Nonetheless, a favorable view of Bush's foreign policy leadership did not emerge until the end of the year, after the well-received Malta summit with Soviet leader Mikhail Gorbachev.

The press perceptions of Bush's foreign policy leadership in 1989 largely reflected the view that the president acted too cautiously in the face of unprecedented international upheavals. With totalitarian regimes in Poland, China, and the Soviet Union under pressure to reform, journalists could not accept what R. W. Apple, Jr., called Bush's "plodding, almost timid foreign policy style." Apple wrote that Bush's "aversion to initiative is earning him mostly brickbats." Apple pointed out that the president's qualities of "caution and moderation" were better suited to "normal times," but not 1989.[78]

It is not possible to detail all of Bush's many foreign affairs activities in 1989. Consequently, I shall focus on press coverage in three major areas: Soviet Union/Eastern Europe, U.S.–Chinese relations, U.S. policy toward Panama.

Soviet Union/Eastern Europe

President Bush liked to refer to his foreign policy as "status quo–plus"— that is, no dramatic change from the Reagan years plus cautious alterations in policy to accommodate changing circumstances. Throughout 1989, circumstances in East–West relations had changed dramatically. For the most part, journalists perceived Bush as moving too slowly to take advantage of unprecedented changes in East–West relations.

In brief, Soviet leader Gorbachev demonstrated quite a flair for the dramatic that year. He embarked upon a series of important domestic and foreign policy reforms. Under his leadership, the Soviet Union held elections, withdrew its forces from Afghanistan, withdrew some troops from Eastern Europe, and made cuts in its short-range nuclear forces (SNF). The Soviet leader's popularity grew in Western European countries, putting the U.S. president under some pressure to accept Gorbachev as a new kind of Soviet leader and negotiate with him for further weapons reductions. As Gorbachev and his foreign minister Eduard Shevardnadze traveled throughout Europe promising *perestroika* and an end to East–West ideological conflict, the Bush administration expressed skepticism about the Soviet leadership's motives and emphasized the need for caution. The Soviet leadership initiatives left the United States and its NATO allies arguing over how to deal with such sudden changes. West German leader Helmut Kohl angered the Bush administration by openly calling on the superpowers to negotiate reductions in short-range nuclear missiles.

Throughout the first four months of the year, journalists lambasted Bush for failing to meet the challenges of revolutionary times. A *Newsweek* story commented that "so far Bush has offered no vision to match the Soviet leader's." The story concluded that "change is coming to Europe; the question is whether Bush will lead it or follow it."[79] Stephen S. Rosenfeld asked, "what is it about George Bush that keeps him from assuming the statesman's role that beckons to him?"[80] Richard Cohen answered that "the Bush administration has spent so much time reevaluating Soviet-American relations that it has become unhinged."[81] Lou Cannon expressed the same view:

Instead of plunging ahead with negotiations . . . Bush opted for the delaying tactic of a policy review, behaving the way new presidents do when replacing someone from the opposing party with different views. . . . The only discernible element of consistency is Bush's preference for reacting to events. This is in notable contrast to the risk-taking Reagan, who was sometimes naive but had a strong sense of mission and of what he wanted to accomplish. . . . [Bush] does not want to go too fast, too far with Gorbachev, and his natural reluctance to take any initiative has left him vulnerable to the initiatives of others.[82]

Stephen S. Rosenfeld added that, in light of Gorbachev's initiatives, "Bush is going to have to demonstrate an awareness of the broad sweep of global change. He must have a compass, and he must show he has a compass." Rosenfeld lamented the "American failure so far to articulate a convincing sense of the new world that almost everyone sees taking shape around them."[83] The *New York Times* criticized Bush's lack of "vision" in East–West relations. "What of the costs of the present do-nothing policy? Mr. Bush and his key advisers are moderates. For most situations, that's a virtue. . . . Their very moderation tends to blind them to the vast changes unfolding around the world, and to the power of language and bold goals."[84] Mary McGrory wrote that "President Bush's judgment is seriously impaired by Mikhail Gorbachev." She lambasted Bush's "incredibly small-minded foreign policy."[85] A *Time* news story added that "faced with a political upheaval in the Soviet Union and its spillover in Europe, Bush seems almost recklessly timid, unwilling to respond with the imagination and articulation that the situation requires."[86] A *U.S. News and World Report* story described Bush's policy toward the Soviets as "stand-pat-diplomacy," "cautious," and, given the context of Gorbachev's major initiatives, more conservative than the policies of the Reagan era. The article further noted Bush's "image of indecision" and "absence of a strategic design" with which to confront Soviet initiatives. "History is not kind to presidents who do not lead," the article warned.[87] Charles Krauthammer summarized all of the press criticism of Bush as follows:

Today's conventional wisdom, repeated daily by the nation's herd of independent minds, is that the administration has been timid, slow, entirely inadequate in responding to the Gorbachev challenge. The cry, left, right and center, is for a foreign policy of boldness and vision. . . . The charge is timidity. Bush is not advancing bold and decisive enough negotiating positions.[88]

Bush received somewhat better press reviews when he changed course by late May. Although Bush had consistently resisted Soviet proposals to eliminate short-range nuclear missiles and had instead proposed deployment of new-generation *Lance* missiles, he changed course just prior to the June NATO summit in Brussels. Bush announced prior to that summit his support for a major disarmament plan, including a reduction of U.S. forces in Europe by 30,000 men. At the summit, Bush presented to Western leaders a plan to reduce short-range nuclear forces. News commentaries both praised Bush's initiative and suggested that he had to be moved to take such action by outside criticism.

Thomas L. Friedman praised Bush's "dazzling initiatives at the NATO summit" which had "won praise from even some of his harshest critics for the boldness of his initiatives." Friedman expressed concern that Bush had produced the initiatives "hastily" and in reaction to criticism "for having no clear-cut idea for how to respond to the thaw in the cold war."[89] Leslie H. Gelb, too, praised Bush's "dashing, concrete proposal." According to Gelb, Bush "was widely and justly criticized for the lack of courage, vision and content in his policy for NATO and East–West relations. Now he has returned as a conquering hero, a world statesman."[90] Richard Cohen also suggested that Bush had responded to "an accretion of criticism in the press and, more significantly, from European leaders."

> He is the worst of play makers, the best of broken field runners—a man almost totally of the moment. . . . Triumphant, he stands where few predicted he would—in the end zone. Whether he got there by executing a plan or simply by running from his critics is, while troubling, at the moment beside the point. Either way, he's a winner.[91]

Stephen S. Rosenfeld praised Bush's change in policy and commitment to a positive relationship with Gorbachev.[92] Tom Wicker commended Bush for a dramatic leadership gesture that calmed the fears among Western leaders that the United States had lost the initiative in international affairs.[93] Dan Goodgame wrote that Bush could claim some credit for the "remarkable progress on balancing Soviet and Western conventional forces."[94]

The constant, earlier press criticism of Bush's Soviet policies reflected a strong journalistic preference for activist over cautious foreign policy making. When Gorbachev demonstrated a penchant for drama and bold policy proposals, journalists criticized Bush for not doing the same. When Bush finally revealed a set of sweeping U.S.–Soviet policy proposals, journalists suggested that he had done so only in response to criticism.

Yet in preparation of the NATO summit, the Bush administration had been engaged in a series of negotiations, as well as a lengthy study of the issues, which led to the U.S. policy proposals. Bush and Secretary of State James Baker preferred quiet diplomatic maneuvering to international grandstanding and consequently sacrificed their short-term press image for more substantive achievements.

Nonetheless, journalists had framed an image of Bush as too cautious for his own good and only willing to act when pushed to do so. This image of cautious and reactive leadership reflected a view of Bush that the administration subsequently could not change.

In mid-July, the president traveled to France, Poland, and Hungary. In Paris he met with European leaders for what many observers termed the "green summit." The international leaders negotiated agreements on various environmental issues. Bush then made largely symbolic trips to Poland and Hungary to encourage the furtherance of democratic reforms. Bush pledged some U.S. financial aid to those countries, although many press commentators criticized the pledges as not substantial enough to help the Polish and Hungarian economies.[95] Bush received more favorable press note for the symbolic importance of the meetings and the gesture of U.S. support for democratic reforms in Eastern Europe.[96]

The most important meeting of foreign leaders in 1989 occurred December 2 and 3 in Malta, as President Bush and Soviet leader Gorbachev held their first summit. During that meeting, the superpower leaders discussed troop cuts in Europe and the futures of Eastern European nations. Bush then flew to Brussels to brief NATO country leaders about the results of the superpower summit in Malta.

Prior to the summit, a number of journalistic accounts speculated about how Bush would display his leadership in Gorbachev's company. The Bush White House went to great lengths to downplay the significance of the summit, to lower expectations of some major accomplishments. Without a clearly articulated, well-advertised U.S. agenda leading up to the summit, journalists again raised critical points about Bush's cautious leadership and lack of foreign policy vision.

For example, the *New York Times* asked whether Bush had called the summit for symbolic reasons—"a photo opportunity summit." According to the *Times*, "Mr. Bush has been slow to deal with the momentous transformations now under way in the East. His cautious policy . . . created widespread doubts about Mr. Bush's leadership."[97] Kenneth T. Walsh assessed that "the whole Malta summit is a microcosm of the Bush presidency: It is tailored largely for domestic politics and inspired by the president's belief that good intentions and personal diplomacy matter more than a carefully prepared agenda."[98] According to Strobe Talbott, "for Bush . . . slow is better than fast and standing pat is often the safest posture."[99] David Broder added that Bush "appears most of the time to be a cautious, plodding, rather unimaginative fellow."[100] George J. Church concluded that

"the vision thing" has never been George Bush's forte. So far, his administration has shown no inclination to do anything except stand on the sidelines and cheer. . . .

Bush is doing only tactical planning, concentrating on getting through the summit without a major substantive mistake or public relations flop.[101]

Washington Post White House correspondent David Hoffman offered the following assessments of Bush. Taken together, these assessments summarize the prevailing press portrait of Bush just prior to the Malta summit.

- Bush [is] down to earth, interested in "what works," but bored by the abstract or theoretical.
- Bush is reactive, but also intensely competitive; he prefers to conciliate but will return fire if pushed to the wall.
- Bush is the most adaptable of American politicians. He may not be a visionary man himself, but he is little burdened by rigid ideology.
- Bush is not an original thinker, but he often responds to criticism and advice.
- Bush believes in evolutionary change. He is not a crusader and does not see himself as leading any kind of revolution.
- He may not possess the vision to chart an innovative response to the upheavals now rending the East, but he will bend to the new reality, in his own careful, cautious way.[102]

One upheaval that Bush did not respond to in dramatic fashion was the crumbling of the Berlin Wall in November. Press critics characterized Bush's response to that event as strangely unenthusiastic, given the enormous import of what had occurred.[103] Nonetheless, some commentators acknowledged that Bush had acted properly by not boastfully proclaiming U.S. victory in the cold war.[104] What credit could Bush possibly have accrued for dramatic events abroad over which he played little or no role?

At the December 2–3 Malta summit, Bush presented to Gorbachev a series of proposals that unsaid the charges that Bush was too cautious and unable to respond to new international realities. Bush proposed that the superpowers conclude the Strategic Arms Reduction Talks and sign an agreement to reduce conventional forces in Europe. He also proposed to help the Soviet economy by lifting trade barriers and granting most-favored-nation status to the Soviet Union in return for an easing of Soviet emigration laws. Bush and Gorbachev discussed their nations' future roles in Europe and the conditions for a reunited Germany. Most press commentaries gave due credit to Bush's initiatives.

Michael Duffy wrote in *Time* that Bush's "chummy session with Mikhail Gorbachev in Malta restored momentum to U.S.–Soviet relations and gave a boost to what Bush called his 'new thinking' about the changes in the communist world."[105] Hugh Sidey added that "the outcome reassured the world and seemed to enhance Bush's presidential stature."[106] Richard Lacayo concluded that "after months of taking criticism for dithering, the U.S. president has made it clear that he too intends to do business with

Mikhail Gorbachev."[107] A *Newsweek* story reported that "Bush has moved a long way from the suspicious, go-slow approach he favored toward the Soviet Union when he took office last January. . . . Bush's program is optimistic and ambitious, a blueprint for what he calls 'a new era.' "[108] John Barry similarly reported that Bush had "endured attacks on his reticent style" for several months. Barry praised Bush's "audacious" strategy for a reunited, democratic Europe.[109] R. W. Apple, Jr., reported that Bush had finally moved the United States beyond Reagan-era, stridently anti-Soviet policies to an era of possible superpower cooperation. In all, "the summit conference generated a sense of momentum, an intangible but important dynamic element, that the Soviet-American relationship had heretofore lacked."[110] The *Washington Post* praised the summit discussions as "a positive and necessary outcome" and supported Bush's willingness to assist Gorbachev's perestroika.[111] The *New York Times* declared that Bush had finally displayed the qualities of a leader.

Firmly and unambiguous, President Bush said on leaving the Malta summit talks what his administration has needed to say with one voice: "We stand on the threshold of a brand-new era of U.S.–Soviet relations." And finally, he demonstrated that he understands the new era's opportunities by sending three strong messages on the Soviet economy, arms control and regional conflicts. . . . Mr. Bush sent the most important message to the Soviet people: The U.S. stands ready to help make Mikhail Gorbachev's economic reforms work, and won't simply sit on the sidelines to gloat or cheer. . . . In the last few days, he's finally brought his leadership into focus.[112]

U.S.–Chinese Relations

A major test of Bush's foreign affairs leadership occurred on June 3–4 when the Chinese military killed hundreds of protesters taking part in a prodemocracy demonstration in Tiananmen Square. In 1974–1975 Bush served for thirteen months as the U.S. envoy to China. He had always maintained a special relationship with the Chinese government, and clearly he did not want to do anything that would undermine long-term United States–China policy.

Nonetheless, the severity of the Chinese government action against mostly young, idealistic students calling for democratic reforms could not be ignored. News coverage of protesters erecting U.S. symbols of liberty and peaceably standing down military tanks provided compelling and moving images to which Americans responded.

During the early stages of the protests, Bush did not offer any stirring rhetoric in defense of the prodemocracy movement. For not doing so, wrote David R. Gergen, "the president was peppered with attacks from the press and politicians for the low-key, cautious approach that has become his trademark." One of those attacks came from A. M. Rosenthal. "At a moment of passion in the story of democracy, [the administration] has been pale and thin." Gergen added that Bush "is almost embarrassed by eloquence and cannot easily give voice to the country's deepest emotions."[113] According to Evans and Novak, "Bush's belated response . . . reinforced the suspicion that there is a small place in the Bush presidency for dramatic initiatives and the imagination that fosters them. . . . [Bush] shows no sign of change."[114]

After the Tiananmen Square massacre Bush responded by condemning the action, suspending high diplomatic and military contacts with China, extending U.S. visas for Chinese citizens studying in the United States, and providing sanctuary for dissident couple Fang Lizhi and Li Shuxian. Bush received a good deal of editorial and commentary support for these actions. The *Washington Post* praised Bush's actions, which strongly expressed U.S. revulsion of the massacre yet maintained official ties with China.[115] A *Time* news story reported that Bush had responded "judiciously" to the events and concluded that Bush's commitment to maintain ties with China "makes sense."[116] Tom Wicker believed that, given long-term U.S. interests in China, Bush had "done about as much as he could in the wake of the awful events in Tiananmen Square."[117] Despite many pleas for "more dramatic steps," the *New York Times* declared that "the president is proceeding in a tough and sensible way." Furthermore,

Mr. Bush has indeed been cautious, as is his style. But in this case at least, principle and effectiveness have been well served. His administration has managed the difficult feat of at once signaling revulsion with present trends and openness to restoring close relations when appropriate. Washington's concern to reach out to future Chinese leaders is only reasonable in view of the advanced age of and broad opposition to, the hard-line junta. . . . Mr. Bush's course sends strong yet nuanced signals, making positive effects more likely.[118]

The Chinese government expressed outrage at Bush's extension of the Chinese students' U.S. visas. Members of Congress believed that Bush had not extended the time of the visas sufficiently. Consequently, Congress passed a bill in November to extend the students' visas for another four years. Bush vetoed the bill, declaring it an infringement on presidential discretionary power. The *Washington Post* lambasted Bush's veto as "a presidential *kowtow*" and expressed its pique at "an American president hastening to accommodate . . . people with blood on their hands up to their armpits."[119] The *Post* added that

it's a sorry spectacle. . . . Why Mr. Bush feels constrained to placate the Chinese six months after they committed the enormous crime of the massacre in Beijing is something that neither he nor anyone else has explained. . . . The Chinese government . . . said that if he signed the bill it would no longer let students come to

American universities—a silly and self-defeating threat. But Mr. Bush caved in. A pity.[120]

The Bush administration received more criticism when National Security Adviser Brent Scowcroft traveled to China as a U.S. emissary and met with government leaders. The *Post* called the U.S. decision to send an emissary to China a "surprise bow to the Chinese government. . . . The president should not be making placatory concessions to a repressive and blood-stained Chinese government."[121] George F. Will called Bush "a Pekingese curled around the ankles of China's tyrants."[122] Mary McGrory intoned, "murderous and unrepentant China is the Willie Horton of nations, and George Bush has just given it a furlough."[123] Haynes Johnson called it "astounding" that Bush would be "embracing a remorseless regime" that had committed such "brutal actions." He concluded that Bush "richly deserves" all of the press criticism for sending an emissary to China.[124] The *Wall Street Journal* rounded out the criticism.

Now, at the very moment when the world is witnessing this century's greatest flowering of democratic courage and hope, Mr. Bush boldly offers absolution to the year's leading anti-democratic miscreant. It has to go down as one of the great tin-ear exercises of our time.[125]

U.S. Policy toward Panama

The brutal Panamanian regime of General Manuel Antonio Noriega posed serious problems for Bush's foreign policy leadership. In May, Bush made clear his desire to see the Panamanian dictator removed from power. Noriega's many human rights violations and notorious international drug dealing had created an atmosphere in the United States in favor of inter-vention in Panama. Although the climate of U.S. opinion had given Bush leeway to take action against Noriega, the reality was that overthrowing the dictator would not be easy.

Bush initially adopted a number of actions to try to encourage Noriega's ouster from power. The president advocated that Panama's defense forces stage a coup d'etat. Bush negotiated with leaders of Latin American coun-tries to attain their support for possible U.S. intervention in Panama. The president dispatched 1,800 troops to Panama to protect U.S. citizens and send a message to the Panamanian dictator about U.S. resolve. Bush's actions won widespread approval. Philip Geyelin praised Bush's multifac-eted approach as a positive departure from previous U.S. policy toward Panama.[126] A *Newsweek* article praised the president's "boldness" in step-ping up pressure against Noriega.[127] R. W. Apple, Jr., wrote that "no one can accuse President Bush of timidity in his dealing with General Manuel Antonio Noriega." Bush had displayed U.S. resolve without "looking like the swaggering gringo imperialist who looms so large in the perfervid Latin imagination."[128]

In October, a government opposition group in the Panamanian military attempted a coup against Noriega. The attempt failed, and the U.S. press blamed the Bush administration for not sufficiently aiding the anti-Noriega forces. Once again, press critics decried Bush's "timid" leadership. A *Newsweek* headline declared "Amateur Hour" and a *U.S. News and World Report* headline described the Bush administration as "The Gang That Wouldn't Shoot." The *New York Times* called Bush's handling of the Panama crisis "a model of incompetence."[129] According to Brian Duffy of *U.S. News*, this event was "the administration's worst foreign-policy embarrassment." Bush had once again displayed a cautious leadership approach that had worked in some foreign policy areas but not in others. "But to lead, a president has to know when to shift gears and act."[130] C. S. Manegold wrote in *Newsweek* that the coup failure "was just the beginning of a crisis of credibility" for Bush, who had shown "an innate caution once again."[131] William Safire observed that, by failing to project U.S. power boldly, Bush had "invited derision from right and left." Richard Cohen and Mary McGrory lambasted Bush's lack of involvement in the coup.[132] Safire concluded that "this pulled punch, so reminiscent of the Carter era, may be a blessing in disguise if it helps the Bush administration separate prudence in policy from hesitancy in execution."[133]

In late December, Bush ordered a military invasion of Panama to overthrow Noriega. The U.S. military eventually captured the Panamanian dictator and brought him to the United States to stand charges on international drug trafficking. Bush's action was at variance with his image of a cautious and even indecisive leader. Paul A. Gigot declared that "by provoking George Bush into decisive action, the Panamanian rogue has taken us back to the future of the uses of American power and the responsibilities of power and the responsibilities of democracy."[134] Evans and Novak cited Bush's initiative as evidence that the president planned to develop an activist foreign policy backed up by the use of force to undermine repressive regimes.[135] Michel McQueen and David Shribman added the following view: "Beyond the foreign policy objectives, [the Panama] invasion provides President Bush with new political momentum, displaying him as decisive and tough and blunting criticism that his sense of prudence precludes bold action."[136]

A NOT READY FOR PRIME-TIME PRESIDENT

That journalists criticized the president for lacking a leadership vision and for not effectively exerting his power at home and abroad was serious enough. They also criticized him for not knowing how to use the media to promote his agenda. *Washington Post* "Outlook" section editor David Ignatius best expressed the problem in an aptly entitled essay, "Press Corps to Bush: Manipulate Us!"[137] Ignatius noted the irony that many journalists who had previously complained about Reagan-era media manipulation had been excoriating Bush for not knowing how to use the media. Ignatius quoted *Wall Street Journal* reporter Gerald F. Seib.

People who did stories about the cynical, manipulative Reagan presidency are now complaining about the unfocused, unpackaged Bush presidency. . . . It truly is a damned-if-you-do, damned-if-you-don't proposition. If you try to manipulate the press, you'll be accused of manipulation. If you don't, you'll be accused of incompetence.[138]

Charles Krauthammer agreed. He explained that "without a blush or a memory, the press is now on Bush's tail for poor Deaverism: no stage presence, weak backdrops, lousy scheduling."[139] Journalists take their cues about a president's leadership acumen from evidence of how he handles the media. Consequently, the failure to effectively manipulate the press becomes perceived as the inability to lead. From this vantage, because the media are so important to a president's success, a chief executive who gives boring speeches, doesn't work hard at staging events, and downplays public relations must not know how to lead.

Ann Devroy of the *Post* wrote that, unlike Reagan, Bush failed to focus his message and grab the public's attention. She noted "the scattershot style of the [Bush] presidency" characterized by "a jumble of public events, tumbling over and into each other with no apparent theme and little success in dominating the news."[140]

Tom Wicker chided Bush for failing "to speak as well as look like a president." Wicker described Bush as a poor communicator, one who "lapses into clichés, leaves sentences hanging . . . relies on, like, you know, the vernacular and slang." Furthermore, "could he not express himself at least in, like, maybe, you know, sixth- or seventh-grade English, rather than speaking as if he were Dan Quayle trying to explain the Holocaust?"[141] As a *New York Times* editorial explained, "articulation is not Mr. Bush's strong point."[142]

Charles Paul Freund identified common press criticisms of Bush: not speaking with a clear point of view, not using rhetoric for political gain, not appreciating the importance of a good line or catch phrase. Freund noted that although the Reagan standard made Bush look bad, too many journalists had "confused content with packaging."[143]

Bernard Weinraub pointed out that, in a cost-cutting measure, George Bush lowered the salaries of the White House speechwriters. "Now the speechwriters seem to be giving the president his money's worth. Hardly a memorable phrase or stirring refrain has passed the president's lips since 'kinder and gentler' last summer." Weinraub repeated the common press criticisms of Bush's rhetoric.

[Bush's] daily remarks, from ceremonial events and brief comments to major speeches, have generally been rambling and themeless. And they have been criticized widely and none too gently for spilling boredom and forgettable oratory across Washington like oil across Prince William Sound.[144]

Bush understood his limitations as a speechmaker. He did not make a prime-time address to the country until he had been in office more than seven months. He preferred informal discussions with journalists over prime-time news conferences. He did not hold a prime-time news conference until after he had been in office for more than five months. Despite these limitations, Bush maintained a high level of personal popularity among the public during his first year in office.[145] A *Time*/CNN poll in October gave Bush a 75 percent approval rating—the highest for any modern president at that stage of the term.[146]

The danger for Bush was that all of the press criticism—both of his leadership and of his handling of the press—would eventually define the man for the rest of the country as not up to the job of being president. As Richard Cohen warned, "a president who muddles his message and fails to build a constituency outside of Washington is soon going to be in trouble. Just ask Jimmy Carter."[147] Kenneth T. Walsh likewise summarized Bush's problem with public relations.

The Republican nightmare is that Bush will end up like Jimmy Carter, a leader who began, like Bush, with very high approval ratings, but whose popularity plummeted when he failed to communicate effectively with the public at crucial moments. Carter lost control of the agenda, and the media filled the vacuum by accentuating the negative.[148]

Bush's press image also suffered somewhat from certain presidential appointments. Press reports hinted that Chief of Staff John Sununu and Budget Director Richard Darman would cause serious problems for the administration's media relations given both men's reputations for being standoffish toward journalists. Reports noted that both men projected big egos and oftentimes arrogant demeanors—traits that made enemies of the people around them. These early reports foreshadowed the more serious and critical press commentary toward these two men later in Bush's term.[149]

Bush's vice presidential selection continued to generate negative press commentary. Nonetheless, Quayle benefited somewhat in press coverage from the common journalistic tendency to create news by identifying something "new" or different about some well-known event or person. After the trashing of Quayle by the press in 1988, it was inevitable that some news reports during the following year would suggest that the vice president had some admirable qualities after all. A good many reports commented somewhat favorably on Quayle's diplomatic travels, including a high-profile trip to Latin America to meet with heads of state, ambassadors, and other national leaders. A. M. Rosenthal praised a Quayle speech on the Middle East as "a lot more than some vice presidents managed to do during a whole administration." Some press reports hinted at the emergence of a new and improved Quayle image.[150] The most positive review came from Paul Gigot, who described the vice president as a major influence on administration policy and as a much more substantive leader than acknowledged by critics.[151]

None of this is to suggest that Quayle underwent a press rehabilitation in 1989. Despite some favorable reports, his image as a man ill-prepared to assume the presidency, if tragedy occurred, remained intact. Quayle's image remained a serious problem for Bush because journalists judge a president in part by the people chosen to serve in the administration.

CONCLUSION

By the end of Bush's first year in office, it had become clear that his leadership generally did not comport with widely held journalistic expectations. In David Broder's words, Bush was merely "a good manager" and "a status quo man." Yet "management is not leadership." Broder maintained that the times called for more creative leadership than Bush offered. "The situation cries out for a president capable of imagining and describing the shape of a new world order and defining America's role in it. Bush has yet to show that he can do that."[152]

A *U.S. News and World Report* article referred to Bush's first year leadership as "the year of living timorously." The article described Bush as "most comfortable as a paint-by-the-numbers leader, dependent on a moment-by-moment strategy that substitutes for a presidential agenda." Furthermore, Bush's leadership earned low marks because he "refused to get off to a running start, rejected the notion of a first hundred–days agenda and has gone out on a limb" for such causes as a capital gains tax cut and a ban on flag-burning.[153]

The *New York Times* recalled that Bush promised to be nothing more than "a competent, cautious steward with a slim agenda . . . [and] a prudent leader in placid times." Bush offered "no grand plan, just a sensible approach to governance." Unfortunately for Bush, the *Times* observed, the times had changed and demanded bolder leadership, "a transformation of American priorities." The *Times* editorial praised certain aspects of Bush's style; in particular, his openness with the media. But Bush had failed to demonstrate a penchant for major domestic policy initiatives. He was merely "a capable shepherd of the status quo."

The sound emanating from Washington is the sound of wind machines. The whirl is intended to make people think America is moving. The education summit . . . was all wind. The housing plan, ditto. The famous War on Drugs, mostly ditto. There's little new money, and no will to find any. . . . Mr. Bush doesn't shout charge! He whispers it.[154]

To summarize the journalists' reviews: in his first year in office, Bush had failed to use his honeymoon period to move forward major policy objectives. He adopted a limited unimaginative domestic policy agenda; could claim some significant achievements in foreign affairs, despite a too cautious response to dramatic developments abroad. He lacked a Reaganesque flair for speech and did not inspire people the way in which his predecessor did.

Bush's leadership approach did not initially bother the public as much as it bothered leading journalists. The president maintained very good public approval ratings throughout much of 1989. Nonetheless, the development of a negative presidential press image promised to become a serious leadership problem for Bush, as this image of the man as lacking vision and a bold policy agenda began to filter down to the public and undermine his ability to be effective.

NOTES

1. Robert L. Bartley, "Scripts for a New President," *Wall Street Journal*, January 20, 1989, p. A22.

2. "Inaugural Address," *Weekly Compilation of Presidential Documents*. Washington, D.C.: Government Printing Office, January 20, 1989.

3. Harrison Rainie, "His Moment Arrives," *U.S. News and World Report*, January 30, 1989, pp. 19–20.

4. "The Inaugural," *Washington Post*, January 21, 1989, p. A24.

5. Michael Kramer, "A New Breeze Is Blowing," *Time*, January 30, 1989, p. 17.

6. Jonathan Alter, "Bush Reaches Out," *Newsweek*, January 30, 1989, pp. 22, 24.

7. Ibid., pp. 24, 25–26.

8. "President Bush's Breeze of Decency," *New York Times*, January 21, 1989, p. 26; see also "Mr. Bush's Hand," *New York Times*, January 22, 1989, sec. 4, p. 24.

9. "Mr. Bush's Lights," *Wall Street Journal*, January 23, 1989, p. A14.

10. "The Bush Presidency," *Washington Post*, January 22, 1989, p. D6.

11. R. W. Apple, Jr., "Bush Offering a Special Mix: Ivy League and Pork Rinds," *Washington Post*, January 20, 1993, p. A11.

12. David R. Gergen, "George Bush's Balky Start," *U.S. News and World Report*, January 30, 1989, p. 34.

13. David Hoffman, "For Bush, the Baton At Last," *Washington Post*, January 20, 1989, p. F3.

14. George F. Will, "Bush Promises Rectitude, but Then What?" *Washington Post*, January 26, 1989, p. A25.

15. Charles Krauthammer, "No More Mr. Nice Guy—Please," *Washington Post*, January 27, 1989, p. A21.

16. Richard Cohen, "Why Have a Press Conference?" *Washington Post*, January 31, 1989, p. A17.

17. George Hackett, "The Frenetic President," *Newsweek*, February 6, 1989, p. 19.

18. David Gergen, "Bush Marching to His Own Beat," *U.S. News and World Report*, February, 20, 1989, p. 20.

19. See E. J. Dionne, Jr., "Waiting for the Resumption of Politics," *New York Times*, February 5, 1989, pp. E1, E3.

20. See R. W. Apple, Jr., "Bush Offering a Special Mix: Ivy League and Pork Rinds;" Russell Baker, "So Grand At The Game," *New York Times*, January 25, 1989, p. A23; David S. Broder, "Will This Easy Style Work?" *Washington Post*, February 1, 1989, p. A23; Charles Paul Freund, "Building Bush, Dismantling Reagan," *Washington Post*, January 31, 1989, p. A15; Charles Paul Freund, "Bush's Surprisingly Soft Images," *Washington Post*, January 24, 1989, p. A21; Charles Freund, "The Pitch to the People," *Washington Post*, January 10, 1989, p. A21; Mary McGrory, "When the Breeze Dies Down," *Washington Post*, January 24, 1989, p. A2; Gerald F. Seib and Michel McQueen, "Bush Sets the Tone for a New Administration, with Bipartisanship and Ethics as Its Bywords," *Wall Street Journal*, January 23, 1989, p. A16; Mark Shields, "Another Brief Honeymoon?" *Washington Post*, January 19, 1989, p. A27.

21. Tom Shales, "The Yawn of an Era," *Washington Post*, February 10, 1989, p. D1.

22. President Bush, televised address before joint session of Congress, February 9, 1989.

23. David S. Broder, "A 'Willie Horton' Budget," *Washington Post*, February 15, 1989, p. A25.

24. David R. Gergen, "Bush Marching to His Own Beat," *U.S. News and World Report*, February 20, 1989, pp. 20–23.

25. See, for example, "Mr. Bush's Bacon," *New York Times*, February 12, 1989, sec. 4, p. 22; Anthony Lewis, "The Empty Government," *New York Times*, February 23, 1989, p. A23; William Raspberry, "The Budget: Bush's Ploy . . . " *Washington Post*, February 16, 1989, p. A23; Hobart Rowen, " . . . And Darman's Package," *Washington Post*, February 16, 1989, p. A23; Tom Wicker, "No More Pretty Flowers," *New York Times*, February 14, 1989, p. A23.

26. "The Bush Priorities," *Wall Street Journal*, February 13, 1989, p. A14.

27. Mark J. Rozell, "Campaign Pledge Can Be a Tripwire," *Houston Post*, March 11, 1989, p. A29; Mark J. Rozell, "Remember Carter—Too Much Ethics Talk Breeds Trouble," *Los Angeles Herald-Examiner*, February 28, 1989, p. A15.

28. Haynes Johnson highly praised Bush's emphasis on ethics as an important departure from Reagan-era practices. See Haynes Johnson, "Strides Toward Higher Standards," *Washington Post*, February 3, 1989, p. A2. George F. Will blasted Bush's efforts as "moral exhibitionism." See George F. Will, "Wallowing in the Fine Print," *Newsweek*, February 27, 1989, p. 82. Two editorials praised Bush's efforts to reform ethics in government but qualified that Bush's efforts were not substantial enough. See "Mr. Bush's Ethics Plan: Big and Thin," *New York Times*, April 13, 1989, p. A26; "The President's Ethics Proposals," *Washington Post*, April 14, 1989, p. A26.

29. See, for example, Jonathan Alter, "Washington Rules," *Newsweek*, February 20, 1989, pp. 16–18; Maureen Dowd, "Bush Finds Old Money Can Be Hard to

Handle," *New York Times*, February 19, 1989, sec. 4, p. 4; "The First Bush Ethics Mistake," *Washington Post*, February 8, 1989, p. A26; Mary McGrory, "No Snickering from the Hill," *Washington Post*, February 7, 1989, p. A2; William Safire, "Bush's Emperor of Ethics Is Wearing No Clothes," *New York Times*, February 6, 1989, p. A15. One editorial criticized the accusations about Gray's behavior as overblown. See "Gerth, Safire and Anonymous," *Wall Street Journal*, February 6, 1989, p. A8.

30. See, for example, Jonathan Alter, "Washington Rules"; Maureen Dowd, "Bush Finds Old Money Can Be Hard to Handle;" "An Odd Way to Raise Ethical Standards," *New York Times*, February 22, 1989, p. A26.

31. "The Credibility Gap That Keeps on Growing," *U.S. News and World Report*, February 13, 1989, p. 12.

32. See, for example, David Broder, "A President Undermines His Own Authority," *Washington Post*, March 8, 1989, p. A23; John Barry, "The Tower Soap Opera," *Newsweek*, February 13, 1989, p. 17; George J. Church, "Towering Troubles," *Time*, February 13, 1989, p. 36; Thomas M. DeFrank, "Bush Risks His Chips on Tower," *Newsweek*, February 20, 1989, p. 19; Rowland Evans and Robert Novak, "The Tower Scorecard," *Washington Post*, March 15, 1989, p. A23; Haynes Johnson, "Towering Blunders," *Washington Post*, March 3, 1989, p. A2; Richard Lacayo, "So Much for Bipartisanship," *Time*, March 13, 1989, pp. 20–21; Walter Shapiro, "Drawing the Line," *Time*, March 13, 1989, pp. 18–19.

The *Wall Street Journal* and William Safire harshly criticized the Democratic senators and others who opposed Tower for conducting a personal smear campaign. In defending Tower, the *Journal* and Safire drew attention to the various accusations. See "Chopping Down the President," *Wall Street Journal*, February 27, 1989; p. A10; "The Nunn Standard," *Wall Street Journal*, February 28, 1989. p. A22; "Nunn's Tower Play," *Wall Street Journal*, February 9, 1989, p. A22; "On Character Assassination," *Wall Street Journal*, March 6, 1989, p. A2; Paul Gigot, "What Evil Lurks in Bashing Tower? The Shadows Know," *Wall Street Journal*, February 10, 1989, p. A12; Peter R. Kann, "Making of the President, 1992," *Wall Street Journal*, March 14, 1989, p. A24; William Safire, "Towering Inferno," *New York Times*, February 13, 1989, p. A21.

33. See Maureen Dowd, "Bush's Fierce Loyalty Raises Debate on Whether It Hinders His Judgment," *New York Times*, March 10, 1989, p. B6; Michael Duffy, "Friendship Has Limits," *Time*, February 20, 1989, pp. 30–31; Mary McGrory, "Meanwhile, Back at the Ranch," *Washington Post*, February 28, 1989, p. A2; Tom Morganthau, "Tower's Troubles," *Newsweek*, March 6, 1989, pp. 16–22; Gerald F. Seib, "Personal Loyalty, Tactical Political Calculations Help Explain Bush's Dogged Support for Tower," *Wall Street Journal*, March 3, 1989, p. A14.

34. Richard Cohen, " . . . Or of His Own Indiscretion?" *Washington Post*, February 8, 1989, p. A27.

35. George J. Church, "Is This Goodbye?" *Time*, March 6, 1989, pp. 18–22.

36. See Dan Balz, "Bush Given Painful Lesson about Divided Government," *Washington Post*, March 10, 1989, pp. A1, A16; Gloria Borger, "In the Wake of the Tower Wars," *U.S. News and World Report*, March 13, 1989, pp. 44–46; Lou Cannon, "Danger Signals for the President," *Washington Post*, March 7, 1989, p. A25; Larry Martz, "Bush's Plea: 'A Lot Is Happening,'" *Newsweek*, March 20, 1989, pp. 26–28.

37. "For Democrats, the Price of Victory," *New York Times*, March 10, 1989, p. A32.

38. David S. Broder, "It's Showtime, George!" *Washington Post*, March 12, 1989, p. D1.

39. Gerald F. Seib and John J. Fialka, "Tower Fiasco Hurts Bush, but It Also Puts Congress on Defensive," *Wall Street Journal*, March 10, 1989, p. A1.

40. Lou Cannon, "Danger Signals for the President," *Washington Post*, March 7, 1989, p. A25.

41. Peter Milius, "Obits for the Administration," *Washington Post*, March 9, 1989, p. A25.

42. "After Tower: High Road and Low," *New York Times*, March 11, 1989, p. 26.

43. David S. Broder, "Good News Cheney." *Washington Post*, March 15, 1989, p. A23.

44. "Kick-starting the Presidency of George Bush," *U.S. News and World Report*, March 20, 1989, p. 10. See also Gerald F. Seib and John J. Fialka, "Selection of Well-liked Cheney for Defense Post Shows Bush's Wish to Put Tower Fight in the Past," *Wall Street Journal*, March 13, 1989, p. A16.

45. Quoted in Ann Devroy, "The First 100 Days, Now and Then," *Washington Post*, April 21, 1989, p. A25. During his first 100 days in office VanBuren presided over a national depression, the collapse of over 900 banks, and food riots in many cities. VanBuren subsequently lost his bid for reelection.

46. Philip Geyelin, "Bush Is No FDR," *Washington Post*, May 2, 1989, p. A15.

47. Kenneth T. Walsh, "Bush's First Quarter," *U.S. News and World Report*, May 1, 1989, pp. 24–25.

48. David R. Gergen, "Looking Back from 2000: What Exactly Did Bush Do?" *U.S. News and World Report*, May 1, 1989, pp.26–27.

49. R. W. Apple, Jr., "The Capital," *New York Times*, April 26, 1989, p. A24.

50. A. M. Rosenthal, "Will This Scourge End?" *New York Times*, January 27, 1989, p. A31.

51. A. M. Rosenthal, "Funny Way to Lead an Army," *New York Times*, June 2, 1989, p. A31.

52. Robert M. Morgenthau, "A Drug War, with Little Ammunition," *New York Times*, September 27, 1989, p. A29.

53. Tom Morganthau, "Now It's Bush's War," *Newsweek*, September 18, 1989, pp. 22–24.

54. "A War on the Cheap," *Newsweek*, September 18, 1989, p. 24.

55. Stanley W. Cloud, "The Can't Do Government," *Time*, October 23, 1989, p. 32.

56. "The President Whispers 'Charge!'" *New York Times*, September 7, 1989, p. A26.

57. Michael Duffy and Glenn Garelik, "Smell That Fresh Air!" *Time*, June 26, 1989, pp. 16–17. See also Gregg Easterbrook, "Clearing the Air: Bush's Plan," *Newsweek*, June 19, 1989, p. 34.

58. "The Air around the President," *New York Times*, June 2, 1989, p. A30; "Mr. Bush Clears the Air," *New York Times*, June 14, 1989, p. A26; "Perfection vs. Cleaner Air," *New York Times*, August 22, 1989, p. A22.

59. "The President's Clean Air Plan," *Washington Post*, June 13, 1989, p. A26; "White House Smog," *Washington Post*, October 13, 1989, p. A18.

60. Cloud, "The Can't Do Government," p. 31.

61. Walter Shapiro, "Reaganomics with a Human Face," *Time*, February 20, 1989, pp. 32–33.

62. "Inflation Again," *Washington Post*, April 19, 1989, p. A18.

63. "Brave Senate," *Washington Post*, May 5, 1989, p. A26.

64. Hobart Rowen, "Fraud in Budgeting," *Washington Post*, April 20, 1989, p. A19.

65. David S. Broder, "Bush's Political Life Preserver Is Sinking Us," *Washington Post*, October 25, 1989, p. A27.

66. George J. Church, "Bill Me Later," *Time*, October 9, 1989, pp. 22–23.

67. Cloud, "The Can't Do Government," p. 31.

68. Robert J. Samuelson, "The 'Maypo Complex,'" *Washington Post*, November 8, 1989, p. A23. See also Samuelson, "Inflation Won't Wait for Bush," *Washington Post*, February 22, 1989, p. A17.

69. Walter Shapiro, "Reaganomics with a Human Face," p. 33.

70. Stanley W. Cloud, "The Can't Do Government," p. 31.

71. George F. Will, "An Unserious Presidency," *Washington Post*, October 12, 1989, p. A23.

72. Ibid.

73. "The Flag War," *Washington Post*, June 29, 1989, p. A24.

74. A. M. Rosenthal, "How to Embarrass Americans," *New York Times*, October 24, 1989, p. A27. See also Tom Wicker, "A President Beholden," *New York Times*, November 21, 1989, p. A25.

75. Mary McGrory, "A Point of Light," *Washington Post*, June 27, 1989, p. A2.

76. Quoted in Stanley W. Cloud, "The Can't Do Government," p. 31.

77. Ibid., p. 32.

78. R. W. Apple, Jr., "The Capital," *New York Times*, May 24, 1989, p. B6. See also Hugh Sidey, "Is Bush Bold Enough?" *Time*, October 16, 1989, p. 28; Louise Lief, "A Shrinking American Role in the World," *U.S. News and World Report*, November 13, 1989, pp. 22, 24, 26.

79. Russell Watson, "Bush's First Foreign Crisis," *Newsweek*, May 8, 1989, pp. 16, 18. See also Kenneth Auchincloss, "The Postwar World Order Is Fading," *Newsweek*, May 8, 1989, p. 18.

80. Stephen S. Rosenfeld, "Drug-store Diplomacy," *Washington Post*, May 19, 1989, p. A27.

81. Richard Cohen, "The 'Nyet' Spirit in Washington," *Washington Post*, May 19, 1989, p. A27.

82. Lou Cannon, "Reagan Is Concerned about Bush's Indecision," *Washington Post*, May 6, 1989, p. A21.

83. Stephen S. Rosenfeld, "Is Bush Being Too Careful?" *Washington Post*, April 14, 1989, p. A27. See also John Barry, "After the Cold War," *Newsweek*, May 15, 1989, pp. 20–25; Anthony Lewis, "Missing the Big One," *New York Times*, April 23, 1989, sec. 4, p. 23.

84. "What East–West Policy?" *New York Times*, May 25, 1989, p. A26.

85. Mary McGrory, "Witlessness as Foreign Policy," *Washington Post*, May 18, 1989, p. A2.

86. George J. Church, "Do-Nothing Détente," *Time*, May 15, 1989, pp. 22–23.

87. Henry Trewhitt, "The Naysayer and New Détente," *U.S. News and World Report*, May 22, 1989, pp. 18–19. See also Steven V. Roberts, "Counterpunching Gorbachev," *U.S. News and World Report*, May 29, 1989, pp. 16–17.

88. Charles Krauthammer, "Why Play Gorbachev's Game?" *Washington Post*, May 19, 1989, p. A27. Krauthammer did not agree with the conventional press wisdom regarding Bush's policies. See also William Safire, "Bush's 'New Path,'" *New York Times*, May 15, 1989, p. A19.

89. Thomas L. Friedman, "How Bush Finally Got Foreign Policy Pizazz," *New York Times*, June 4, 1989, sec. 4, p. 2.

90. Leslie H. Gelb, "Mr. Bush's Leap toward Leadership," *New York Times*, June 4, 1989, sec. 4, p. 30.

91. Richard Cohen, "Crazy Legs Bush," *Washington Post*, June 1, 1989, p. A25.

92. Stephen S. Rosenfeld, "Bush: A Big Hit . . . ," *Washington Post*, June 2, 1989, p. A25.

93. Tom Wicker, "Now for the Hard Part," *New York Times*, June 2, 1989, p. A31.

94. Dan Goodgame, "A NATO Balancing Act," *Time*, June 5, 1989, p. 39.

95. See, for example, Walter Isaacson, "From Patrons to Partners," *Time*, July 24, 1989, p. 19; Larry Martz, "The Green Summit," *Newsweek*, July 24, 1989, pp. 13–14; Hugh Sidey, "High-wire Act," *Time*, July 24, 1989, p. 17. Numerous other commentaries criticized Bush for not taking stronger action in 1989 to promote noncommunist alternatives in Poland and Hungary. See "The Passive President," *New York Times*, September 17, 1989, sec. 4, p. 22; Jonathan Alter, "As the World Turns, Where's George?" *Newsweek*, September 4, 1989, p. 30; Cloud, "The Can't Do Government," p. 31; Richard Cohen, "Don't Ask Us—We're Broke," *Washington Post*, September 15, 1989, p. A31; Rowland Evans and Robert Novak, "Bush Fears to Seize the Moment for Poland," *Washington Post*, August 23, 1989, p. A27; Stephen S. Rosenfeld, "Kissinger's Path Or Brzezinski's?" *Washington Post*, April 21, 1989, p. A27.

96. See, for example, "Mr. Bush's Polish Question," *Washington Post*, July 9, 1989, p. B6; David S. Broder, "Playing a Subtle Hand," *Washington Post*, July 18, 1989, p. A23; Rowland Evans and Robert Novak, "Marshmallow Diplomacy," *Washington Post*, July 21, 1989, p. A21; Walter Goodman, "The President's European Tour," *New York Times*, July 17, 1989, p. C16; Walter Isaacson, "From Patrons to Partners," *Time*, July 24, 1989, p. 19; Martz, "The Green Summit," pp. 12–15; Hugh Sidey, "High-wire Act," pp. 16–18.

97. "The Summit: Just a Photo Op?" *New York Times*, November 1, 1989, p. A28.

98. Kenneth T. Walsh, "Gentlemen Prefer Bland," *U.S. News and World Report*, December 4, 1989, p. 21.

99. Strobe Talbott, "The Road to Malta," *Time*, December 4, 1989, p. 32.

100. David S. Broder, "Who Says George Bush Is Boring?" *Washington Post*, November 8, 1989, p. A23.

101. George J. Church, "In Search of Vision," *Time*, November 27, 1989, p. 20.

102. David Hoffman, "What the KGB Should Tell Gorby about Bush," *Washington Post*, November 19, 1989, pp. D1, D2.

103. See, for example, George J. Church, "In Search of Vision," pp. 20–23; Mary McGrory, "Berlin and Bush's Emotional Wall," *Washington Post*, November 14, 1989, p. A2; William Raspberry, "When Prudence Is the Boldest Stroke," *Washington Post*, November 15, 1989, p. A21.

104. See, for example, Haynes Johnson, "No Time for the Slows," *Washington Post*, November 17, 1989, p. A2; Strobe Talbott, "The Road to Malta," pp. 32, 37–38.

105. Michael Duffy, "Easier Said Than Done," *Time*, December 18, 1989, p. 36.

106. Hugh Sidey, "A Game of One-on-One," *Time*, December 18, 1989, p. 38.

107. Richard Lacayo, "Turning Visions into Reality," *Time*, December 11, 1989, p. 39.

108. Thomas M. DeFrank and Ann McDaniel, "Designing 'A New Era,'" *Newsweek*, December 18, 1989, p. 22.

109. John Barry, "A Design after All," *Newsweek*, December 11, 1989, p. 33.

110. R. W. Apple, Jr., "New Spur for a New Journey Together," *New York Times*, December 4, 1989, p. A1. See also Andrew Rosenthal, "At the Malta Meeting, West Met West, Too," *New York Times*, December 10, 1989, sec. 4, p. 2; Tom Wicker, "Plenty Of Credit," *New York Times*, December 5, 1989, p. A35.

111. "A Useful Meeting," *Washington Post*, December 4, 1989, p. A18.

112. "Mr. Bush, Talking Like a Leader," *New York Times*, December 5, 1989, p. A34. Two columnists diverged from the generally positive reviews of Bush's summit activity. See A. M. Rosenthal, "Life Support for Moscow," *New York Times*, December 5, 1989, p. A35; William Safire, "Doormat Diplomacy," *New York Times*, December 4, 1989, p. A23.

113. David R. Gergen, "A Cautious Man Plays China by the Book," *U.S. News and World Report*, June 5, 1989, p. 27. Rosenthal is quoted by Gergen.

114. Rowland Evans and Robert Novak, "Bush's Beijing Caution," *Washington Post*, May 24, 1989, p. A25.

115. "Signals to China," *Washington Post*, June 6, 1989, p. A22.

116. George J. Church, "Saving the Connection," *Time*, June 19, 1989, pp. 30–32.

117. Tom Wicker, "Darkness in China," *New York Times*, June 6, 1989, p. A31. See also Rowland Evans and Robert Novak, "China: Why Bush Hesitated," *Washington Post*, June 7, 1989, p. A21.

118. "Firm, Not Just Angry, toward China," *New York Times*, June 22, 1989, p. A22. Another *Times* editorial praised Bush's actions but expressed disappointment with his "half-hearted" efforts to rally public support behind this approach. See "On China: Right Words, No Music," *New York Times*, June 27, 1989, p. A22. Thomas L. Friedman similarly wrote that Bush's declarations "contained no poetry, no memorable language, nothing seems to have stuck in the public's mind." See his "Taking the Measure of a 'Measured Response,'" *New York Times*, July 2, 1989, sec. 4, p. 3. Richard Cohen also criticized Bush for not strongly enough declaring the China regime's actions "an outrage." See his "Bush Should Proclaim Our Revulsion to China," *Washington Post*, June 27, 1989, p. A23.

119. "Will Mr. Bush *Kowtow?*" *Washington Post*, November 30, 1989, p. A26. See also Mary McGrory, "Playing the Nixon Card," *Washington Post*, November 30, 1989, p. A2.

120. "On China: A *Kowtow*," *Washington Post*, December 3, 1989, p. C6.

121. "The China Mission," *Washington Post*, December 11, 1989, p. A14.

122. Quoted in Haynes Johnson, "China and Double Standards," *Washington Post*, December 15, 1989, p. A2.

123. Mary McGrory, "Patting the Dragon," *Washington Post*, December 12, 1989, p. A2.

124. Haynes Johnson, "China and Double Standards." See also Rowland Evans and Robert Novak, "Bush's Bow to Beijing," *Washington Post*, December 13, 1989, p. A25.

125. "Indecent Interval," *Wall Street Journal*, December 12, 1989, p. A20.

126. Phil Geyelin, "A Promising Panama Policy," *Washington Post*, May 16, 1989, p. A21.

127. Larry Martz, "A Test of Wills," *Newsweek*, May 22, 1989, p. 34.

128. R. W. Apple, Jr., "The Capital," *New York Times*, May 17, 1989, p. A24.

129. "On Panama: Luck and Incompetence," *New York Times*, October 8, 1989, sec. 4, p. 20.

130. Brian Duffy, "The Gang That Wouldn't Shoot," *U.S. News and World Report*, October 16, 1989, pp. 26–27.

131. C. S. Manegold, "Amateur Hour," *Newsweek*, October 16, 1989, p. 30.

132. Richard Cohen, "What Went Wrong? Almost Everything," *Washington Post*, October 10, 1989, p. A21. Mary McGrory, "Panama: Where Was George?" *Washington Post*, October 8, 1989, p. C1.

133. William Safire, "The Man with No Plan," *New York Times*, October 9, 1989, p. A17.

134. Paul A. Gigot, "Get Ready to Use Democracy's Gunboats Again," *Wall Street Journal*, December 22, 1989, p. A6.

135. Rowland Evans and Robert Novak, "Toughening Up," *Washington Post*, December 22, 1989, p. A19. See also Mary McGrory, "The Panamanian Intervention," *Washington Post*, December 21, 1989, p. A28.

136. Michel McQueen and David Shribman, "Bush Wins Praise for Ordering Panama Invasion," *Wall Street Journal*, December 21, 1989, p. A20.

137. David Ignatius, "Press Corps to Bush: Manipulate Us!" *Washington Post*, May 7, 1989, pp. B1, B4.

138. Ibid., p. B1.

139. Krauthammer, "Why Play Gorbachev's Game?" p. A27.

140. Ann Devroy, "For This President, the Medium Is Not the Message," *Washington Post*, April 30, 1989, p. A18.

141. Tom Wicker, "Like Too Bad, Yeah," *New York Times*, February 24, 1989, p. A33. See also "Ode to a Silver Foot: A Sampler of Bushspeak," *Newsweek*, May 29, 1989, p. 40.

142. "The Thing Thing," *New York Times*, June 28, 1989, p. A22.

143. Charles Paul Freund, "Bush Speeches: No Glitz, No Glory," *Washington Post*, March 28, 1989, p. A17.

144. Bernard Weinraub, "White House," *New York Times*, April 7, 1989, p. A14.

145. Laurence I. Barrett, "Giving the Public What It Wants," *Time*, October 23, 1989, p. 34.

146. Robin Toner, "Cracks Appear in Facade Of Bush's Rating in Poll," *New York Times*, December 4, 1989, p. A20.

147. Richard Cohen, "A Newspaper President," *Washington Post*, November 10, 1989, p. A27.

148. Kenneth T. Walsh, "The Not-Playing-for-Prime-Time Presidency," *U.S. News and World Report*, April 17, 1989, p. 23.

149. See Donald Baer, "The Trying Times of John Sununu," *U.S. News and World Report*, March 13, 1989, pp. 49–50; David R. Gergen, "Bush Marching to His

Own Beat," pp. 20–21; Ari L. Goldman, "Sununu Is Called Smart, Decisive and Impatient," *New York Times*, November 20, 1988, p. 28; William Safire, "Sununu's 'Different Template,'" *New York Times*, April 3, 1989, p. A23; Eleanor Clift, "Darman: The Collapse of a Grand Strategy," *Newsweek*, November 20, 1989, p. 54; Thomas M. DeFrank and Ann McDaniel, "Say Hello to Charmin' Darman," *Newsweek*, June 5, 1989, p. 24.

150. A summary of the somewhat favorable commentaries is contained in Mark J. Rozell, "Quayle Is Succeeding in His Quest for Respect," *Houston Post*, May 11, 1989, p. A37. See also George J. Church, "The Education of a Standby," *Time*, January 30, 1989, p. 27; Robert Pear, "Quayle Abroad: Cheers for the Right," *Wall Street Journal*, June 15, 1989, p. A3; Eloise Salholz, "Dan Quayle Hits the Road," *Newsweek*, February 13, 1989, p. 18.

151. Paul A. Gigot, "The Veep's Getting Better on the Job," *Wall Street Journal*, December 15, 1989, p. A14.

152. David S. Broder, "Being a Good Manager Isn't Enough," *Washington Post*, December 6, 1989, p. A29.

153. Gloria Borger, "The Year of Living Timorously," *U.S. News and World Report*, November 13, 1989, pp. 26–27.

154. "A Second Chance for Vision," *New York Times*, December 17, 1989, p. E20.

4

The Two George Bushes: Masterly Abroad, Ineffectual at Home (1990)

During Bush's second year in office, the press discovered that there were two different sides to the man: one was politically savvy, compelling, experienced, and effective. That was the foreign policy Bush. The other was directionless, uninspired, reactive, and ineffectual. That was the domestic policy Bush. The contrasting sides of George Bush became most evident later in the year when the president effectively put together an international coalition to defeat Iraqi aggression against Kuwait and when he agreed to an ill-advised budget deal that included the tax increases that he had pledged never to accept.

Timing. Journalists expected Bush to begin the new year with a better-defined, more active domestic policy agenda than he put forth in 1989. The State of the Union address offered the president the opportunity to renew his domestic policy agenda. Journalists assessed that Bush had failed to take advantage of the opportunity when he offered only marginal policy changes.

In international affairs, some said that Bush benefited from fortunate timing. Events abroad—especially the collapse of communism—made him look good. Bush did not "seize the moment," but he acted responsibly, cautiously, even prudently, to the major events of his time.

Symbolism/Rhetoric. Journalists continued to emphasize Bush's lack of eloquence. They criticized him for rejecting the public relations tasks that Ronald Reagan had so effectively used as president. *New York Times* reporter Maureen Dowd summarized the views of many.

What good is integrity if your failure to offer a coherent strategy and message hurts your ability to push your agenda and rends your party? What good is it to strip governing of public relations if it allows your opponents to paint you as a protector of the rich and a politician of convenience? . . . In the era of mass communications, is it smart to resist the notion—as President Bush does—that perception can quickly harden into reality?[1]

The press analyzed Bush's muddled syntax, some suggesting that it evidenced the man's lack of clear thought, others perceiving it as a part of his public charm. According to the latter view, citizens related to a president who spoke like them.[2] In any case, journalists assessed that Bush had failed to offer the kind of inspiring rhetoric that presidents need to rally the nation around a program or to suit the occasion of such a major event as the collapse of communism.

Agenda. In his State of the Union address, the president enunciated broad goals in such policy areas as education, transportation, the economy, housing. His budget proposal did not offer large spending increases in these areas. Consequently, journalists reported that he lacked a serious domestic policy agenda. He articulated worthy goals but did not want to put the full weight of the federal government behind achieving them.

Journalists harshly criticized his proposal to outlaw flag burning as a diversion from serious issues. They lambasted his veto of a civil rights bill as racially insensitive. They attributed Bush's agreement to raise taxes in return for a budget plan as evidence of his lack of policy convictions and willingness to negotiate away anything, if convenient at the time.

In foreign affairs, press reviews of Bush's leadership were somewhat less critical. Journalists did not credit him with having an innovative agenda, but they did generally praise his handling of international events and crises.

Policy Development. Journalists continued to criticize the president for lacking an effective strategy to promote policy change. According to the press view, Bush was content to be a status quo president. He failed to use the State of the Union address to rally the nation behind a forward-looking agenda. Throughout the year, he reacted to the initiatives of others rather than push forward his own programmatic vision. Journalists maintained that his veto strategy did not constitute real leadership. He merely negated the initiatives of others.

In foreign affairs, journalists credited Bush with admirable leadership acumen. Although critical of Bush's response to human rights abuses in China, they praised his military action in Panama, U.S.–Soviet summit initiative, and especially his efforts to create the international coalition against Iraq. Indeed, many reports marveled that Bush had displayed superb leadership acumen abroad but very little initiative at home.

Staff. With some conspicuous exceptions, journalists praised Bush's staff as competent, dedicated public servants. The leading exceptions were chief of staff John Sununu and OMB director Richard Darman, both of whom had reputations for being abrasive, arrogant, and sometimes devious. Both received blame—within and without the White House—for persuading Bush to negotiate a budget deal with congressional Democrats. For the most part, journalists agreed with *Newsweek*'s description of Bush's key advisers as "much like him—proven public servants with an aversion to flamboyance."[3]

Although the press gave high marks for professionalism to Bush's White House and Cabinet appointees, the media image of Vice President Quayle tarnished Bush's reputation. News accounts made much of the vice president's misstatements and inability to be taken seriously.[4] One report even castigated Bush for allegedly risking his safety by traveling abroad and closed, "the voters did not elect President Quayle."[5] A *Time* cover story on Quayle beamed, "No Joke: This Man Could Be Our Next President."[6] Despite all of the White House's best efforts, journalists still portrayed the vice president as a national joke.

EARLY EVALUATIONS/STATE OF THE UNION

Bush's foreign affairs actions during his first year in office earned some good press reviews. Nonetheless, reporters were quick to point out the contrast between Bush's international leadership and apparent lack of action at home. *Newsweek* reported that because of the Panama invasion and other foreign policy decisions, "suddenly Bush seems bold and decisive." Although Bush had shown himself to be "in charge," he had not changed from being a "reactive" rather than visionary leader.[7] Kenneth T. Walsh agreed that although in foreign policy Bush had "revealed a new capacity for audacity," the president still displayed in domestic affairs a "troubling lack of vision." Therefore, "as he begins his second year as president, Bush will need more boldness."[8] R. W. Apple, Jr., observed that Bush had become a "foreign-policy president." Apple asked, "will George Bush, in 1990, turn to the detailed domestic policies that he avoided in 1989?"[9] Mary McGrory added that although the Panama invasion "was a big hit," in domestic affairs there was "no-call to action," only "presidential passivity."[10] And George F. Will not only agreed with his colleagues but also panned the president's foreign affairs leadership. "An enthralled assessment of George Bush's first year as president is this: his campaign showed little promise, and he has kept his promise."[11]

The president used the occasion of the State of the Union address on January 31 to articulate a programmatic vision. He spoke about the need for action in such areas as education, health care, the economy, the environment, and housing. But journalists were quick to point out that the president had submitted a budget that failed to reflect a bold domestic agenda.

Michael Kramer wrote that Bush's message "could have been delivered by Lyndon Johnson." Kramer liked the president's Democrat-like bold policy pronouncements but disapproved of Bush's trim Republican-like budget.[12] Richard Cohen noted that Bush had articulated worthy goals but failed to back them up with a call for higher taxes. Hence, "his speech amounted to a wish list, an inadvertent admission that much needs to be done but that he can't do it."[13] The *New York Times* characterized Bush's address as "a lofty speech about domestic goals, full of oratory and lacking substance . . . bright shining goals . . . but few new programs, and little new money for reaching them."[14] The *Washington Post* concluded that Bush didn't have "any large new departures in mind for domestic politics."[15] George F. Will again took shots at the president. "The address, following the budget, further defined the Bush administration as a limousine without a transmission, nothing connecting motor (mind) with wheels (action)."[16] Finally, David R. Gergen noted the danger "that voters will decide there is too much of a gap between Bush's rhetoric and his reality." Gergen warned that "the Washington press is already on that trail."[17]

Other press criticisms of the speech focused on style. William Safire called the speech "unfocused" and "verbose."[18] *Washington Post* television critic Tom Shales cited the "blandness" of the speech and called Bush "a pretty dull president."[19] And Michael Kramer added that "no one will ever say of George Bush what someone once said of Winston Churchill, that 'he mobilized the English language and sent it into battle.' "[20] Mary McGrory wrote that "Bush communicates in a kind of fractured English that reassures the public that the Andover-Yale graduate has overcome his advantages in life."[21]

BUSH MEETS THE WORLD

In 1990, the press continued to credit Bush with leadership acumen in foreign affairs—a distinct contrast to the portrait of the man as lacking "vision" in domestic politics. Jim Hoagland summed up very well the press portrayal of Bush with the assessment that the president needed a prime minister: someone to handle the messy affairs of domestic politics while Bush was "out building the new international order."[22] Tom Wicker marveled that a president without a bold domestic agenda remained popular merely because of foreign policy achievements.[23]

Of course not all agreed that Bush deserved accolades for his foreign affairs leadership. Many criticized him for not capitalizing quickly enough on the end of the cold war and for not giving the "peace dividend"—money that would have been spent on defense—to domestic programs.[24] Bush called his cautious response to the close of the cold war "prudent." The *New York Times* differed. "Meanwhile, the nation wallows in Mr. Bush's prudence—and awaits his leadership."[25] Many suggested that Bush acted on problems abroad in order to avoid thorny domestic problems.[26]

The late 1989 Panama invasion and later the capture of Manuel Noriega gave Bush's reputation for foreign policy leadership a temporary boost. Philip Geyelin did not agree that Bush deserved the boost, but the columnist summarized his colleagues' assessments. "Presto, chango: No more Mr. Wimp. Rather, the pundits and pollsters tell us, from now on it's going to be Officer Bush, the world policeman who . . . pretty much wrapped up a second presidential term."[27] George J. Church indeed wrote that the Panama invasion marked a stage in Bush's "monumental transformation" from a cautious to a vigorous leader.[28] Eloise Salzholz enthused that "Bush can bask in the glow of a great victory."[29] The *New York Times* lauded Bush's success but also warned that his actions were only the beginning of a resolution to Panama's troubles.[30]

The press strongly rebuked Bush for his handling of United States–China policy. Against popular opinion, the president successfully vetoed legislation aimed at protecting Chinese students in the United States from deportation and extended China's trade privileges. A. M. Rosenthal blasted the president for "betrayal" of the democratic movement in China and for allegedly coddling a repressive regime.[31] Numerous of Rosenthal's colleagues agreed.[32] David S. Broder summarized Bush's dilemma. "I doubt anyone can explain to the American people why we cheered on the demonstrators in Gdansk and Dresden, Prague and Bucharest—but chose to toast the rulers who crushed the students in Beijing."[33] Nonetheless, Bush's policies prevailed earning him recognition for political effectiveness on an issue about which he felt strongly.[34]

Bush's caution earned him more favorable comments regarding U.S.–Soviet policy. To be sure, certain journalists argued that Bush responded too cautiously to major developments in the Soviet Union.[35] Some criticized his unwillingness to pressure Soviet leader Mikhail Gorbachev into supporting independence movements in the Baltic nations.[36] But most depicted Bush's leadership as effective under difficult circumstances.

Andrew Rosenthal described Bush's "innate caution" and "restraint" as unsettling to those who wanted bold presidential pronouncements and actions in U.S.–Soviet policy. Yet, "the evidence shows that Mr. Bush's brand of quiet diplomacy can pay off."[37] Margaret Warner noted that Bush "blows in the political wind on domestic issues" but maintains a steady compass in foreign affairs. Despite Bush's propensity for foreign policy secrecy, "his go-it-alone policies have brought success."[38] A *Time* news story assessed that "George Bush may lack Gorbachev's grand vision, but he and his advisers proved their mastery of creative diplomacy."[39] Even the *New York Times* praised Bush for being cautiously courageous in not speaking out in favor of the Lithuanian independence movement.[40]

Bush and Gorbachev staged a summit meeting in Washington, D.C., beginning on May 31. Because of domestic unrest, Gorbachev appeared politically vulnerable, though highly regarded in the U.S. media as the kind of visionary leader that Bush could never become.[41]

George J. Church wrote that Gorbachev was a "revolutionary" man. By contrast, "Bush is a cautious politician dedicated largely to making relatively minor adjustments in the status quo."[42] No major agreements on arms control or the Baltic states emerged from the summit. Yet a number of journalists reported favorably on Bush's performance. The *Washington Post* praised Bush's "personal grace" and "unprovocative but clear statement" of U.S. interests.[43] Flora Lewis added that the president "was firm but considerate, careful not to humiliate and to avoid gloating . . . focusing on substance instead of prestige or personality, an admirably presidential performance."[44] Anthony Lewis weighed in with an equally kind review of the president's summit diplomacy.[45]

In December, as the Soviet Union suffered from food and provisions shortages due to an unusually harsh winter, Bush lifted trade restrictions and offered $1 billion of food on official credit to the Kremlin. Journalists praised Bush's decision, none more so than Haynes Johnson: "It's to Bush's great credit that he is responding to the new relationship positively and imaginatively. His latest moves toward the Soviet Union reinforce a sense that, when it comes to foreign affairs, he is one of the most accomplished presidents in years."[46]

Operation Desert Shield

After the August 2, 1990, Iraqi invasion of Kuwait, Bush effectively forged an international coalition against the Iraqi government of Saddam Hussein. Bush secured economic sanctions against Iraq and then U.N. resolutions authorizing the use of military force to restore Kuwait's freedom. Even the Soviet Union joined the coalition after Bush convinced Saudi Arabia to give $1 billion aid to the Kremlin. The president's earlier overtures to the Chinese government ultimately aided his efforts to forge the international coalition.

Press coverage initially focused on Bush's diplomatic acumen. Haynes Johnson wrote that "Bush has performed with skill and sureness of purpose . . . [and] demonstrated presidential leadership of high order."[47] Stephen S. Rosenfeld opined that Bush had finally achieved a "grand new post-cold war 'vision.' "[48] David S. Broder added that "the speed and skill with which Bush has moved command nearly unanimous respect."[49] Jim Hoagland contrasted Bush's actions to those of Jimmy Carter early in the 1979–1980 Iran hostage crisis and concluded that "the Bush principle looks like a winner."[50] Richard Cohen praised "Bush's total mastery of the presidency in this crisis." He declared, "stand up and take a bow, Mr. President."[51] Carl Bernstein applauded "Bush's remarkable progress" in forging the coalition. Unlike in domestic affairs, Bernstein wrote, Bush showed that he could "take huge risks, make tough decisions, spend money quickly" to achieve the administration's goals.[52] Many others similarly praised Bush's actions, agreeing with Paul Gigot's assessment: "Toward Iraq, Mr. Bush has literally spoken softly but wielded a big stick. The "pastel president . . ." has acted in primary colors. . . . It's clear Washington still hasn't taken the measure of George Bush."[53]

On September 11, Bush addressed a joint session of Congress to announce his resolve to drive Iraq out of Kuwait. Bush proclaimed his willingness to use military force if diplomatic measures and economic sanctions failed to achieve his goal. An almost uniform press corps praised the president's televised address. R. W. Apple, Jr., wrote that "it was perhaps the hardest hitting and the best-delivered speech" of Bush's presidency.[54] The *New York Times* praised Bush's "right strategy" and "clear-eyed purpose." The president "did well in his address before the nation."[55] Bruce W. Nelan offered more praise.

No one, not even the president's most loyal supporters, would confuse a Bush speech and its delivery with a performance by Churchill. Last week, however, George Bush gave a speech—no, make that an oration—that riveted listeners and left absolutely no doubt he meant every word he uttered.[56]

The accolades continued to pour in. Russell Watson called Bush's international coalition building "a stunning diplomatic achievement."[57] Mortimer B. Zuckerman declared that "George Bush has looked great so far. His leadership in establishing consensus was a major diplomatic triumph."[58]

Yet many marveled at such leadership acumen from a president who appeared uncomfortable building domestic policy coalitions. A *Newsweek* story described Bush as a "bold world leader" who evoked "confidence" and as a "modest domestic problem solver" who lacked "passion."[59] Paul Gigot declared that Bush had a "split personality."

On foreign and domestic policy, Mr. Bush can seem like two different men. The one is decisive and cool under pressure. The other is detached and quick to give in. Foreign Bush can be stubborn about China, deft toward Europe and Mikhail Gorbachev, gutsy in taking out Manuel Noriega. Domestic Bush trades his tax pledge for nothing, treats Democratic leader George Mitchell as if he were Sam Rayburn, turns the other cheek to those who sandbagged John Tower.

According to Gigot, Bush had failed to recognize that leadership "starts before the water's edge."[60] Others echoed Gigot's sentiment.[61]

Bush's early diplomatic efforts and international economic sanctions did not force Iraq out of Kuwait. Consequently, the president had to make a convincing case for a continued and ultimately expanded U.S. military presence in the Persian Gulf. The trouble was, Bush had to make his pitch to different audiences—some domestic and some international—with different goals. As the crisis prolonged, he presented numerous objectives of the U.S. policy: restoring Kuwait's sovereignty, protecting the U.S. national interest, preserving U.S. economic interests, defeating a Hitler-like dictator, stopping international aggression.

By November, press coverage of Bush's handling of the crisis had changed from bouquets to brickbats. The *New York Times* editorialized that Bush had "vacillated in declaring his objectives" and failed to make "a solid case" for his Persian Gulf policies.[62] *Time* also reported that Bush had failed "to explain his goals clearly."[63] Mary McGrory declared that "incoherence is the theme of our Middle East policy."[64] According to *U.S. News and World Report*, "Bush's 'Skull and Bones' diplomacy is causing confusion and undermining his Gulf policy."[65] Charles Krauthammer agreed with the substance of Bush's actions but blamed the president for "the muddiness of the debate" over U.S. objectives.[66] George F. Will added that Bush's "incoherence is a substantive, not merely stylistic, defect."[67]

Some journalists expressed their reservations about the U.S. military getting involved in a deadly Middle East conflict.[68] Some suggested that Bush used the Middle East crisis to avoid thorny domestic issues.[69]

Bush insisted that his goals remained clear, his commitment to achieve them unchanged. In December he issued an ultimatum to the Iraqi government: leave Kuwait by January 15, 1991, or be forced to do so.

BUSH'S CHALLENGES AT HOME

On the domestic front, journalists continued to portray Bush as a reactive, do-nothing president. No proposal stirred such press contempt for Bush's apparent lack of a serious agenda than his call to amend the Bill of Rights to outlaw flag burning. The president expressed contempt for a Supreme Court decision that gave First Amendment protection to a form of protest that he considered reprehensible.

A *Time* headline best summarized the criticisms of Bush's actions: "Hiding in the Flag." The article said that "Washington has more important things to do than posture about Old Glory." Walter Isaacson lamented that, as budget agreements failed, scandals pervaded Washington, an environmental disaster hit the Texas coast, and "not one serious education reform" came out of Washington, the president decided to focus on flag burning.[70] Both the *Washington Post* and George F. Will charged the president with demagoguery over the flag issue.[71] Tom Wicker and others merely said that Bush was "playing politics with the Bill of Rights."[72]

On a host of domestic policy issues, journalists gave Bush's leadership low marks. His education initiatives "offered more symbols than dollars."[73] His housing initiative did not include enough funding for new public housing.[74] He lacked commitment to solving environmental problems.[75] He had "no domestic agenda," only "spare" legislative accomplishments, and was "a caretaker with no vision."[76] Finally, he failed the "fairness" test by refusing to offer expensive programs to help the needy while pursuing the goal of a capital gains tax cut.[77]

In October the Congress presented Bush with one of the most difficult dilemmas of his presidency by passing a new civil rights act. Bush maintained that he wanted to support a new civil rights law.[78] Because the bill placed the onus on employers to prove nondiscrimination in situations where few minorities had been hired, Bush declared it a "quota bill" and vetoed it. Congress upheld the veto by a one-vote margin. Numerous columns and editorials blasted the president's opposition to the bill as racially insensitive.[79] The *New York Times* alone weighed in with six editorials against Bush on this issue.[80] Anthony Lewis summed up the sentiments of many: "For the man with a sure sense of how to bring people together in foreign policy was unsure and unconvincing on this most delicate domestic issue, dividing instead of healing."[81]

The press did not respond so negatively to Bush's choice of conservative jurist David Souter to replace the retired William Brennan on the Supreme Court. At most, some journalists determined that Bush had purposefully chosen a relatively unknown, noncontroversial person over better-known, highly distinguished jurists to avoid a confirmation battle.[82] As Richard Lacayo maintained, "if there is anything George Bush dislikes more than eating broccoli, it is taking risks." Bush therefore selected a "stealth candidate."[83]

The Budget Fiasco

Despite all of the press criticism of Bush in 1988 for running a meaningless campaign, he did make one notably unequivocal pledge: "Read my lips. No new taxes." Bush wasn't comfortable with making such a pledge. By many accounts, he didn't believe in it, but he made the pledge anyway to help win the election.

Polls revealed that few believed that Bush would fulfill the pledge. It was just a matter of time when he decided to consider negotiating with Congress on tax increases.

Bush's break with the tax pledge occurred during the lengthy 1990 budget negotiations. It became clear that the government had to send a signal of seriousness about deficit reduction to the financial markets. Congressional Democrats forced the president to consider tax increases in return for budget cuts. In June, Bush signed a statement agreeing that "tax revenue increases" would be a part of the deficit reduction plan. A *New York Post* headline screamed: "READ MY LIPS—I LIED."[84] Headlines from inner-circle publications during the budget negotiations also told the story:

"Eating His Words"

"Lip Balm for Bush"

"He Moved His Lips and Said Nothing"

"Bush Moves His Lips But Not His Troops"

"Political Ineptitude"

"The President: Read His Slips"

"Bush Trips, Capital Reels"

"Read My Lips II: The Horror Continues"

"Bush League"

"Read Their Flips"

The contents of the articles were no less critical. A "flip flop," wrote George J. Church, and "a pledge [Bush] should never have made."[85] "Bush's retreat" from "a great political slogan . . . [that] proved a poor guideline for running the government," according to Steven V. Roberts.[86] Russell Baker called Bush's no-taxes pledge "malarkey."[87] The "wound" that Bush suffered from the broken tax pledge according to David R. Gergen, was "the worst of his presidency." Consequently, Bush "looked like just another politician who neither says what he means nor means what he says. Now he must act to restore both his presidency and the economy."[88] E. J. Dionne, Jr., asked "if a man can change his position on abortion and Reaganomics . . . why expect consistency on something so mundane as taxes?"[89]

In early October, the House of Representatives rejected the budget plan that the administration and Congress had been working on for months. Bush pressed on to get a budget agreement. In so doing, Bush conceded his bargaining positions to congressional Democrats, believing that an objectionable budget package was more responsible than none at all. By the end of the month, the president and Congress had agreed upon a deficit reduction package that included some tax increases and few real budget cuts. Congressional Democrats prevailed in getting Bush to accept their taxing and spending priorities.

Much of the press portrayed the budget negotiations as Bush's most conspicuous leadership failure. According to R. W. Apple, Jr., "by giving the impression that he could easily be pushed around . . . Bush revived talk of him as a political wimp, a description he seemed to have shaken two years ago." Consequently, "[Bush's] credibility trickled away in Washington."[90] George F. Will asked, "how can a president so popular be so powerless?"[91] Bush's tax policy reversal proved that he was "a flaming hypocrite," according to Richard Cohen.[92] Paul A. Gigot called Bush's performance one of the "defining moments" of his presidency. That is, Bush was defined as a president who "can be had."[93] A *Wall Street Journal* editorial summarized the implications of Bush's actions. "The president finds himself going into the midterm elections at war with his own party, giving up the issues that won him the presidency, and in fact sounding the themes of his opposition."[94]

Bush didn't help his own case. He failed to effectively communicate to the public that circumstances had changed from 1988, that he could not act unilaterally on budget policy but had to achieve the politically possible while working with an opposition party–led Congress. He never appeared to try to make a case for his actions. Then during his daily jog on October 11, the president responded to a query about the budget deal by pointing to his backside and yelling, "read my hips."[95] The embarrassing photograph along with a caption explaining Bush's dismissive retort appeared on newspaper front pages across the country. Bush continued to take a beating in the press.[96]

It's not that nobody believed that Bush had done the right thing. Economics columnist Hobart Rowen defended Bush's policy reversal as a move toward responsible leadership. The *New York Times* and the *Washington Post* also agreed that new taxes were needed.[97] But Bush never made the case that what he had done was both substantively correct and politically courageous. Congressional Democrats received credit for taking control of the budget agenda, and Bush looked like a feckless leader.

Bush's approval rating dropped from 67 percent in September to 54 percent in October. The Gallup poll also showed that only 29 percent of the public approved of Bush's handling of the economy.[98] A *Newsweek* cover screamed "Bush League." Regarding the budget deal, the news story noted that "Bush took no stand on principle and didn't seem to know what he wanted. . . . As in the bad old days, he looked goofy."[99]

Others raised the issue of whether Bush lacked core principles. Dan Goodgame concluded that "[Bush] has never had firm convictions on domestic issues. . . . Bush has always regarded domestic policy as 'deep doo-doo,' not to be stepped in if at all possible."[100] Richard Cohen too picked up the theme that Bush lacked a core of beliefs. "Neither a liberal nor a conservative—and sometimes not much of a moderate either—he is the darling of no constituency."[101] According to Tom Wicker, presidential leadership entails establishing a policy direction for the country. "Mr. Bush appeared, instead, to have no central conviction for which he was willing to fight . . . and to be more concerned about escaping blame than asserting leadership."[102] David Broder's article, "An Absence of Guiding Principle," agreed.

The president has revealed to the nation's voters that you can't have the courage of your convictions if you lack any convictions. . . . Bush has reached the White House without ever pausing to reflect on what principles or beliefs guide his approach to that inescapable domestic bargaining process. He not only appears to be rootless, he is rootless. He occupies a philosophical ground as ill-defined as his geographic home bases in Connecticut, Maine and Texas.[103]

The timing of this negative presidential coverage could hardly have been worse for Bush and the Republicans. Going into the 1990 midterm elections,

Bush had forfeited the GOP political advantage on the tax issue. Many Republican congressional candidates feared they would suffer the electoral consequences.

Symbols of Bush's political weakness abounded. An incumbent Republican Congressman, Representative Alfred McCandless (California), requested that his picture be taken with the president. McCandless used the picture in a campaign commercial as a prop to make the point that he stood up to Bush on the tax issue. Representative Peter Smith (Vermont) used a joint campaign appearance with Bush to lecture the president about taxes and other issues. One Republican senatorial candidate stood up the president at a campaign event. The cochair of the National Republican Congressional Committee, Ed Rollins, advised GOP congressional candidates to openly oppose the president. In Arizona, GOP leaders canceled a presidential campaign appearance because of the budget deal.

Bush nonetheless went on the campaign trail and used anti-Washington rhetoric to attack the Democrats. Journalists pointed out that a man who had spent his professional life as a public servant had no credibility when attacking the "inside-the-beltway crowd."[104] Richard Cohen called Bush a cynical politician, willing to say anything politically advantageous on the campaign trail and then ignore his rhetoric when governing. Cohen considered Bush "a politically hollow man . . . without ideology or commitment."[105] Other journalists agreed that Bush's campaign rhetoric evidenced a lack of philosophical convictions.[106]

Although many had predicted large-scale Republican defeats in the midterm elections, the Democrats picked up only one seat in the Senate and eight in the House. Nonetheless, Bush became the first president in over half a century to have lost party seats in Congress in both his own election year and in the midterm elections. Most of the congressional candidates for whom Bush campaigned lost their races.

The Democrats had seized the domestic policy agenda, Bush's popularity plummeted, and "the election results only worsened his problems," reported Steven V. Roberts. According to Roberts, it had become evident that Bush needed "to adopt a real domestic agenda and invigorate his staff."[107] Michael Duffy and Dan Goodgame reported that "for the first time in his presidency, Bush seemed vulnerable." The elections results showed that "the U.S. does not need more 1988–style partisanship. It needs more leadership."[108] David Gergen and Kenneth T. Walsh said the results and a new campaign strategy for 1992 "will force the White House to decide—as it never has before—what it is really trying to accomplish and why voters should eventually support another four years of GOP rule."

The Bush presidency . . . still has no underlying mission and therefore no message. . . . Why couldn't the president use a familiar refrain from other midterm elections, such as "Stay the Course" or "Let us continue"? For good reason: Stay what course? Continue what? No one can say, especially on domestic issues.[109]

BUSH AND PRESIDENTIAL LEADERSHIP

Several themes emerged in the 1990 press assessments of Bush's leadership. First, in foreign affairs, he had the benefit of good luck. Paul Taylor wrote that Bush had "the good fortune of being on duty when communism collapsed."[110] According to Mary McGrory, Bush had "been touched by magic." World events had merely made "him look good."[111] Second, Bush evidenced strong foreign policy skills. He had successfully devised "creative techniques for disparate situations" and his "'don't gloat'" response to communism's demise was the statesmanlike one.[112] In the diplomatic arena, he was "well-briefed, engaged and self-confident."[113] His success at putting together an international coalition to oppose Iraq was "remarkable."[114] Third, on the domestic front, Bush continued to show a lack of leadership vision. Press evaluations both before and after the budget agreement made that point.

Prior to the agreement, many noted a disconnect between presidential rhetoric and action in domestic affairs. According to Tom Wicker, Bush had not displayed "the political courage and the 'vision thing' to face the necessity for national action and national investment to meet national needs." Wicker strongly rebuked the president's efforts to shift the focus of domestic policy action from the federal government to the states.[115] Margaret Carlson called Bush's domestic agenda "long on rhetoric, short on dollars": "Like a teenager promising a night on the town without a dime in his pocket, the Bush administration is beginning to look a little silly issuing long reports outlining national problems without coming up with any funds for the solutions."[116]

Jack Anderson and Dale Van Atta wrote that "Bush behaves like a man whose only worry is maintaining the status quo. The president practiced management instead of leadership. Bush was a "'maintenance president'" and "the perfect president for a time in which nothing important is happening."[117] Richard Cohen asked "what does this man stand for?" Cohen concluded, "no question about it, when it comes to convictions, this man travels light."[118]

A number of journalists said that there really were "two George Bushes." As Mary McGrory determined, "in George Bush, the American people got two presidents for the price of one. . . . The foreign policy president is cool, measured, tough, coping. The domestic policy man is strident, petulant, self-pitying."[119] Kenneth T. Walsh added that "Bush seems increasingly a split personality. In international affairs, he is a bold Commander in Chief and effective diplomat. . . . On the domestic front, he is a reluctant warrior." Bush had "not dramatized or focused the nation's attention" on domestic programs. Walsh's report featured a summary of Bush's foreign and domestic policy attributes. In foreign policy: "a leader we don't have to train," "a leader in touch," "a power player." In domestic policy: "a man with a lot to learn," "the wanderer," "the vulnerable pragmatist."[120] Carl Bernstein agreed that Bush had been surefooted and commanding in foreign affairs, "low profile, low risk and largely ineffectual" in domestic affairs.[121]

Even on the domestic front, Bush displayed two different sides: one "kinder and gentler," the other unabashedly partisan. Dan Goodgame's report entitled "Two Faces of George Bush" identified this apparent contradiction. "The president woos Democrats while his evil twin fights them."[122] A drawing of Bush's face split into three different appearances accompanied a James Reston article, "The Conflict within George Bush." Reston called Bush's internal conflict "a wrestling match between the gentleman from Connecticut and the politician from Texas."[123]

Post-budget deal analyses of Bush's leadership were even more negative. George Will declared Bush's leadership "Carteresque." According to Will, "presidential ascendancy is necessary. However, it may be beyond Bush's capacities."[124] Eleanor Clift said that Bush had been "Carterized," that is, "weakened to the point of ridicule."[125] Tom Wicker wrote of "a suddenly floundering presidency." Bush practiced a "managerial approach to an office that demands persuasiveness and vision."[126] Kenneth T. Walsh's report declared Bush's presidency as "foundering" and "in danger."

There is a growing realization that the president's domestic agenda is basically nonexistent. His "governing" strategy, which is based vaguely on getting things accomplished rather than articulating a forceful program, is fatally flawed. . . . [Bush] is a man without a mission leading an administration without a purpose.[127]

CONCLUSION

By the end of Bush's second year in office, the press consistently gave his leadership low marks. All agreed—liberal, conservative, and nonpartisan alike—that Bush did not exhibit certain leadership qualities: core convictions, a clearly articulated policy agenda, a strategy for enacting key programs, a vision for the future. The *New York Times* referred to Bush as "the Dr. No of modern presidents," a man who was "much more energetic in reacting to the initiatives of others than in offering a coherent domestic agenda of his own." Rather than assert positive leadership, Bush wielded the veto to stop the momentum of Congress. He was "a president all too devoted to obstruction."[128] The *Wall Street Journal* fundamentally agreed.

The second year of his term has been an establishment, white shoe, inside-the-beltway year. . . . The choice we see is nothing less than whether Mr. Bush wants simply to be president or to accomplish something. If he is satisfied simply to preside over Washington, he can continue on the recent path with the same team, issuing vetoes now and then but largely playing defense. . . . Mr. Bush needs to seize the domestic initiative.[129]

Newsweek's Jonathan Alter too said that Bush merely presided over the government but did not offer real leadership. He too characterized Bush as a Carter-like leader.

Bush mocked the Democrats' aspirations to mere competence in 1988, but he is governing with the same cramped vision. Like Carter, Bush is the inverse of Ronald Reagan: knowledgeable, but unable to conjure the magic that remains essential to leadership. . . . [Reagan's] heavily scripted presidency tended to lead the country backward. But at least he was leading it somewhere.[130]

Consequently, the test of leadership was whether the president established a policy direction for the nation, even if that course was harmful. At midterm, journalists determined that Bush needed to act quickly to show that he could give the country a domestic policy road map to follow. Otherwise, Bush would have to stake his presidency on foreign policy triumphs and hope that the economy did not deteriorate.

NOTES

1. Maureen Dowd, "Lost for Words," *New York Times*, October 21, 1990, sec. 4, p. 1.
2. See, for example, Maureen Dowd, "Bush Stumps in 1990, Looking for 1988s Beef," *New York Times*, July 27, 1990, p. A10; Maureen Dowd, "The Language Thing," *New York Times Magazine*, July 29, 1990, pp. 32, 48; Maureen Dowd, "Not Pretty. Seems to Work, Though," *New York Times*, March 9, 1990, p. A14; Maureen Dowd, "President and the Press: A Clash of 2 Obsessions," *New York Times*, February 21, 1990, p. A16; David Hoffman, "How Bush Drives His Message Home to Us," *Washington Post*, March 18, 1990, pp. B1, B5.
3. "Point Men," *Newsweek*, January 29, 1990, p. 32. See also Michael Barone and David R. Gergen, "The High-flying Plans of Sam Skinner," *U.S. News and World Report*, March 12, 1990, p. 32; Thomas M. DeFrank, "From Pit Bull to President," *Newsweek*, November 12, 1990, p. 30; Maureen Dowd and Thomas L. Friedman, "The Fabulous Bush and Baker Boys," *New York Times Magazine*, May 6, 1990, pp. 34, 36, 58, 62, 64, 67; Rowland Evans and Robert Novak, "Bush's Raging Bull," *Washington Post*, December 3, 1990, p. A15; William Safire, "Bush's Cabinet: Who's Up, Who's Down," *New York Times Magazine*, March 25, 1990, pp. 31–33, 63, 66–67; Kenneth T. Walsh, "Bush's Cautious Alter Ego," *U.S. News and World Report*, March 26, 1990, pp. 26–27; "Educating the Education President," *New York Times*, December 18, 1990, p. A24.
4. Thomas M. DeFrank and Ann McDaniel, "Quayle's Quandary: Can He Fix His Image?" *Newsweek*, February 19, 1990, pp. 34–35.
5. Thomas M. DeFrank and Ann McDaniel, "Bush Plays Macho Man," February 5, 1990, p. 20. To be accurate, in 1988 Democrats made Bush's vice presiden-

tial choice a key campaign issue. People elected Bush fully aware that Quayle could become president.

6. *Time* cover page, April 23, 1990.

7. Thomas M. DeFrank and Ann McDaniel, "Bush: The Secret Presidency," *Newsweek*, January 1, 1990, pp. 26, 27.

8. Kenneth T. Walsh, "America's Born-again Swashbuckler," *U.S. News and World Report*, January 8, 1990, p. 26.

9. R. W. Apple, Jr., "For Bush in 1989, the Focus Was Foreign Policy," *New York Times*, January 1, 1990, p. A11.

10. Mary McGrory, "Bush Is a Hit, Despite Misses," *Washington Post*, January 16, 1990, p. A2.

11. George F. Will, "This Empty Presidency," *Washington Post*, January 21, 1990, p. B7.

12. Michael Kramer, "Lyndon Baines Bush?" *Time*, February 12, 1990, p. 23.

13. Richard Cohen, "Wish List," *Washington Post*, February 2, 1990, p. A23.

14. "The President's Two Worlds," *New York Times*, February 2, 1990, p. A30. The editorial nonetheless praised Bush's foreign policy vision in the speech.

15. "The State of the World," *Washington Post*, February 2, 1990, p. A22.

16. George F. Will, "Unconnected Motor," *Washington Post*, February 2, 1990, p. A23.

17. David R. Gergen, "The Rush to Glory of 'Crazy Legs' Bush," *U.S. News and World Report*, February 12, 1990, p. 30. Among the others who cited a disjunction between Bush's rhetoric and budget proposals were David S. Broder, "A Budget from a Great Nibbler," *Washington Post*, January 30, 1990, p. A19; George J. Church, "How Much Is Too Much?" *Time*, February 12, 1990, pp. 16–21; "Mr. Bush on Defense: Too Much, Too Late," *New York Times*, January 30, 1990, p. A22; "Mr. Bush's Budget," *Washington Post*, January 30, 1990, p. A18. One editorial blasted Washington reporters for equating leadership vision with the size of budget proposals. See "Epoxy Apostasy," *Wall Street Journal*, February 2, 1990, p. A14.

18. William Safire, "The Bush Style," *New York Times*, February 2, 1990, p. A31.

19. Tom Shales, "From George Bush, Something Borrowed, Something Bland," *Washington Post*, February 1, 1990, p. C1.

20. Kramer, "Lyndon Baines Bush?"

21. McGrory, "Bush Is a Hit, Despite Misses."

22. Jim Hoagland, "President Bush Needs a Prime Minister," *Washington Post*, October 23, 1990, p. A21.

23. Tom Wicker, "Beyond the Jackpot," *New York Times*, January 22, 1990, p. A15.

24. See, for example, "$150 Billion a Year," *New York Times*, March 8, 1990, p. A24.

25. "Why Not Prudence Plus Leadership?" *New York Times*, February 11, 1990, sec. 4, p. 24.

26. See, for example, Russell Baker, "Look Who's Coming!" *New York Times*, December 11, 1990, p. A27.

27. Philip Geyelin, "The John Wayne Way," *Washington Post*, January 19, 1990, p. A21. Geyelin cited columns by Charles Krauthammer as well as Jack W.

Germond and Jules Witcover. But Richard Cohen ("Bush: No Class as Coach," *Washington Post*, January 5, 1990, p. A19) agreed with Geyelin.

28. George J. Church, "Showing Muscle," *Time*, January 1, 1990, pp. 20–23.

29. Eloise Salzholz, "Noriega's Surrender," *Newsweek*, January 15, 1990, p. 18.

30. "Operation Just Begun," *New York Times*, January 5, 1990, p. A30.

31. See A. M. Rosenthal, "Chronology of Betrayal," *New York Times*, January 14, 1990, sec. 4, p. 23; Rosenthal, "Bush Won. Who Lost?" *New York Times*, February 1, 1990, p. A23.

32. See, for example, Anthony Lewis, "Trahison Des Clercs," *New York Times*, March 9, 1990, p. A35; Hobart Rowan, "Dollars before Principle," *Washington Post*, May 24, 1990, p. A23; "On China, Trust Is Not Enough," *New York Times*, January 24, 1990, p. A22; "In China, No Sign of Spring," *Washington Post*, February 26, 1990, p. A10. One editorial agreed with the policy of renewing China's trade privileges but expressed disappointment that Bush had not condemned China's human rights abuses. "Half Right on China Trade," *New York Times*, May 25, 1990, p. A26.

33. David S. Broder, "China: Making Bush Look Bad," *Washington Post*, February 21, 1990, p. A21.

34. See R. W. Apple, Jr., "Getting Mad, Getting Even," *New York Times*, January 26, 1990, pp. A1, A9; Dan Goodgame, "China Breach," *Time*, February 5, 1990, pp. 16–18.

35. See George J. Church, "Clinging to the Cold War," *Time*, June 18, 1990, p. 20; Anthony Lewis, "The Bush Disaster," *New York Times*, February 9, 1990, p. A31; Mary McGrory, "The Most Happy President," *Washington Post*, July 15, 1990, pp. B1, B2; "How to Fulfill the Promise of Malta," *New York Times*, January 16, 1990, p. A26.

36. See Rowland Evans and Robert Novak, ". . . A Hunting License for Gorbachev," *Washington Post*, March 30, 1990, p. A25; Evans and Novak, "My Pal, Mikhail," *Washington Post*, June 4, 1990, p. A15; Evans and Novak, "'Soft' on the Baltics," *Washington Post*, February 19, 1990, p. A19; "The Lithuanian Case," *Washington Post*, April 25, 1990, p. A26.

37. Andrew Rosenthal, "Bush Yields to an Impulse to Stay Cautious about the Soviets," *New York Times*, February 11, 1990, sec. 4, p. 2.

38. Margaret Garrard Warner, "Defying the Politicians and the Pundits," *Newsweek*, April 16, 1990, pp. 32–33.

39. Michael Kramer, "Anger, Bluff—and Cooperation," *Time*, June 4, 1990, p. 38.

40. "Cautious Courage about Lithuania," *New York Times*, March 28, 1990, p. A28.

41. See, for example, Jim Hoagland, "Still a Serious Leader," *Washington Post*, May 31, 1990, p. A23; A. M. Rosenthal, "Warmth and Ice," *New York Times*, June 7, 1990, p. A23.

42. George J. Church, "The Last Picture Show," *Time*, June 11, 1990, p. 17.

43. "The Summit on Day One," *Washington Post*, June 1, 1990, p. A18; see also, "On the Summit Track," *Washington Post*, May 20, 1990, p. D6; "Summit Assessment," *Washington Post*, June 4, 1990, p. A14.

44. Flora Lewis, "The Right Shoulder," *New York Times*, June 5, 1990, p. A29.

45. Anthony Lewis, "Bush Vindicated," *New York Times*, June 15, 1990, p. A29.

46. Haynes Johnson, "Statesman and Hit Men," *Washington Post*, December 14, 1990, p. A2. Nonetheless, Johnson blasted Bush's domestic record as divisive. See also "A Hand to Mr. Gorbachev," *Washington Post*, December 14, 1990, p. A26; Nancy Gibbs, "Rescue Mission," *Time*, December 24, 1990, pp. 16–18.

47. Haynes Johnson, "The Mideast Challenge," August 10, 1990, p. A2.

48. Stephen S. Rosenfeld, "Bush's 'Vision,'" *Washington Post*, August 31, 1990, p. A27.

49. David S. Broder, "Maine Breezes, Arabian Furnace," August 26, 1990, p. C7.

50. Jim Hoagland, "Saddam's Last Fantasy," *Washington Post*, August 21, 1990, p. A23.

51. Richard Cohen, "Mr. Bush's Understudy," *Washington Post*, August 30, 1990, p. A23.

52. Carl Bernstein, "Bush's Other Summit," *Time*, September 17, 1990, p. 24. Many other journalists noted the contrast between Bush's leadership in foreign and domestic affairs. See David S. Broder, "Reactive President," *Washington Post* August 19, 1990, p. C7.

53. Paul A. Gigot, "George Bush—A Good Man on a Tiger Shoot," *Wall Street Journal*, August 10, 1990, p. A10. See also George J. Church, "A New World," *Time*, September 17, 1990, pp. 20–23; Michael Kramer, "Read My Ships," *Time*, August 20, 1990, pp. 16–22; Steven V. Roberts, "George Bush, Diplomat," *U.S. News and World Report*, September 10, 1990, pp. 26–29; Hugh Sidey, "Bush's Balancing Act," *Time*, September 10, 1990, p. 28; Hugh Sidey, "Networking Pays Off," *Time*, August 27, 1990, p. 21; Strobe Talbott, "The Search for Supervillains," *Time*, September 3, 1990, p. 40; "Opportunity for Mr. Bush," *Wall Street Journal*, August 8, 1990, p. A10; "Resistance and Appeasement," *Washington Post*, August 7, 1990, p. A18.

54. R. W. Apple, Jr., "Bush's Two Audiences," *New York Times*, September 12, 1990, p. A1.

55. "A Good Gulf Pep Rally," *New York Times*, September 13, 1990, p. A26.

56. Bruce W. Nelan, "Call to Arms," *Time*, September 24, 1990, p. 32.

57. Russell Watson, "The Price of Success," *Newsweek*, October 1, 1990, p. 20.

58. Mortimer B. Zuckerman, "Are We Willing to Act Alone?" *U.S. News and World Report*, September 24, 1990, p. 100.

59. Ann McDaniel and Evan Thomas, "'The First Test of Our Mettle,'" *Newsweek*, September 24, 1990, p. 27.

60. Paul A. Gigot, "Two Faced Bush—Tough Abroad, Squishy at Home," *Wall Street Journal*, September 14, 1990, p. A14.

61. See, for example, Melinda Beck, Ann McDaniel, and Russell Watson, "The Burden of Decision," *Newsweek*, October 29, 1990, pp. 32–33; David S. Broder, "The Sands in Bush's Hourglass," *Washington Post*, October 21, 1990, p. C7; Charles Krauthammer, "The Great Cooperator," *Washington Post*, October 19, 1990, p. A23.

62. "Desert Sword: Time for Answers," *New York Times*, November 14, 1990, p. A28.

63. Otto Friedrich, "Time for Doubt," *Time*, November 26, 1990, p. 30.

64. "Incoherent Mideast Policy," *Washington Post*, November 6, 1990, p. A2.

65. Carla Anne Robbins, "Lonely at the Top," *U.S. News and World Report*, November 26, 1990, p. 26.

66. Charles Krauthammer, "The Case for Destroying Saddam," *Washington Post*, November 25, 1990, p. C7. See also George J. Church, "Raising the Ante," *Time*, November 19, 1990, pp. 48–51.

67. George F. Will, "Did You Ever See a Policy Go This Way and That?" *Washington Post*, November 7, 1990, p. A23. See also Jim Hoagland, "The Gulf: Right Policy, but Wrong President?" *Washington Post*, November 4, 1990, p. C1.

68. See, for example, Anthony Lewis, "No Thanks," *New York Times*, November 23, 1990, p. A37; Anthony Lewis, "Patience Is Strength," *New York Times*, November 2, 1990, p. A35; William Raspberry, "Americans Don't Want War," *Washington Post*, November 26, 1990, p. A11; James Reston, "It's Still Wiser to Jaw Than to War," *New York Times*, November 30, 1990, p. A33; "The Gulf Buildup," *Washington Post*, November 11, 1990, p. B6.

69. See, for example, Haynes Johnson, "Politics and Presidential Signals," *Washington Post*, November 2, 1990, p. A2; Tom Morganthau, "Should We Fight?" *Newsweek*, November 26, 1990, pp. 26–27.

70. Walter Isaacson, "Hiding in the Flag," *Time*, June 25, 1990, p. 16.

71. "Flag Games," *Washington Post*, June 14, 1990, p. A22; George F. Will, "This Empty Presidency," *Washington Post*, January 21, 1990, p. B7.

72. Tom Wicker, "Home of the Brave?" *New York Times*, June 14, 1990, p. A27. See also Dan Balz, "The President and Politics of the Flag," *Washington Post*, June 17, 1990, p. A12.

73. "Cavazos and Bush: A Shared Failure," *New York Times*, December 13, 1990, p. A30.

74. "More Hype than Hope," *New York Times*, February 18, 1990, sec. 4, p. 18.

75. Steven V. Roberts, "Is Bush in Nature's Way?" *U.S. News and World Report*, March 19, 1990, pp. 20–22; Philip Shabecoff, "In Thicket of Environmental Policy," *New York Times*, July 1, 1990, sec. 1, p. 20; "Too Cool on Global Warning," *New York Times*, February 8, 1990, p. A28.

76. Richard Cohen, "Secretary of State Bush," *Washington Post*, May 8, 1990, p. A27; "The Rest of the Agenda," *Washington Post*, October 9, 1990, p. A20; Kenneth T. Walsh, "Bush's Veto Strategy," *U.S. News and World Report*, July 2, 1990, pp. 18–20.

77. Michael Kinsley, "Capital Gains Dementia," *Washington Post*, October 11, 1990, p. A23; "Yes: Drive Down the Deficit. No: Don't Punish," *New York Times*, March 18, 1990, sec. 4, p. 18.

78. Larry Martz, "Bush's Pledge: 'I Want to Do the Right Thing,'" *Newsweek*, May 28, 1990, pp. 20–21.

79. See, for example, Jack Anderson and Dale Van Atta, "Stains on Bush Civil Rights Record," *Washington Post*, July 3, 1990, p. D14; Alain L. Sanders, "A Quota-vs.-Voters Dilemma," *Time*, October 29, 1990, p. 42; "The Civil Rights Bill," *Washington Post*, October 2, 1990, p. A18; "Sign the Civil Rights Bill," *Washington Post*, October 18, 1990, p. A22.

80. See the following *Times* editorials: "Mr. Bush against the Tide," October 15, 1990, p. A18; "Mr. Bush, the Wagon's Leaving," May 16, 1990, p. A26; "Mr. Bush's Loaded Label for Fairness," October 20, 1990, p. A22; "On Civil Rights: No Steps Back," August 6, 1990, p. A12; "Precious Days for Civil Rights," September 14, 1990, p. A32; "A Veto Mr. Bush Can Still Avoid," October 1, 1990, p. A20.

81. Anthony Lewis, "Who Is George Bush?," *New York Times*, October 26, 1990, p. A35.

82. See, for example, David S. Broder, "The Next Three Court Nominees," *Washington Post*, July 27, 1990, p. A27; Richard Cohen, "No Paper Trail," *Washington Post*, July 26, 1990, p. A27; David Gergen and Steven V. Roberts, "The Hidden Perils of Souter's Nomination," August 6, 1990, p. 25; Ed Magnunson, "Right Turn Ahead?" *Time*, July 30, 1990, pp. 16–18; "The President Proposes," *New York Times*, July 24, 1990, p. A20.

83. Richard Lacayo, "A Blank Slate," *Time*, August 6, 1990, p. 16.

84. Cited in George F. Will, "He Moved His Lips and Said Nothing," *Washington Post*, June 29, 1990, p. A27.

85. George J. Church, "Eating His Words," *Time*, July 9, 1990, p. 16.

86. Steven V. Roberts, "Who Will Pay the Tab?" *U.S. News and World Report*, July 9, 1990, p. 18.

87. Russell Baker, "And Yet They Rise," *New York Times*, April 11, 1990, p. A25.

88. David R. Gergen, "Lip Balm for Bush," *U.S. News and World Report*, July 9, 1990, p. 84.

89. E. J. Dionne, Jr., "Read Their Flips," *Washington Post*, July 1, 1990, p. C1. See also Rowland Evans and Robert Novak, "Tax Storm," *Washington Post*, July 2, 1990, p. A11; David E. Rosenbaum, "Bush Moves His Lips but Not His Troops," *New York Times*, July 1, 1990, sec. 4, pp. 1–2; Robin Toner, "On Taxes, Bush Shows None of His '88 Agility," *New York Times*, July 4, 1990, p. A9; George F. Will, "He Moved His Lips and Said Nothing," *Washington Post*, June 29, 1990, p. A27.

90. R. W. Apple, Jr., "Bush Trips, Capital Reels," *New York Times*, October 11, 1990, pp. A1, D22.

91. George F. Will, "Deals and Delusions," *Washington Post*, October 11, 1990, p. A23. See also George F. Will, "It's Not Modesty, It's Arrogance," *Washington Post*, October 12, 1990, p. A21.

92. Richard Cohen, "The Politics of Cynicism," *Washington Post*, October 5, 1990, p. A25.

93. Paul A. Gigot, "The Capital Captures a President," *Wall Street Journal*, October 26, 1990, p. A14.

94. "Political Ineptitude," *Wall Street Journal*, October 10, 1990, p. A18. See also "To the People," *Wall Street Journal*, October 9, 1990, p. A22; Rowland Evans and Robert Novak, "Capital Gains, Political Losses," *Washington Post*, December 24, 1990, p. A15.

95. According to *Time*'s White House correspondents, Bush really meant "Kiss My Ass." Michael Duffy and Dan Goodgame, *Marching in Place: The Status Quo Presidency of George Bush* (New York: Simon and Schuster, 1992), p. 238.

96. See, for example, Maureen Dowd, "The Patrician's Way," *New York Times*, October 10, 1990, p. A19; Michael Kinsley, "Read My Lips II: The Horror Continues," *Washington Post*, November 29, 1990, p. A23; Mary McGrory, "Trouble on the Home Front," *Washington Post*, October 11, 1990, p. A2; Tom Morganthau, "The Art of the Deal," *Newsweek*, November 5, 1990, pp. 20–22; "Government by Cabal-Again," *New York Times*, November 3, 1990, p. A24.

97. Hobart Rowen, "Bush's Shift on Taxes," *Washington Post*, June 27, 1990, p. A19; Hobart Rowen, "Wrong Then, Right Now," *Washington Post*, July 19, 1990, p.

A23; "The Deficit, without Pretense," *New York Times*, June 28, 1990, p. A24; "The Balanced Budget Vote," *New York Times*, July 17, 1990, p. A18; "If They're Serious about the Deficit," *New York Times*, May 15, 1990, p. A24; "Yes to Taxes," *Washington Post*, June 27, 1990, p. A18.

98. "D.C. Disgust: A *Newsweek* Poll," *Newsweek*, October 22, 1990, p. 23.

99. Larry Martz, "Bush League," *Newsweek*, October 22, 1990, p. 20. This article listed phrases from other negative headlines: "Clowns," "Waver," "Waffle." *Newsday*'s headline yelled "READ MY FLIPS." The *New York Times* called Bush "a political wimp" (p. 21).

100. Dan Goodgame, "Read My Hips," *Time*, October 22, 1990, p. 27.

101. Richard Cohen, "A President without a Constituency," *Washington Post*, October 12, 1990, p. A21.

102. Tom Wicker, "Bush: No Mo Big Mo," *New York Times*, October 21, 1990, sec. 4, p. 19. See also James Reston, "The President: Read His Slips," October 21, 1990, sec. 4, p. 19.

103. David S. Broder, "An Absence of Guiding Principle," *Washington Post*, October 12, 1990, p. A21.

104. See, for example, Edwin M. Yoder, Jr., "The Blame Extends beyond the Beltway," *Washington Post*, October 23, 1990, p. A21.

105. Richard Cohen, "Treating Voters as Children," *Washington Post*, October 26, 1990, p. A27.

106. See also Dan Goodgame, "Plain Squeaking," *Time*, November 12, 1990, p. 38; Juan Williams, "George Bush and the Politics of Confusion," *Washington Post*, October 28, 1990, pp. C1, C2.

107. Steven V. Roberts, "Election Hangover," *U.S. News and World Report*, November 19, 1990, pp. 26, 28.

108. Michael Duffy and Dan Goodgame, "Nothing to Cheer," *Time*, November 19, 1990, p. 31.

109. David Gergen and Kenneth T. Walsh, "The Bush Presidency: Running on Empty," *Washington Post*, November 11, 1990, p. B1.

110. Paul Taylor, "Why Bush Should Start Worrying About '92," *Washington Post*, June 24, 1990, p. C4.

111. Mary McGrory, "Bush's Charmed Presidency," *Washington Post*, April 10, 1990, p. A2.

112. Michael Kramer, "The Vision Is in the Details," *Time*, March 19, 1990, p. 18.

113. David S. Broder, "The Negotiator," *Washington Post*, May 9, 1990, p. A27.

114. Bernstein, "Bush's Other Summit."

115. Tom Wicker, "Don't Read His Lips," *New York Times*, March 12, 1990, p. A17.

116. Margaret Carlson, "Déjà Voodoo?" *Time*, March 26, 1990, p. 17.

117. Jack Anderson and Dale Van Atta, "The 'Maintenance President,'" *Washington Post*, March 18, 1990, p. B7.

118. Richard Cohen, "What Does Bush Stand For?" *Washington Post*, May 11, 1990, p. A27.

119. Mary McGrory, "Two Contrasting Bushes," *Washington Post*, August 16, 1990, p. A2.

120. Kenneth T. Walsh, "Bush's Split Personality," *U.S. News and World Report*, September 17, 1990, pp. 26–27.

121. Bernstein, "Bush's Other Summit."

122. Dan Goodgame, "Two Faces of George Bush," *Time*, July 2, 1990, p. 23.

123. James Reston, "The Conflict within George Bush," *New York Times*, July 8, 1990, sec. 4, p. 17.

124. George F. Will, "'Let Congress Clear It Up,'" *Newsweek*, October 22, 1990, p. 84.

125. Eleanor Clift, "The 'Carterization' of Bush," *Newsweek*, October 22, 1990, p. 28.

126. Tom Wicker, "Bush's Midterm Crisis," *New York Times*, November 21, 1990, p. A23.

127. Kenneth T. Walsh, "Can Bush Come Back?" *U.S. News and World Report*, October 29, 1990, pp. 24, 26; See also Evan Thomas, "An Infusion of Vision," *Newsweek*, December 3, 1990, pp. 24–25.

128. "The Energetic Naysayer," *New York Times*, December 9, 1990, sec. 4, p. 16.

129. "Bring Back the New Bush," *Wall Street Journal*, November 13, 1990, p. A22.

130. Jonathan Alter, "Leadership," *Newsweek*, December 31, 1990, p. 25.

5

The New World Order and
Domestic Gridlock (1991)

Because of the impending war with Iraq and possibility of a recession, a *New York Times* column and *Wall Street Journal* editorial declared 1991 a "make or break" year for Bush's presidency.[1] War in the Middle East could become as protracted and damaging to the presidency as Vietnam, or it could lead to Bush becoming known as the creator of a new world order. The domestic economy could slip into recession, or the president could be credited with keeping the nation prosperous. To many, the stakes appeared no less than the choice between international humiliation and recession or peace and prosperity.

Timing. Key events in 1991 drove the policy agenda. The Gulf War dominated the early months of the year, and journalists credited the president with having seized the opportunity to demonstrate leadership. Many praised Bush's responses to dramatic events in the Soviet Union and Eastern Europe, although some maintained that he needed to have done more to support democratic movements in the Baltic states.

Because of the U.S. victory in the Gulf War, Bush's popularity rose dramatically. He had an extraordinary opportunity to capitalize on the favorable political environment. By not taking advantage of a second presidential honeymoon to promote an aggressive domestic agenda, Bush had failed to meet a journalistic criterion for leadership: the willingness to turn presidential popularity into national support for an activist agenda.

Symbolism/Rhetoric. Journalists continued to give Bush low marks for his use of political theater and speechmaking. He did not use inspiring rhetoric to articulate a national vision and move the country toward bold policy goals. His administration gave short shrift to new, innovative policy ideas from such figures as Housing and Urban Development secretary Jack Kemp. Even during wartime, when the country rallied behind its president, journalists reported that Bush's words did not inspire. A *Newsweek* story summed up the views of many. "George Bush is a poor public speaker. In his formal televised addresses, he can sound tinny and false, and he has a way of grinning at precisely the wrong moment."[2]

Agenda. A *Time* cover story and many other reports again analyzed the "two George Bushes." According to the press, Bush projected a bold and innovative vision in foreign affairs. Although the beneficiary of the collapse of communism and the Soviet Union, he responded effectively to change and protected United States interests abroad. Press coverage of Bush's leadership during the Persian Gulf War could hardly have been more flattering. He demonstrated astute leadership in developing an international coalition against Iraq. Press coverage nonetheless turned negative after the cease-fire, when reports of the slaughter of Kurdish refugees in northern Iraq gave evidence of the terrible consequences of the postwar situation. Many blamed Bush for not acting forthrightly to protect the refugees.

Although journalists credited Bush with an impressive agenda abroad, they said that he had no plans for his own country. Accordingly, Bush showed little energy or initiative on the domestic front. He only had a "defensive agenda"—to stop Democratic initiatives. Even when he proposed domestic initiatives such as his "America 2000" education plan, journalists decried the lack of additional federal funding. Bush received almost no credit for signing a civil rights law because he had not championed the plan from the outset. By the end of the year, when the economy appeared to be headed toward recession, journalists decried the lack of broad-based federal initiatives to stimulate economic growth.

Policy Development. On the foreign policy front, according to the press, Bush displayed his adroit consensus-building skills. A leader who proceeded with masterly skill at protecting U.S. interests, Bush had created the conditions for a brave new world order freed from the old cold war assumptions.

On the domestic front, to the contrary, Bush displayed his weaknesses as a leader: inability to build consensus, unwillingness to promote innovative and far-reaching programs. A leader who proceeded only cautiously, if at all, Bush had failed to translate his Gulf War victory and unprecedented popularity into an action-oriented domestic program. Journalists expressed amazement that a president with all of Bush's political advantages in 1991 would not use his assets to make a major impact on American public life. They accused the president of merely "playing politics" with such contentious issues as civil rights as well as with education, health care, and the economy.

Staff. Although press profiles of Bush's foreign policy team were flattering, many stories focused on internal White House squabbling and controversies surrounding Chief of Staff John Sununu.[3] Those stories that assessed Sununu's actions caused a great deal of difficulty for the president. Bush relied heavily on Sununu's counsel and willingness to be the White House "bad cop." But allegations of various improprieties by the chief of staff troubled a president who had promised to run an administration of high ethical standards. Stories reported the contrast between Bush's standards and Sununu's actions.

These negative stories particularly were harmful to a president who fashioned an image of competence, experience, and professionalism. For many journalists, Sununu and Vice President Dan Quayle were twin presidential embarrassments whose very presence in the administration reflected poorly on the man who had chosen them.

EARLY EVALUATIONS/STATE OF THE UNION

Time magazine caused something of a stir with its 1991 "Man of the Year" issue. The issue cover declared "Men of the Year: The Two George Bushes." Others already had written about the two sides of Bush, but not so prominently. Author of one of the cover pieces, George J. Church, described two different presidents in one man. "One finds a vision on the global stage; the other displays none at home."[4] Furthermore,

One was a foreign policy profile that was a study in resoluteness and mastery, the other a domestic visage just as strongly marked by wavering and confusion. . . . [Bush] raised a vision of a new world order. . . . But domestic policy! What could have been more baffling, at times ludicrous, than Bush's performance on taxes. . . . His domestic policy, to the extent that he has one, has been to leave things alone until he could no longer avoid taking action.[5]

This issue of the magazine contained two lengthy pieces entitled "In the Gulf: Bold Vision" and "At Home: No Vision." The first was generally laudatory toward Bush's efforts "to shape a brave new world order."[6] The second described "Bush's feckless approach to America's ills." Michael Duffy criticized the president's "shilly-shallying performance on domestic issues." According to Duffy, the president devoted his energies "to thwarting Democratic initiatives" rather than to articulating an agenda; Bush had been "inactive, if not silent" regarding domestic ills; "tinkered at the margins" and preferred to "manage" rather than lead.[7] A caption accompanying the story stated "Read his hips: Is this any way to lead a nation?" Pictures next to the caption showed homeless people, drug pushers, young blacks out of school, environmental waste, and George Bush jogging past the mayhem pointing at his hips. The implication was clear: Bush was crassly indifferent to the suffering of others.[8]

A *U.S. News* story too was not sympathetic to Bush's domestic agenda. It referred to the White House as "George Bush's idea-free zone." Kenneth T. Walsh reported that original thinkers within the administration had no influence because of "the White House's peculiar aversion to ideas." The White House fostered a "do-nothing atmosphere" where the president "refuse[d] to infuse life into his domestic agenda."[9]

Even the conservative *Wall Street Journal* echoed the call for Bush to offer a bold domestic agenda. The *Journal* praised Bush's strong leadership abroad and implored him "to translate his foreign policy momentum into similarly energetic leadership on the home front." It was time to "take the political offensive on [such] national priorities" as the economy and social problems. "Any president who established a commanding position in foreign, we should think, would want to lead his nation on domestic issues as well."[10]

On January 16, one day after Bush's deadline for Iraq to withdraw from Kuwait had expired, the United States launched a massive air attack on the city of Baghdad, targeting strategically crucial Iraqi command and communications centers. In unprecedented fashion, the events of that evening were captured live on television for millions of Americans to see.

In typical rally-round-the-flag fashion, the president's popularity dramatically increased. On January 29 Bush spoke to the nation in his annual State of the Union address. Although the president focused on the Middle East crisis and received an enthusiastic reception from members of Congress in the audience, he disappointed the many critics who expected him to use his wartime popularity to promote a bold domestic agenda. Margaret Carlson reported that

Bush spoke convincingly of a cause that is just, moral and right. . . . But when Bush moved from the state of the world to the state of the country, he left his vision at the border. The domestic side of the speech . . . sounded as if it had been cobbled together by a committee of tightfisted accountants.[11]

Jim Hoagland declared that Bush's address had completed the "transformation of the Republican party" from a formerly isolationist party to the internationalist one. While Bush displayed strong international leadership, he could claim "no domestic accomplishments."[12]

Michael Kinsley maintained that a popular wartime president had an obligation to persuade the nation to accept such domestic sacrifices as income and gasoline taxes. "If ever there was a moment to call on citizens to sacrifice for their country's long-range good, this was it. But President WASP funked it" [*sic*].[13]

Mary McGrory said that Bush's speech only appeared to be a "smashing success" because the nation was at war and rallied behind its president. After he presented a progress report on the war, "[Bush] moved into a dispirited discussion of a subject that plainly bores him, the state of the union." McGrory added that "the speech had been a kind of empty sandwich, two great chunks of bread about the war, nothing in between."[14]

The *New York Times* noted that Bush had failed to give adequate attention in the address to homelessness, AIDS, drug abuse, poverty, health care, and other "intractable problems" that were "not part of Mr. Bush's union. Instead, he offer[ed] bromides." Bush made "no clarion calls," he avoided "bold rhetoric and ambitious goals."

The contrast between Mr. Bush the military leader and Mr. Bush the domestic leader was never more stark. No listener could miss his resolve when discussing war in the Persian Gulf. And no listener could find resolve when he discussed problems at home. . . . In the Middle East, President Bush stands up to lead the world. At home, he waits to manage each crisis as it happens to come along.[15]

Joining such voices of liberalism as Kinsley, McGrory, and the *Times* in criticizing the address was conservative columnist George F. Will, who maintained that Bush had ignored the nation's "gravest problems" at home. According to Will,

The nation, meaning its domestic conditions and its sense of collective effort for improvement as a single community, received scant attention from [Bush]. . . . His tone was perfunctory—even the timber of his voice diminished—when he turned to domestic matters. Clearly he is most comfortable in the role of commander in chief, attending to the hard work of freedom abroad.[16]

A good many commentaries judged Bush's rhetoric harshly. Mary McGrory wrote that "there were no words that sing or sting, or sentences that march or paragraphs that advance like armies. Bush is almost aggressively not the orator. He is more at home with the telephone than the megaphone."[17] Jonathan Yardley called the address "a bromidic homily distinguished only for its utter poverty of language and imagination." The address "didn't inspire and it didn't clarify. . . . On and on it went, banality following banality in a succession not once interrupted by an original or interesting phrase or idea."[18] The *New York Times* agreed that the "speech clanked with banalities" except when Bush addressed the topic of war.[19]

Not every judgment was so harsh. David S. Broder noted that for a man with a "barely adequate" career, Bush had given "a superb performance" and achieved "a Reagan-size triumph."[20] The *Wall Street Journal* added that "for a president who is not known as the great communicator, Mr. Bush came through loud and clear."[21]

BUSH'S WARTIME LEADERSHIP: FROM BOUQUETS TO BRICKBATS

From the initiation of the U.S. missile attacks on Baghdad on January 16 until the cease-fire on February 28, the nation—including many leading journalists—rallied behind allied troops and the president. Bush's popularity soared. It reached 86 percent—the highest level for any president in thirty years—on the day after the war against Iraq had begun.[22] After the cease-fire, Bush's approval rating soared to 91 percent.[23] During most of the conflict, the president could hardly have asked for kinder press coverage.

R. W. Apple, Jr., said it was "surely apt" that press secretary Marlin Fitzwater's January 16 statement—"the liberation of Kuwait has begun"—was reminiscent of Dwight Eisenhower's D-day message that "the liberation of Europe" had begun. "President Bush harked back to one of the great days in American military history—June 6, 1944."[24]

A. M. Rosenthal maintained that Bush had succeeded by facing down Saddam Hussein, politicians who opposed military intervention, and critical journalists. The Democrats had become so marginalized that "maybe they can get George McGovern to run again" for president. Rosenthal glowed that Bush had saved many from the murderous Hussein and closed, "I have just four words for [Bush]: Thank you Mr. President."[25]

Suddenly, the press corps transformed Bush from a feckless and vacillating executive to an adroit, commanding world leader. According to the *Wall Street Journal*, Bush's Gulf crisis leadership was "truly spectacular."[26] World leaders accepted the "rightness" of the U.S. cause "in large part because George Bush worked adroitly to assemble that consensus."[27]

Paul A. Gigot wrote that Bush had dispelled criticism for lacking convictions. "It turns out he has at least one very large conviction—a belief in the worth and purposes of American power." Bush even displayed "conviction, timing, and some guile" in dealing with congressional opponents. In a statement revealing of press standards applied to modern presidents, Gigot added that "Mr. Bush has been underestimated because he lacks the rhetorical skills that journalists prize."[28]

A *Newsweek* report agreed that "Bush was firm and formidable" and had shown "his basic decency." Furthermore, "Bush [didn't] really need to be an inspirational spokesman as long as the war" succeeded.[29] Bush displayed his "resolve" and showed that he was "tough." Unfortunately, Bush had difficulty communicating such qualities.[30]

Charles Krauthammer argued that Bush had succeeded in the war despite being "devoid of rhetorical skill." Bush accomplished his goals by "bold" decisions and making an unarguable case for U.S. action in the Persian Gulf.[31]

Dan Goodgame added that Bush had failed in the past to display strong convictions, but in the Gulf War the president "had finally found something that he was willing to defend in the face of withering criticism and at a terrible cost in human life." It made Bush look "like a winner."[32]

David Gergen, a frequent Bush critic, offered glowing praise. Bush had "turn[ed] the Persian Gulf crisis into a triumph of American leadership."

He had "seized the initiative to create a more peaceful and just world." For the president,

Praise is in order. The United States today enjoys greater respect around the world than at any time since an American stepped onto the moon. Its men and women in uniform serve with renewed pride. The prospects for peace and justice are rising again. And most of the credit belongs to one man.[33]

Mortimer B. Zuckerman offered similarly high praises for the president. Zuckerman credited the president with having

managed this whole complicated process brilliantly. He formed and led an international coalition. He retained and built popular support at home. He carried enough bipartisan support in Congress. He gave appropriate leeway and support to America's military planners and our fighting men and women.[34]

Some reports suggested that Bush had shown himself to be a thoughtful and principled world leader. Accordingly, he elaborated a "just war theory" for going to war, studied history and learned valuable lessons from working with some of his predecessors.[35] Mary McGrory wrote that the man who was "once dismissed as hapless, wimpy, weak" commanded the world's respect.[36] Journalists perceived Bush's stature as so commanding, his success so complete, that many suggested the Democratic party would not be able to put up a viable challenge in the 1992 presidential campaign.[37]

After the cease-fire Bush boasted, "by God, we've kicked the Vietnam syndrome once and for all." Three *Time* pieces reflected on Bush's achievement. Stanley W. Cloud praised the president's "meticulous" efforts to achieve the military victory.[38] Strobe Talbott credited Bush's "personal determination" and the effective alliance that the president created.[39] Hugh Sidey offered the most glowing praise.

Never before has an American president stood so grandly astride this capricious world as George Bush does these days. . . . The widespread notion that Bush would forever remain in the charismatic shadow of Ronald Reagan or be viewed as a foreign policy amateur compared with Richard Nixon has evaporated. It will probably never rise again.[40]

For many, Bush's public standing provided a unique opportunity to also promote an aggressive domestic agenda. Some said that Bush needed to apply the same level of energy and commitment to problems at home as he had to those abroad.[41]

Unfortunately for Bush, it was not long after the cease-fire when presidential press coverage turned from bouquets to brickbats. Some suggested that the president and leading Republicans gloated too much about the military success.[42] Others maintained that any military success in the Gulf had to be considered tainted by Republican policies under Reagan and Bush that had created the conditions for Iraq's invasion of Kuwait.[43] Some argued that Bush ignored human rights abuses in Kuwait—a hypocritical stance given his justifications for U.S. military action.[44]

The most vociferous criticisms concerned Bush's response—or lack thereof—to the Iraqi slaughtering of Kurdish and Shiite rebels. Many considered the allied victory in the Gulf soiled because of the failure to get Hussein out of power and the lack of intervention in the Iraqi civil war. Numerous commentaries blamed Bush for the disastrous postwar situation in Iraq, even though he said on numerous occasions that the objective of the allied effort was not to settle a protracted civil war. As *Newsweek* reported, "the columnists who extolled the president for rescuing Kuwait from Saddam were now accusing him of moral perfidy. What happened to the president who sent a half-million troops into the desert to 'stand up for what's right and condemn what's wrong?' "[45] Consequently, Bush achieved "an incomplete victory."[46] Headline titles made the point.

"Bush's Bay of Pigs"

"The Iraqi Kurds: Tiananman II"

"The Iraqi Kurds: A Moral Failure"

"Suckering the Kurds, Again"

"Neither Moral nor Smart"

"A Confused Strategy"

"White House Failure?"

"Too Cautious in Iraq"

"Bush's Peace Problems"

Charles Krauthammer summed up the views of many in a column that argued Bush had failed the test of leadership after the war. That is, Bush refused to risk any popularity or political capital to avert the "Kurdish catastrophe."

After seven months of brilliant, indeed heroic, presidential leadership, George Bush's behavior after the gulf war—his weak and vacillating hands-off, I'm-out-of-here policy—is a puzzle. . . . A man of pathological prudence, having just risked everything on one principled roll of the dice, was not about to hang around the gaming room a second longer. . . . The willingness to risk political capital is not just a sign of greatness in a leader, it is almost a definition of it. . . . And having had his brush with greatness, Bush would rather not risk it again.[47]

Krauthammer also criticized Bush's failure to define the concept "New World Order." Bush did not infuse that concept with some underlying set of values to justify American intervention abroad. Consequently, "Americans will not rally to some desiccated notion of international stability or balance of power."[48]

Others echoed that harsh analysis. *U.S. News and World Report* described the president as "prudent, and a Scrooge when it comes to investing his precious political capital." Furthermore, Bush preferred "the status quo to the risky business of promoting change."[49] George F. Will was unimpressed with Bush's postwar leadership.

The administration's post–Desert Storm hubris regarding the external world, and its congenital lack of imagination regarding problems at home, are now reinforcing each other. The administration has a swollen sense of its potency on the world stage and an inability to imagine things to do domestically.[50]

Criticism of Bush's postwar foreign policy focused on two areas—U.S. relations with China and the Soviet Union. Regarding China, most of the press criticism was directed at the administration's extension of most-favored-nation status to that country, despite continuous human rights abuses.[51] For example, Mary McGrory said that Bush refused to adopt a moral posture regarding human rights abuses against Tibet because, unlike in the Middle East, no marketable commodity such as oil was at stake.[52] Jack Anderson and Dale Van Atta described Bush National Security Adviser Brent Scowcroft and Deputy Secretary of State Lawrence Eagleburger, as "men who hear no evil, see no evil and speak no evil when it comes to China. . . . It is Bush's nature to *kowtow* to China."[53]

Bush's late July U.S.–Soviet summit in Moscow produced a Strategic Arms Reduction Treaty (START), the hallmark of which was an agreement to limit superpower nuclear arsenals. Press reviews favorably noted Bush's diplomatic skills as instrumental in bringing the agreement about.[54] Some used the occasion to criticize the president's constant focus on international affairs. Strobe Talbott wrote that "it is no secret that this most peripatetic of presidents prefers diplomacy to what he sometimes calls the 'domestic stuff.' "[55] George F. Will called Bush's "frenetic diplomacy . . . a national embarrassment." Bush had "virtually abandon[ed] presidential responsibilities regarding affairs within America's borders." Unlike Ronald Reagan, Bush had failed to accept "the presidency as an engine of domestic change."[56] Stephen S. Rosenfeld wrote that "Bush has his priorities upside down."

Bush, a devoted pro when he sits down at the foreign policy keyboard, often conveys indifference and boredom at the domestic console. Sometimes he seems dizzied by the success of the values of freedom in the world, as though ideological triumph on a global scale—a condition he inherited on taking office—had relieved him of a requirement to do everything within his power to build a good society.[57]

While vacationing in Kennebunkport, Maine, on August 18, the president learned of a coup attempt against the Soviet government. Bush initially adopted a cautious approach to this disturbing event, refusing to condemn it as illegal. Clearly the president wanted to protect U.S. interests whatever the outcome. Although some believed that Bush had been too reluctant to endorse Russian Republic President Boris Yeltsin's gestures against the coup plotters, many praised the cautious, flexible U.S. response.[58] In the end, when the plot failed, Bush's actions appeared successful. Strobe Talbott gave "two cheers" for Bush's crisis leadership. "In other contexts, Bush's obsession with prudence and caution sometimes makes him seem like a stick-in-the-mud. But recently . . . Bush's go slow instincts were welcome." Talbott withheld a third cheer because the president had not displayed "active, articulate and innovative" leadership in response to profound changes in the Soviet Union and Eastern Europe.[59] Some reports suggested that Bush's deft foreign policy leadership had left his Democratic opponents at a major disadvantage going into the next year's election season.

Newsweek: Loopy and flappable when forced to play street politician, Bush gathers himself into a sure-footed presence when the tanks roll abroad. . . . For now, Bush has all the excuse he needs to dwell on his first love, foreign policy—and the more global a stage he plays on, the more parochial the Democrats look in comparison.[60]

Time: Bush's continuing popularity is clearly bad news for the Democrats, whose 1992 election chances have been further dimmed by the dramatic events in the Soviet Union. . . . Democrats face a chilling worst-case scenario: that the party of F.D.R. and J.F.K. may one day join the party of Lenin and Stalin on the ash heap of history.[61]

Favorable press coverage also attended Bush's October arms reduction initiative to which Soviet leader Mikhail Gorbachev responded positively. Bush offered to eliminate ground-launched short-range nuclear warheads. Gorbachev not only agreed; he offered to cut Soviet long-range nuclear warheads well below the START treaty requirements. The *New York Times* praised Bush's initiative.[62] Tom Wicker wrote that the president's actions had displayed both "courage" and "vision."[63] Strobe Talbott called Bush's actions both "prudent" and "bold." The president had "demonstrat[ed] real leadership."[64] *Newsweek* lauded Bush's "bold proposal" and concluded that he "ha[d] laid down his marker to history."[65]

To a certain extent, Bush's critics said that he merely had the luck to preside during the end of the cold war and then the dissolution of the Soviet Union in late 1991.[66] They also claimed that Bush had failed to seize the occasion of the end of the Soviet Union to offer bold pronouncements and policy initiatives. According to Mary McGrory, it took "an activist Democrat," Bush's ambassador to the former Soviet Union, Robert S. Strauss, to articulate the importance of that event and the dangers that it potentially posed to the world. As for Bush, he didn't recognize "the dangers of inaction." A "bewildered" president responded "as he did to the fall of the Berlin Wall."[67] Many criticized Bush for not immediately offering substantial new aid to the former Soviet republics to encourage a more stable

Democratic transition.[68] Charles Krauthammer blasted Bush for "respond[ing] to the greatest Eurasian upheaval of the half-century with Gorby-clutching silence." The columnist offered the familiar criticism.

Ronald Reagan ran for president on ideas and promises. George Bush did not. Bush had no agenda. He promised only to be an adequate steward for the country. . . . George Bush does not believe in very much. He never pretended to. . . . Take away George Bush's belief in internationalism and free trade, and what's left?[69]

THE PRESIDENT AT HOME: ALL BRICKBATS

Throughout 1991, journalists consistently criticized Bush for failing to promote an activist domestic agenda. The *Washington Post* said that he offered "no urgent agenda" but rather a "defensive agenda" at home while he focused on foreign policy.[70] The *Post* opined that Bush's advocacy of the marketplace and volunteerism did not amount to an adequate strategy to combat social problems.[71]

Numerous *Post* columnists echoed that view. In a piece entitled "Activist Government Works, Mr. President," David S. Broder lambasted Bush's critical view of LBJ's Great Society. According to Broder, Bush could not understand or empathize with the problems of economically marginal Americans because of a privileged background.[72] Furthermore, Bush's thinking on domestic issues was characterized by "fuzziness" and "ambivalence": "But the fundamental problem is that the American situation does not allow the minimalist approach to domestic policy that Bush brought to the presidency."[73]

Meg Greenfield implored the president to promote "positive programs and decisions." She considered his foreign policy leadership of "much superior quality" to what he tried to do at home. Greenfield declared that "conventional political wisdom is right: the president doesn't seem to have a strong interest in or focus on domestic issues at all."[74]

William Raspberry agreed. He wrote that Bush appeared "surefooted and resolute in foreign policy" but directionless in domestic affairs. Bush proved himself a "statesman" in the international arena and a "bumbler" at home.[75]

Haynes Johnson added that Bush had demonstrated an "exemplary record in foreign affairs" and an "ineffectual" one at home. According to Johnson the president exhibited leadership characteristics abroad: political will, clearly articulated goals, talent and perseverance. Such "strong presidential leadership" evaded Bush in the face of domestic problems.[76]

New York Times columnists Leslie Gelb, James Reston, and Russell Baker expressed similar views. Gelb wrote that the president could effectively lead only by "reordering [his] priorities and paying more attention to America than the world."[77] Reston's article highlighted in bold type, "George Bush's moral urge to remake the world echoes Woodrow Wilson's but ignores the need for an overhaul at home."[78] Baker rhetorically asked whether the administration *should* do something about the domestic "wrack and ruin" and answered "Sure, but you can bet this crowd won't. They hate domestic problems. Press them about people sleeping in the streets or 34 million Americans without medical care, and they talk public-relations cant about 'points of light.' "[79]

Wall Street Journal columnists Albert R. Hunt and Paul A. Gigot joined the presidential criticism. According to Hunt, the president was "either ignorant or insensitive" when it came to the plight of the inner-city poor.[80] Gigot joked that Bush had many domestic policy goals—for Kuwait, not the United States. "George Bush could finish his first term having done more for the world than he has for his country."[81]

The news magazines weighed in with equally negative reviews. Bush had "a puny agenda" marred by "aimlessness."[82] He offered "virtually no legislative program."[83] He displayed "no interest in announcing any break-through domestic initiatives."[84] Bush promised "no plans for bold, new domestic programs," only a conservative "minimalist approach" to governing.[85] A *Newsweek* report stated that Bush's points-of-light program evidenced "an almost 19th-century approach to social ills" rather than real "presidential leadership."[86]

The Economy

The declining state of the economy in 1991 was the basis for much press and public disgruntlement with Bush's leadership. In October a *Newsweek* column described Bush's greatest challenge as "not the Democrats, but the economy."[87]

Indeed, whenever the public focus on foreign affairs lifted, Bush was in trouble. During the Persian Gulf War, *Newsweek* declared that "by all rights, George Bush's economic advisers should be goners." But Bush's economic policies had been temporarily "spared the withering criticism" because of the war.[88]

The withering criticism returned. In a mocking reference to former president Jimmy Carter's leadership during a recession, the *Wall Street Journal* called Bush's policies a "new spin on Jimmynomics." The *Journal* blasted Bush's "feckless" policymaking and declared his advisers "economic incompetents."[89] According to the *Journal* editors, Bush's policies did not promote the creation of capital and jobs; he relied too heavily on budget director Richard Darman's advice; the administration had failed to set clear economic priorities.[90] *Journal* columnist Paul A. Gigot offered similar assessments.

The scent of Carterism is wafting from Pennsylvania Avenue. The floundering, the abandonment of principles like used clothes—these are signs of a president in trouble. . . . On the economy, he cannot make up his mind because he does not really know what to believe. . . . He does not believe in anything enough to fight for it.[91]

Although the business daily was a natural critic of presidential economic policy, other sources joined the *Journal*. Reports in the news weeklies referred to the contrast between Bush's international leadership and "hands-off" response to the recession.[92] Many suggested that Bush adopted economic themes—sensitivity to the underclass, the need for a new tax break, protecting U.S. trade interests—mostly for political reasons while he failed to offer positive programs.[93]

Civil Rights

Bush received the worst press coverage in 1991 for his handling of the proposed Civil Rights Act. The president initially expressed strong reservations about signing the Act, which he claimed would require businesses to adopt racial hiring quotas. Bush insisted that he wanted to sign a civil rights bill, as long as the legislation did not create quota requirements. Advocates of the Act insisted that it did not mandate quotas. Despite his earlier stated objections, in October Bush signed a slightly revised version of the Act. He did so, he said, because the compromised version had overcome his earlier objections.

Throughout most of the year, when Bush opposed the Civil Rights Act, press coverage emphasized racial insensitivity and political opportunism by the president. David S. Broder speculated that Bush would eventually veto the bill and then exploit racial divisions in 1992 for political gain.[94] The *New York Times* and the *Washington Post* agreed that Bush's major motivation was to exploit the race issue for political gain, and they argued that the bill had nothing to do with quotas.[95] Anthony Lewis wrote that Bush was not interested in "alleviating this country's corrosive race relations." Rather, the president cared more about "gaining political advantage."[96] Tom Wicker maintained that the president was incapable of recognizing historical injustice against blacks in the United States. Wicker said that black leaders had no reason to believe that Bush cared about racial justice.[97] Richard Cohen accused the president of "exploiting the widespread fear of quotas." According to Cohen, the president preferred the "quota issue" over real civil rights progress.[98]

The president won over very few critics by signing the revised bill in October. The *New York Times* praised the president's decision to sign the bill but largely credited congressional Democrats and moderate Republicans for the legislative success. Furthermore, "after insisting for two years that the measure was a 'quota bill,' Mr. Bush suddenly discovered that a new draft, barely distinguishable from old ones, was not a quota bill. His instant revision of history fooled nobody."[99] A *Time* report blasted the president's "feckless efforts to have it both ways on civil rights."[100] Anthony Lewis dwelled on the costs of the president having taken so long to agree to the civil rights bill.[101] Both Paul A. Gigot and the *Wall Street Journal* editors cited Bush's policy reversal as further evidence of a lack of principles. Gigot asked, "how many more belly flops can this president stand?"

Because he sends out no clear signals, everyone believes everything with Mr. Bush is negotiable. He is paralyzed by his own pragmatism. Perhaps an historian will be able to explain how a man who was so sure-footed in the Gulf War can be so flat-footed on so much else.[102]

The *Journal* editors asked, "Earth to 1600 Pennsylvania Avenue: Who's in charge?" "By compromising at every turn," they said, "the president's real beliefs on this subject are muddled beyond recognition and Mr. Bush wakes up this morning as the Quota President."[103]

Many questioned Bush's motivations for signing the Civil Rights Act of 1991. For example, the Louisiana GOP had nominated an ex-Klansman for governor, fueling enormous negative coverage of the national state of race relations. According to a common view, Bush wanted to be seen as rising above that climate by adopting a conciliatory position on civil rights.[104]

Furthermore, Bush had taken a beating on his nomination of Clarence Thomas to the Supreme Court. What especially bothered many is that the president had chosen Thomas, a forty-three-year old conservative without a distinguished judicial or scholarly background, to replace the retiring Justice Thurgood Marshall, the man who stood as the strongest symbol of American judicial commitment to civil rights. Some suggested that Bush's selection of Thomas was cynical because liberals allegedly would have enormous political difficulties making the case against a black appointee to replace Marshall. Furthermore, critics suggested that Bush would be able "to pull back on civil rights programs" by appointing a conservative black jurist to the Court.[105] Bush's choice was "the new front in the 'quota' war."[106]

When Professor Anita Hill, a former subordinate of Thomas at the EEOC, stepped forward during the nomination hearings to accuse him of sexual harassment, the nomination process turned into an ugly political battle. Without specific facts about what had transpired between Thomas and Hill in the past, ideological conservatives and liberals took opposing stands on the controversy, using the nominee and his accuser as vehicles to promote political agendas. The White House adopted a confirmation strategy that called attention to Thomas's personal triumphs against poverty and racism. That strategy turned public opinion in Thomas's favor and probably saved his confirmation by the Senate. Civil rights leaders who already had opposed Thomas's confirmation became especially angry with what they perceived as Bush's crass use of a racial appeal to save the nomination.

Some columnists suggested that Bush was responsible for the increasingly disturbing racial climate that attended Thomas's selection and controversial confirmation.[107] That Bush reversed his course on the Civil Rights Act soon after the Thomas confirmation did not appear to be strictly coincidental.

Other Issues

Bush clearly did not win press plaudits for his domestic policy leadership. In addition to the economy and civil rights, journalists perceived a lack of strong presidential leadership—that is, calls for bold, innovative and ultimately costly programs in health care, AIDS policy, energy, drug abuse, conservation, and education.[108]

The press reaction to Bush's education policy initiatives provides the best example. Bush offered what he considered a bold education initiative entitled "America 2000: An Education Strategy." The initiative called for a series of elementary and secondary school reforms, including national testing, experimental schools, and support for vouchers. David S. Broder called the initiative "an invitation to cynicism" and a "scam." Why? Because the program did not call for an increase in the Department of Education budget.[109] A *Time* report extolled Bush's objectives as laudatory but maintained that he couldn't achieve them "without the money that might really make a difference."[110] A *New York Times* editorial agreed that only a significant increase in federal funding for education would demonstrate that Bush was serious about his goals.[111] *Newsweek* considered Bush's proposal a better-late-than-never effort and noted that federal inaction had put the country into the position of needing a major education "revolution."[112]

BUSH AND PRESIDENTIAL LEADERSHIP

To a press corps focused on the conventional wisdom of the moment, Bush looked unbeatable for reelection after the Gulf War victory. Laurence I. Barrett mused that perhaps the Democrats should also nominate Bush in 1992—it was the only way that they could win. In that case, the Democrats would nominate someone other than Dan Quayle for vice president. Voters would then choose, for example, between the Republican Bush-Quayle ticket and the Democratic Bush-Gore ticket. Barrett said that the Democrats were "so discombobulated" that they would probably foul up the ploy and nominate Tom Eagleton for vice president![113] More seriously, Barrett discussed the Democrats' plight: "Running against an incumbent president is hard enough; running against a triumphant Commander in Chief is nearly impossible, no matter how much bunting a candidate drapes himself in."[114]

Numerous articles commented on the lack of enthusiasm within the Democratic party to challenge Bush in 1992.[115] Howard Fineman described the "funereal air" surrounding the party's efforts to find a good presidential candidate. He added that "dead Whig Zachary Taylor gets more respect than most live Democrats."[116] According to Fineman, Democrats had few viable options in running against the president who presided over the first major U.S. war victory since 1945: they could "play for 1996," "agree on a good soldier," hope for an act of God, hope for a turnaround in political cycles, make a statement with some "liberated long shot" such as L. Douglas Wilder who was the nation's first elected black governor.

If you are a Democrat with a compulsion to run for president, this would be a good time to find a detox program for the ambition-addicted. President Bush's popularity is at Founding Father levels. . . . Running for president requires an unshakable faith in your chances of victory. But this time it may require what theater critics call "the willing suspension of disbelief."[117]

Many others as well maintained that Bush was unbeatable in 1992. Some suggested that the Democrats were reduced to hoping for a deep recession as their only chance to win the presidency. Others said that Bush had the leeway—unlike in 1988—to run an issue-oriented campaign in 1992.[118]

According to the *Wall Street Journal*, Bush's Gulf War victory also provided him a unique opportunity to become an activist president and a major historical figure. The victory "almost certainly will secure for Mr. Bush a second term in office. We wonder whether the president plans to do anything with this authority." The *Journal* editors fundamentally agreed with the progressive notion of activist presidential leadership.

The opportunity is at hand for George Bush to alter the politics of this country for a generation. As did Teddy Roosevelt, FDR and John Kennedy . . . [who] offered the nation a political model that launched ideas and initiatives at every level of government. . . . The Bush presidency represents a new era of U.S. global leadership. . . . If the Bush presidency is to push its achievements into the next century, it will have to shape a domestic agenda as well.[119]

The *Journal* implored Bush to use his stature to assert presidential prerogatives in the face of "a power-grabbing president." Throughout the Bush presidency, the *Journal* made the case for presidential ascendancy and the case against legislative impositions on the executive branch.[120]

Bush did not live up to such expectations of domestic policy activism. Andrew Rosenthal wrote that Bush preferred "an incremental, small-bore approach" to domestic issues.[121] Michael Kramer wrote that Bush's likely 1992 victory would merely result in "four more years of governmental paralysis."[122] David S. Broder argued that Bush would likely be reelected, but the president still did not offer a positive domestic program. The president expected to be rewarded for past accomplishments, not for future plans, according to Broder.[123] Howard Fineman suggested a Democrat's "fantasy" scenario for 1992: Bush suffers the same fate as British Prime Minister Winston Churchill in 1945. That is, a wartime leader loses reelection when the public focuses on domestic concerns in the postwar environment. Although Bush gave rise to such a "fantasy" by not proposing a positive domestic program, Fineman considered such a scenario in 1992 unlikely to occur.[124]

By November, press assessments of Bush's reelection prospects changed, although the assessments of his leadership acumen had not. In a November 5 special election in Pennsylvania for the U.S. Senate, Bush's former attorney general, Richard Thornburgh, lost decidedly to a political neophyte, Democrat Harris Wofford. During the campaign, Thornburgh stressed his Washington experience and close relationship with the president. Bush actively campaigned for his former attorney general. The underdog candidate Wofford also emphasized Thornburgh's Washington experience and close relationship to the president. Wofford made domestic issues, especially health care and the economy, the focus of his appeals. The press widely interpreted Wofford's victory as a protest vote against Bush. Why such a repudiation of Bush? Because he was a Washington insider and he had failed to offer domestic policy leadership.

Time magazine declared the Pennsylvania election a "wake-up call" to Bush to start moving aggressively on domestic policy. The faltering economy and key domestic issues had finally made Bush electorally vulnerable in 1992.[125] The *Wall Street Journal* implored Bush to take action on the economy. "Bush can't stand above this debate without becoming another Dick Thornburgh."[126] The *New York Times* also perceived Bush as electorally vulnerable because of a lack of emphasis on domestic issues. "However admirable his achievements abroad, he appears singularly inattentive to problems at home. That's probably the most important message the voters sent [on November 5]; he better be listening."[127]

Indeed, many agreed that Bush had caused his own political decline with inaction on the home front. A *U.S. News* report stated that Bush offered the country "no clear answers" to domestic problems. He lacked a "forward-looking vision" and his presidency was a "muddle." Bush's "inertia" put him into political trouble.[128] According to Haynes Johnson, "Bush ha[d] failed by not addressing problems candidly and offering practical solutions." The president failed to "inspire confidence" such as Franklin Roosevelt had inspired during the Great Depression. Johnson predicted that Bush would "pay a heavy political price for his inaction."[129] The *New York Times* revised the "two George Bushes" theme. The *Times* described the president as "shrewd and energetic in foreign policy and just the reverse—clumsy and irresolute—at home."

The foreign Bush has been exemplary. . . . The domestic Bush is a strange figure, a man with no clear idea of how to convert triumph abroad into renewal at home. The domestic Bush flops like a fish, leaving the impression that he doesn't know what he thinks or doesn't much care, apart from the political gains to be extracted from an issue.[130]

The *Wall Street Journal* agreed:

The president needs to show, that in domestic policy as in foreign policy, he knows where he wants to go. . . . Americans now see that the man who confidently led a global coalition against Saddam Hussein is utterly adrift on the . . . economy. What the public senses it has to fear most is the president's fear of acting. He has to show he's in command by showing he knows how to get the country moving again.[131]

Numerous others made similar assessments. Tom Wicker criticized the president's "lack of a coherent economic program" and said that Bush lacked "vision, bold leadership [and] intuitive understanding."[132] Kenneth T. Walsh wrote that "[Bush] and his advisers show little interest in taking the offensive or setting the agenda."[133] David Gergen maintained that Bush needed to show the same aggressive presidential leadership in domestic affairs as demonstrated in the Gulf War.[134] James Reston maintained that it was the president's responsibility to set national priorities, but Bush cared "more about order abroad than disorder at home."[135]

THE PRESIDENT'S MEN

Substantial negative press coverage in 1991 centered on Vice President Dan Quayle and Chief of Staff John Sununu. Criticism of these two men reflected negatively on Bush's judgment.

On May 4, while taking a routine jog at Camp David, the president experienced an irregular heartbeat and shortness of breath. After doctors examined Bush at Bethesda Naval Hospital, they diagnosed him with Graves' disease, a thyroid ailment. At one point, Bush had considered temporarily transferring his powers to Vice President Quayle under the 25th amendment before being treated with anesthesia. The doctors determined that such a measure was unnecessary.

Any presidential illness seemingly as serious as a heart condition worries the country. For journalists who had excoriated Bush's vice presidential selection in 1988, the president's health scare again raised the issue of the wisdom of that selection. What if Bush had experienced a life-threatening complication? What if Quayle actually had become president? According to the *Washington Post*, the lingering question of Quayle's fitness for the presidency was a fair one and the answer "far from reassuring." The *Post* editorial not too subtly raised the question of whether Bush should replace Quayle on the 1992 ticket when it suggested that the president would be forced to confront allegations that he had "put the country at risk" by having a weak vice president.[136]

David S. Broder revisited the other lingering question of why Bush chose Quayle. Bush had not "given a full or persuasive answer to that question." Broder speculated about Bush's decision and argued that too much evidence existed in 1988 that Quayle wasn't presidential. "Why Bush—one of the world's great consulters and kibitzers—made this decision without such checking is the great mystery of the matter."[137]

Haynes Johnson expressed relief that Bush's diagnosis and recovery were both good.

Far better a medically treatable overactive thyroid gland than a heart condition that at any moment could force a change in presidents from George Bush to Dan Quayle. . . . The intriguing question is not so much about Quayle as about Bush. Does the president really believe that Quayle is the person most qualified to lead America through the closing years of this turbulent century?[138]

Dan Goodgame wrote that with the Gulf War victory and other accomplishments, Bush had "made it possible to forget about Dan Quayle." After the presidential health scare, "hearts across the nation and around the world began to fibrillate at the thought that Quayle might suddenly be thrust into the most powerful position on earth." The president recovered but "the rest of the country continued to suffer from the shakes." More devastating, Goodgame said that Bush had endangered the national interest by choosing Quayle.[139] Following this article in *Time* was a long piece entitled "Five Who Fit the Bill." It featured profiles of five GOP figures who were "competent and capable" of replacing Quayle and serving as vice president.[140] The same edition featured an article about Quayle entitled "Is He Really That Bad?" Although the article sought to bring balance to the reporting on Quayle by highlighting some of his accomplishments, overall it was as damaging as the others. It featured a series of embarrassing photographs of Quayle with captions describing various humiliations he had experienced. About the president, the article stated that, "once derided as a wimp, Bush can sympathize with Quayle's dilemma."[141]

Leslie H. Gelb also damned the vice president with faint praise. Quayle was "[no] more than a nice and competent guy." Quayle was "no buffoon" as widely reported, but "an average American and an average politician who . . . strikes people as a kid." Gelb implored Bush to "review his judgment" in choosing Quayle and "think of America first."[142]

Perhaps aware that Bush would not consider replacing Quayle on the 1992 ticket, some implored the president not to take any unnecessary health risks; for example, strenuous sports activities. To a nation frightened at the prospect of Quayle becoming president, Bush needed to demonstrate that he was in good health. He resumed his normal activities soon after being released from the hospital.[143]

Bush's controversial chief of staff, John Sununu, caused different presidential troubles. Sununu had the reputation of being the president's "bad cop." He often deflected presidential criticism by taking blame for unpopular and controversial decisions within the White House. Reporters intensely disliked him. They considered him brilliant, yet arrogant and devious. Sununu had many enemies within the administration who did not like his heavy-handed decision making and temperamental demeanor. To be sure, Sununu had acquired so many enemies throughout political Washington that most eagerly awaited his inevitable downfall.

The downfall occurred in late 1991. It was the culmination of a series of allegations of unethical conduct that resulted in a deluge of negative publicity and caused the president great embarrassment. *U.S. News* reported in April that Sununu had flown in government aircraft 148 times in twenty-seven months, oftentimes combining personal recreation with business on the trips.[144] Additional stories reported too that Sununu had used military planes to travel to the family dentist and to take skiing vacations.

These reports were especially troubling to Bush because he had promised to run an administration of high ethical conduct, permitting not even the appearance of impropriety. The press reminded Bush of his high standard and noted the hypocrisy of tolerating Sununu's actions.[145]

Sununu resigned in early December at the president's request. With a tough reelection challenge ahead, Bush could not afford all of the political trouble that attended Sununu's presence in the administration. Press coverage of the resignation generally was favorable. That is, reporters were glad to be rid of the man. But many pointed out that Bush could not solve his political problems merely by changing personnel. They said that he had to do something about a faltering economy.[146]

Samuel Skinner replaced Sununu as the chief of staff. After one week as chief of staff, according to Tom Wicker, Skinner had failed to rescue the White House from its December doldrums.[147]

CONCLUSION

By the end of the year that many had reported as the make-or-break period for the Bush presidency, the administration was more vulnerable electorally than journalists had reported. Indeed, the first signs of this vulnerability appeared as the economy headed into recession, and many blamed the president for lacking a domestic program. The glitter from the Gulf War victory appeared to be wearing off as the public turned its attention to problems at home. Nonetheless, what many doubted was that the Democrats could offer a strong challenger for the 1992 presidential election.

Press commentary and public perceptions of the Bush presidency in 1991 reveal the importance of developing a media strategy that is linked to a policy agenda plan. Bush maintained high levels of public support when the economy appeared healthy or when the country was at war and people rallied behind their president. But his support dropped dramatically in response to changing unfavorable circumstances. Bush's critics often charged that, unlike Reagan, he lacked a core constituency that would support him through both good times and bad. Bush did not inspire such passion and therefore his standing with the public was favorable only when circumstances made people feel comfortable.

There undoubtedly was much truth to this charge, but many of the White House insiders interviewed for this book added that the president paid insufficient attention to image-building and commanding the media. They perceived the president as especially vulnerable to media criticism because, again unlike his predecessor, he did not do enough to try to control how the public perceived him and his administration's goals.

The following election year provided the White House its final opportunity to try to change course and offer the public a compelling reason to re-elect the president. In what follows, it becomes clear just how difficult it is for an administration at this late stage to change course and fundamentally alter its perception in the press and among the public.

NOTES

1. R. W. Apple, Jr., "Presidency on the Brink of Make or Break Year," *New York Times*, January 1, 1991, p. A10; "Decks Cleared?" *Wall Street Journal*, January 2, 1991, p. A6.

2. Ann McDaniel and Evan Thomas, "Bush the Communicator," *Newsweek*, October 14, 1991, p. 28.

3. Leslie H. Gelb, "Mr. Bush's Three Trios," *New York Times*, August 14, 1991, p. A19; Anthony Lewis, "Government by Cabal," *New York Times*, November 25, 1991, p. A19.

4. George J. Church, "A Tale of Two Bushes," *Time*, January 7, 1991, p. 18.

5. Ibid., p. 20.

6. Dan Goodgame, "In the Gulf: Bold Vision," *Time*, January 7, 1991, p. 22.

7. Michael Duffy, "At Home: No Vision," *Time*, January 7, 1991, pp. 28–29.

8. Ibid., p. 29.

9. Kenneth T. Walsh, "George Bush's Idea-free Zone," *U.S. News and World Report*, January 14, 1991, p. 34.

10. "The Big Mo," *Wall Street Journal*, January 28, 1991, p. A10.

11. Margaret Carlson, "So Who's Minding the Store?" *Time*, February 11, 1991, p. 54.

12. Jim Hoagland, "Taking Up Kennedy's Torch," *Washington Post*, January 31, 1991, p. A19.

13. Michael Kinsley, "Dink Stover Goes to War," *Washington Post*, January 31, 1991, p. A19.

14. Mary McGrory, "Martial Arts," *Washington Post*, January 31, 1991, p. A2.

15. "Meanwhile, Back in the Union," *New York Times*, January 31, 1991, p. A22.

16. George F. Will, "Hard Work Avoided," *Washington Post*, January 31, 1991, p. A19.

17. McGrory, "Martial Arts."

18. Jonathan Yardley, "The Sad State of the Presidential Address," *Washington Post*, February 4, 1991, p. B2.

19. "The Third Year: State of the War," *New York Times*, January 31, 1991, p. A22.

20. David S. Broder, "A Gipper-like Kind of Win," *Washington Post*, February 1, 1991, p. A21.

21. "The Union's Leadership," *Wall Street Journal*, January 31, 1991, p. A16.

22. Michael B. Kagay, "Approval of Bush Soars," *New York Times*, January 19, 1991, p. A9.

23. "The President's Popularity," *New York Times*, March 5, 1991, p. A20.

24. R. W. Apple, Jr., "Defining the Issue," *New York Times*, January 17, 1991, p. A16.

25. A. M. Rosenthal, "The First Battle," *New York Times* January 18, 1991, p. A31.

26. "On the Home Front," *Wall Street Journal*, January 17, 1991, p. A10.

27. "The Bush Coalition," *Wall Street Journal*, January 17, 1991, p. A10.

28. Paul A. Gigot, "Bush's View: This is Still America's Century," *Wall Street Journal*, January 25, 1991, p. A12.

29. Evan Thomas, "'Strong and Steady,'" *Newsweek*, January 28, 1991, p. 34.

30. Evan Thomas, "The One True Hawk in the Administration," *Newsweek*, January 7, 1991, p. 19. See also Evan Thomas, "Bush and the Generals," *Newsweek*, February 4, 1991, p. 27.

31. Charles Krauthammer, "Bush's March through Washington," *Washington Post*, March 1, 1991, p. A15.

32. Dan Goodgame, "Bush's Biggest Gamble," *Time*, January 28, 1991, p. 32.

33. David Gergen, "The President's Finest Hour," *U.S. News and World Report*, March 4, 1991, p. 64.

34. Mortimer B. Zuckerman, "Hussein's Many Miscalculations," *U.S. News and World Report*, January 28, 1991, p. 70.

35. See, for example, Kenneth T. Walsh, "Bush's 'Just War' Doctrine," *U.S. News and World Report*, February 4, 1991, pp. 52–53; Kenneth T. Walsh, "Commander in Chief," *U.S. News and World Report*, December 31, 1990/January 7, 1991, pp. 22–25; Kenneth T. Walsh, "A President's True Mission," *U.S. News and World Report*, February 11, 1991, pp. 46–47.

36. Mary McGrory, "Bush's Winning Ways of War," *Washington Post*, February 21, 1991, p. A2.

37. See, for example, Stanley W. Cloud, "Exorcising an Old Demon," *Time*, March 11, 1991, pp. 52–53; Robin Toner, "Bush's War Success Confers an Aura of Invincibility in '92," *New York Times*, February 27, 1991, p. A1; Robin Toner, "Democrats Don't Need Sacrificial Lamb for '92," *New York Times*, March 11, 1991, p. A12; Tom Wicker, "Victims of War," *New York Times*, March 2, 1991, p. A23; "Digging Out from the Gulf War Rubble," *U.S. News and World Report*, March 25, 1991, pp. 26–28.

38. Stanley W. Cloud, "Exorcising an Old Demon."

39. Strobe Talbott, "White Flags in the Desert," *Time*, March 11, 1991, p. 21.

40. Hugh Sidey, "Of Force, Fame and Fishing," *Time*, March 11, 1991, p. 55.

41. See, for example, Leslie H. Gelb, "Dear Mr. President . . . " *New York Times*, March 3, 1991, sec. 4, p. 17; Dan Goodgame, "Bush's Republican Guard," *Time*, March 11, 1991, p. 54; Robin Toner, "Did Someone Say 'Domestic Policy'?" *New York Times*, March 3, 1991, sec. 4, p. 1; "On the Home Front," *Wall Street Journal*, January 17, 1991, p. A10; "The President's Petulance," *New York Times*, June 12, 1991, p. A26.

42. See, for example, Haynes Johnson, "Multiplying the Divisions," *Washington Post*, March 8, 1991, p. A2; Mary McGrory, "The Real 'Vietnam Syndrome,'" *Washington Post*, March 7, 1991, p. A2.

43. Stephen S. Rosenfeld, "Put the Knives Away," *Washington Post*, March 8, 1991, p. A21. See also Mary McGrory, "Coddling Saddam: A History," *Washington Post*, January 27, 1991, pp. C1, C2; Tom Wicker, "A Foolish Decade," *New York Times*, February 23, 1991, p. A25.

44. See, for example, Richard Cohen, "Lynch Law in Kuwait," *Washington Post*, March 7, 1991, p. A23.

45. Evan Thomas and Ann McDaniel, "Where Was George This Time?" *Newsweek*, April 15, 1991, p. 31. Among the many columns critical of Bush's actions are Russell Baker, "The Manly Joy of Anguish," *New York Times*, April 9, 1991, p. A25; Richard Cohen, "The Iraqi Kurds: A Moral Failure," *Washington Post*, April 5, 1991, p. A19; Rowland Evans and Robert Novak, "Bush's Big Mistake," *Washington Post*, April 8, 1991, p. A17; Leslie H. Gelb, "A Unified, Weak Iraq," *New York Times*, March 20, 1991, p. A29; Leslie H. Gelb, "Iraq: Drawing the Line," *New York Times*, April 3, 1991, p. A21; Leslie H. Gelb, "White House Guilt?" *New York Times*, April 14, 1991, sec. 4, p. 19; Jim Hoagland, "Back on Track in Iraq," *Washington Post*, April 18, 1991, p. A21; Jim Hoagland, "Neither Moral nor Smart," *Washington Post*, April 9, 1991, p. A21; Jim Hoagland, "Too Cautious in Iraq," *Washington Post*, April 2, 1991, p. A21; Mary McGrory, "Bush's Problems," *Washington Post*, March 26, 1991, p. A2; Mary McGrory, "Suckering the Kurds, Again," *Washington Post*, April 4, 1991, p. A2; William Raspberry, "The Iraqi Kurds: Tempting to Insurrection," *Washington Post*, April 5, 1991, p. A19; A. M. Rosenthal, "Reverse the Reversals," *New York Times*, March 29, 1991, p. A23; A. M. Rosenthal, "The Way Out," *New York Times*, April 23, 1991, p. A21; William Safire, "Bush's Bay of Pigs," *New York Times*, April 4, 1991, p. A23; William Safire, "The Kurds' Dilemma," *New York Times*, September 12, 1991, p. A25; Tom Wicker, "A Confused Strategy," *New York Times*, March 30, 1991, p. A19; "What's the Point?" *Wall Street Journal*, April 4, 1991, p. A14.

46. Charles Lane, "What Did Bush Win?," *Newsweek*, May 13, 1991, p. 27.

47. Charles Krauthammer, "In the Casino," *Washington Post*, May 3, 1991, p. A25. See also Charles Krauthammer, "The Iraqi Kurds: Tiananmen II," *Washington Post*, April 5, 1991, p. A19.

48. Charles Krauthammer, "Which New World Order?" *Washington Post*, May 17, 1991, p. A25.

49. "Call Retreat," *U.S. News and World Report*, May 13, 1991, p. 28.

50. George F. Will, "Bad Advice from Washington," *Washington Post*, July 7, 1991, p. B7.

51. See, for example, Richard Cohen, "One Nation That Should Not Be Favored in Any Way," *Washington Post*, May 30, 1991, p. A19; Leslie H. Gelb, "Breaking China Apart," *New York Times*, November 13, 1991, p. A25; A. M. Rosenthal, "For China: Action Now," *New York Times*, May 14, 1991, p. A19; Hobart Rowen, "Bush Is Just Plain Wrong on China," *Washington Post*, June 2, 1991, pp. H1, H4; "How to Advance China's Freedom," *New York Times*, May 29, 1991, p. A22.

52. Mary McGrory, "Reminders of Bush's Blinders," *Washington Post*, April 18, 1991, p. A2. See also Mary McGrory, "China and an Imperial President," *Washington Post*, May 30, 1991, p. A2; Mary McGrory, "Least Favored Nation Status," *Washington Post*, June 20, 1991, p. A2.

53. Jack Anderson and Dale Van Atta, "Deng: Making a Monkey Out of Bush," *Washington Post*, October 27, 1991, p. C7.

54. See, for example, Charles Lane, "Let's Shake on It," *Newsweek*, July 29, 1991, pp. 14-17; Michael S. Serrill, "Tag-team Diplomacy," *Time*, August 12, 1991, pp. 24-26; Strobe Talbott, "Goodfellas," *Time*, August 5, 1991, pp. 20–24.

55. Strobe Talbott, "The Delicate Balancing Act," *Time*, July 29, 1991, p. 32.

56. George F. Will, "President Odysseus," *Newsweek*, August 12, 1991, p. 68.

57. Stephen S. Rosenfeld, "Up until 3 A.M.," *Washington Post*, August 2, 1991, p. A25.

58. Reports critical of Bush's initial "tepid" response were Michael Duffy, "Let's Stay in Touch," *Time*, September 2, 1991, p. 48; A. M. Rosenthal, "Fear of Victory," *New York Times*, August 27, 1991, p. A23; Kenneth T. Walsh, "Bush's Brand-new Phone Pal," *U.S. News and World Report*, September 2, 1991, pp. 53–55; "The Gorbachev Restoration," *Wall Street Journal*, August 21, 1991, p. A12.

59. Strobe Talbott, "Journey without Maps," *Time*, September 23, 1991, p. 34.

60. Howard Fineman, "'This Is What Bush Does Best,'" *Newsweek*, September 2, 1991, p. 56.

61. Stanley W. Cloud, "After the War," *Time*, September 9, 1991, p. 18.

62. "Breathtaking Progress on Arms," *New York Times*, October 7, 1991, p. A16.

63. Tom Wicker, "Courage and Vision," *New York Times*, October 3, 1991, p. A25.

64. Strobe Talbott, "Toward a Safer World," *Time*, October 7, 1991, pp. 18–20.

65. Tom Morganthau, "Will Bush's Plan Work?" *Newsweek*, October 7, 1991, p. 26.

66. Charles Krauthammer, "The Man Who Loved Dictators," *Time*, October 14, 1991, p. 93.

67. Mary McGrory, "Passivity amid Crisis," *Washington Post*, December 12, 1991, p. A2.

68. See, for example, "Help Russia; Push Russia," *New York Times*, November 26, 1991, p. A20; "Hesitating on Moscow," *Washington Post*, December 29, 1991, p. C6.

69. Charles Krauthammer, "Where's the Rest of Bush?" *Washington Post*, December 27, 1991, p. A21.

70. "The Domestic Agenda," *Washington Post*, January 31, 1991, p. A18.

71. "Mr. Bush on Social Policy," *Washington Post*, June 14, 1991, p. A26.

72. David S. Broder, "Activist Government Works, Mr. President," *Washington Post*, May 19, 1991, p. D7.

73. David S. Broder, "It's Not All Sununu's Fault," *Washington Post*, December 1, 1991, p. C7.

74. Meg Greenfield, "Still Waiting, for the President," *Washington Post*, November 19, 1991, p. A21.

75. William Raspberry, "Bush's Missing Drummer," *Washington Post*, November 25, 1991, p. A21.

76. Haynes Johnson, "Less Will than Wallet," *Washington Post*, June 14, 1991, p. A2.

77. Leslie H. Gelb, "Memo for Mr. Bush," *New York Times*, June 12, 1991, p. A27.

78. James Reston, "A Persistent Yearning," *New York Times Magazine*, June 16, 1991, p. 18.

79. Russell Baker, "Let 'Em Eat Photo Ops," *New York Times*, July 9, 1991, p. A19.

80. Albert R. Hunt, "Two Dispatches from America's Poverty War," *Wall Street Journal*, April 15, 1991, p. A14.

81. Paul A. Gigot, "Bush at Home: Not Exactly Stormin' Norman," *Wall Street Journal*, March 15, 1991, p. A12.

82. Kenneth T. Walsh, "Bush's Drive Back Home," *U.S. News and World Report*, April 22, 1991, pp. 20–22.

83. Michael Barone and Steven V. Roberts, "The Democrats' Veto Strategy," *U.S. News and World Report*, August 5, 1991, p. 20.

84. "Bush: Unworried and Unhurried," *U.S. News and World Report*, August 26/September 2, 1991, p. 13.

85. Kenneth T. Walsh, "Bush's Domestic Cul-de-sac," *U.S. News and World Report*, March 18, 1991, p. 17.

86. Ann McDaniel and Evan Thomas, "Bush's No-risk Policy," *Newsweek*, June 24, 1991, p. 20. See also Richard Lacayo, "Back to Reality," *Time*, April 22, 1991, pp. 28–29.

87. John Schwartz, "Runnin' Scared of Recession," *Newsweek*, October 21, 1991, p. 54.

88. Marc Levinson and Rich Thomas, "Is Bush's Team Up to It?" *Newsweek*, February 18, 1991, p. 53.

89. "New Spin on Jimmynomics," *Wall Street Journal*, November 15, 1991, p. A14; "Economic Incompetents," *Wall Street Journal*, November 18, 1991, p. A16.

90. "Are They Serious?" *Wall Street Journal*, December 9, 1991, p. A14; "Listless Economy—II: A Diffident Administration," *Wall Street Journal*, October 8, 1991, p. A22; "President Darman," *Wall Street Journal*, November 6, 1991, p. A18; "Why Not Jobs?" *Wall Street Journal*, September 24, 1991, p. A18.

91. Paul A. Gigot, "Without Beliefs, Bush Stumbles into Carterism," *Wall Street Journal*, November 22, 1991, p. A12.

92. See, for example, Dan Goodgame, "A Time for Leadership," *Time*, December 9, 1991, pp. 22–24; John Greenwald, "Crawling Out of the Slump," *Time*, June 17, 1991, pp. 48–50; Ann McDaniel, "From Triple K to Capital R," *Newsweek*, November 11, 1991, p. 27.

93. See, for example, Hobart Rowen, "Restoring American Superiority," *Washington Post*, December 26, 1991, p. A23; John E. Yang, "Bush Assumes a Caring Theme, but Quibbling Hurts His Cause," *Washington Post*, December 7,

1991, p. A4; "The President's Inept Tax Plan," *New York Times*, November 29, 1991, p. A34.

94. David S. Broder, "Bush's Favorite Victim," *Washington Post*, June 9, 1991, p. D7.

95. "The President's New Pretext," *New York Times*, August 4, 1991, sec. 4, p. 14; "Quota? No, More like a Canard," *New York Times*, May 28, 1991, p. A20; "Tossing Around the 'Quota' Bomb," *New York Times*, April 7, 1991, sec. 4, p. 18; "More Civil Rights Slogans," *Washington Post*, August 4, 1991, p. C6; "Stonewalling on Civil Rights," *Washington Post*, September 27, 1991, p. A28.

96. Anthony Lewis, "Nixon and Bush," *New York Times*, June 7, 1991, p. A35.

97. Tom Wicker, "Justice or Hypocrisy?" *New York Times*, August 15, 1991, p. A23; Tom Wicker, "'Pounding' Mr. Bush," *New York Times*, July 14, 1991, sec. 4, p. 19.

98. Richard Cohen, "Exploiting Quotas," *Washington Post*, May 28, 1991, p. A19.

99. "Thumbing His Nose at Congress: Mr. Bush Signs—and Undermines— the Rights Bill," *New York Times*, November 22, 1991, p. A30. See also "The Death of an Ugly Slogan," *New York Times*, October 27, 1991, sec. 4, p. 14.

100. Dan Goodgame, "Nervous and Nasty," *Time*, December 2, 1991, p. 18.

101. Anthony Lewis, "Winners and Losers," *New York Times*, October 28, 1991, p. A17.

102. Paul A. Gigot, "With Beliefs, Bush Stumbles into Carterism."

103. "It's a Quota Bill," *Wall Street Journal*, November 22, 1991, p. A12. See also Rowland Evans and Robert Novak, "It Was a Surrender on Quotas," *Washington Post*, October 30, 1991, p. A23.

104. See, for example, Bob Cohn, "A Turnabout on Civil Rights," *Newsweek*, November 4, 1991, p. 32; William Raspberry, "Bush, Civil Rights and the Specter of David Duke," *Washington Post*, October 30, 1991, p. A23.

105. Margaret Carlson, "Marching to a Different Drummer," *Time*, July 15, 1991, p. 19. See also Nancy Gibbs, "Filling a Legal Giant's Shoes," *Time*, July 8, 1991, pp. 22–24; Jim Hoagland, "A Tale of Two Nominees," *Washington Post*, October 8, 1991, p. A19; David A. Kaplan, "Where Are the Giants?" *Newsweek*, July 15, 1991, p. 20; Anthony Lewis, "Lessons of Thomas," *New York Times*, September 30, 1991, p. A17; Mary McGrory, "A Tale of Two Nominees," *Washington Post*, August 11, 1991, p. A2; "Even without Judge Thomas," *New York Times*, October 7, 1991, p. A16.

106. David S. Broder, "Thomas: Dilemma for Democrats," *Washington Post*, July 7, 1991, p. B7. See also David S. Broder, "October Fiasco," *Washington Post*, October 20, 1991, p. C7.

107. See, for example, Russell Baker, "The Process Baloney," *New York Times*, October 19, 1991, p. A23; Leslie H. Gelb, "Mr. Bush Packs the Court," *New York Times*, October 13, 1991, sec. 4, p. 15.

108. See, for example, Eleanor Clift, "The Scary Politics of Health," *Newsweek*, June 24, 1991, pp. 18–19; Leslie H. Gelb, "Yet Another [Drug] Summit," *New York Times*, November 3, 1991, sec. 4, p. 15; Michael Kramer, "The Voters' Latest Ailment: Health Care," *Time*, November 11, 1991, p. 51; A. M. Rosenthal, "Silence Is a Lie," *New York Times*, October 8, 1991, p. A25; Steven Waldman, "Will Bush Be

Bold?," *Newsweek*, January 7, 1991, pp. 28–29; "National Forests: Going, Going . . ." *New York Times*, October 5, 1991, p. A20.

109. David S. Broder, "Alexander: The Cynics Are Wrong," *Washington Post*, April 28, 1991, p. C7.

110. Richard N. Ostling, "A Revolution Hoping for a Miracle," *Time*, April 29, 1991, p. 52.

111. "American Education Gets a C," *New York Times*, October 4, 1991, p. A30.

112. Barbara Kantrowitz, "Playing Catch-up," *Newsweek*, April 22, 1991, p. 28.

113. Laurence I. Barrett, "If You Can't Beat Bush . . . " *Time*, April 15, 1991, p. 34.

114. Laurence I. Barrett, "No Donkeys in This Horse Race," *Time*, March 25, 1991, p. 24.

115. See, for example, Michael Kinsley, "What Democrats Need . . . " *Washington Post*, March 7, 1991, p. A23.

116. Howard Fineman, "The Democrats' Mr. Right," *Newsweek*, July 22, 1991, p. 23.

117. Howard Fineman, "Dream On, Democrats," *Newsweek*, March 18, 1991, pp. 40–41.

118. See, for example, E. J. Dionne, Jr., "Staying Awake Through '92," *Washington Post*, August 4, 1991, pp. C1, C4; Tom Wicker, "A Tale of Two Faces," *New York Times*, sec. 4, p. 17.

119. "The President's Leadership," *Wall Street Journal*, March 6, 1991, p. A8.

120. "A Presidency President," *Wall Street Journal*, May 15, 1991, p. A14.

121. Andrew Rosenthal, "Low Key Supplants Grandeur for Bush," *New York Times*, March 13, 1991, p. A16.

122. Michael Kramer, "Fears and Choices on the Road to '92," *Time*, September 23, 1991, p. 24.

123. David S. Broder, "What Bush's Ambivalence Costs Him," *Washington Post*, September 29, 1991, p. C7.

124. Howard Fineman, "Bush: The Churchill Scenario," *Newsweek*, September 16, 1991, p. 41.

125. Michael Duffy, "Wake-up Call," *Time*, November 18, 1991, pp. 22–24.

126. "Martin Van Bush," *Wall Street Journal*, November 7, 1991, p. A14.

127. "The Voters Said: What About Us?" *New York Times*, November 7, 1991, p. A28.

128. Kenneth T. Walsh, "Presiding over Disorder," *U.S. News and World Report*, November 11, 1991, pp. 32–34.

129. Haynes Johnson, "The Price of Political Promises," *Washington Post*, November 22, 1991, p. A2.

130. "The Partial President," *New York Times*, November 24, 1991, sec. 4, p. 16. See also James Reston, "The Puzzling George Bushes," *New York Times*, September 20, 1991, p. A27: "[Bush] loves to fight at home and concentrate on making peace and refereeing fights abroad."

131. "The Vision Thing," *Wall Street Journal*, December 14, 1991, p. A16.

132. Tom Wicker, "After the Storm," *New York Times*, December 19, 1991, p. A31.

133. Kenneth T. Walsh, "Which Way Does He Lean Today?" *U.S. News and World Report*, December 2, 1991, p. 24. See also Kenneth T. Walsh, "The Man of the Moment," *U.S. News and World Report*, September 23, 1991, pp. 31–33.

134. David Gergen, "How to Deal with Problems in Panic Central," *U.S. News and World Report*, December 2, 1991, p. 24.

135. James Reston, "A Jerky Start toward '92," *New York Times*, August 7, 1991, p. A21.

136. "The President's Illness," *Washington Post*, May 7, 1991, p. A20.

137. David S. Broder, "The Quayle Question," *Washington Post*, May 7, 1991, p. A21.

138. Haynes Johnson, "Will Bush Have a Change of Heart?" *Washington Post*, May 10, 1991, p. A2.

139. Dan Goodgame, "Why Not the Best?" *Time*, May 20, 1991, pp. 16–17.

140. "Five Who Fit the Bill," *Time*, May 20, 1991, pp. 18–20.

141. Michael Duffy, "Is He Really That Bad?" *Time*, May 20, 1991, pp. 21–22.

142. Leslie H. Gelb, "The Quayle Factor," *New York Times*, May 8, 1991, p. A23. One opposite-editorial column legitimately defended Quayle. See William Safire, "After the Flutter," *New York Times*, May 20, 1991, p. A15.

143. See, for example, James Reston, "'A Lot of Hoopla about Nothing'? No Way," *New York Times*, May 6, 1991, p. A15; Andrew Rosenthal, "Bush Resumes Hyperspeed; Is He Up to It?" *New York Times*, June 2, 1991, sec. 4, pp. 1, 5; Evan Thomas, "Bush's Heart Scare," *Newsweek*, May 13, 1991, pp. 28–29.

144. Kenneth T. Walsh, Stephen J. Hedges, and Bruce A. Auster, "John Sununu's Flight Plans," *U.S. News and World Report*, April 29, 1991, p. 48.

145. Among the stories and commentaries detailing Sununu's actions and criticizing White House ethics were Michael Duffy, "A Bad Case of the Perks," *Time*, July 1, 1991, p. 26; Michael Duffy, "On a Slippery Slope," *Time*, May 6, 1991, pp. 20–22; Rowland Evans and Robert Novak, "Sununu Bashed," *Washington Post*, June 24, 1991, p. A11; Dan Goodgame, "Fly Free or Die," *Time*, May 13, 1991, pp. 16–18; Ann McDaniel, "The Reign of 'King John,'" *Newsweek*, May 13, 1991, pp. 31–32; Larry Martz, "Headed for the Exit," *Newsweek*, July 1, 1991, pp. 22–24; Larry Martz, "Sununu and the Jews," *Newsweek*, July 8, 1991, p. 27; William Safire, "In Deep Sununu," *New York Times*, June 20, 1991, p. A23; Hugh Sidey, "Why Bush Has Trouble Firing Sununu," *Time*, July 8, 1991, p. 26; Kenneth T. Walsh, "The Flights of Air Sununu," *U.S. News and World Report*, May 6, 1991, p. 28; "Taking Favors in the White House," *New York Times*, June 21, 1991, p. A26.

146. See, for example, David S. Broder, "Presidential Staff Changes, Signaling Trouble Rarely Deliver Cure," *Washington Post*, December 4, 1991, p. A15; Eleanor Clift, "After Sununu, The Challenge on the Right," *Newsweek*, December 16, 1991, pp. 28–30; Ann McDaniel, "The Man Called 'Nunu,'" *Newsweek*, December 2, 1991, pp. 30–31; Michael McQueen and David Shribman, "Sununu Quits as Bush's Chief of Staff; Ouster May Not Solve President's Woes," *Wall Street Journal*, December 4, 1991, p. A18; Kenneth T. Walsh, "Changing the Guard," *U.S. News and World Report*, December 16, 1991, pp. 44–45, 48; Jack E. White, "Clearing the Decks," *Time*, December 16, 1991, pp. 33–34; "The President's Man," *New York Times*, December 4, 1991, p. A26.

147. Tom Wicker, "Mr. Bush's Socks," *New York Times*, December 15, 1991, sec. 4, p. 15.

6

The New Two George Bushes:
Magnanimous President,
Mean-Spirited Campaigner (1992)

Bush entered this actual make-or-break year with declining popularity, a public anxious for presidential action on the economy, and a press corps ready to avoid a repeat of their 1988 practice of allowing campaign attacks to often go uncorrected. For his part, Bush had to prove that he was sensitive to national concern about the economy, ready to adopt forthright action, and that he would conduct a more positive campaign than he did in 1988.

Timing. The presidential election was the key influence in the press evaluations of Bush's leadership in 1992. The campaign context provided the basis for broader judgments about Bush's performance as president and whether he deserved a second term. Furthermore, the press often judged Bush's presidential actions in 1992 according to their implications for his reelection campaign. In an election year in which the incumbent seeks a second term, journalists oftentimes do not judge a presidential initiative on its own merits. Rather, they examine possible political motives. In addition to the pressures of electoral politics, the wearing off of the Persian Gulf War victory afterglow put additional demands on the president to generate new and bold policy initiatives.

Symbolism/Rhetoric. Journalists had never credited the presidential Bush with being strong at the use of symbols and language. But they reviled candidate Bush for shrill, negative attacks on opponents that sometimes degenerated into name-calling and demeaned the presidency. Journalists accused Bush of distorted charges against opponents and a mean-spirited tone.

Regarding Bush's major addresses, the press described his State of the Union speech as lacking a visionary plan or integrating theme. It was, many reported, a grab bag of tinker-at-the-margins initiatives that did not add up to an action agenda. Journalists had a kinder view of his nomination acceptance speech, but the message in that address was drowned out by critical coverage of the "family-values" speeches by other leading Republicans.

Agenda. Unlike the two George Bushes of 1990 and 1991—masterly abroad, inept at home—evaluations of the president's domestic and foreign policies in 1992 tracked fairly consistently. That is, the evaluations were consistently negative, focusing on the criticism that had previously been reserved for his domestic agenda: reactive, slow to embrace change, not forward looking. Many suggested that Bush was too slow to embrace change in the former Soviet Union; that his pre–Persian Gulf War actions toward Iraq had failed to avert conflict and possibly even had caused it; that he did not show leadership in promoting democratic and human rights movements. In the domestic sphere, Bush still had no agenda, according to the press. Journalists considered the lack of a bold economic plan the president's major failing—and the one that had made him politically vulnerable.

Policy Development. There was less emphasis on the theme of Bush as the master of building international consensus. Instead, journalists emphasized that his foreign policy approach was mired in the old cold war conventional wisdom. Unable to reach beyond those blinders, Bush could not develop innovative responses to a dramatically changed world. Furthermore, he continued to display an inability to fashion forward-looking domestic programs and lacked the leadership acumen at home to break legislative gridlock. Some journalists characterized his claim to bring new energy to domestic policy as election-year rhetoric geared to rebut the major criticism of his presidency.

Staff. The leading story about Bush's staffing was his decision to move Secretary of State James Baker to the White House to direct both the administration and the reelection campaign. Although reputed as a solid manager and campaign strategist, Baker's move struck many as inappropriate given his handling of important international negotiations. For many, his changed role signaled a politically desperate presidency that had relegated diplomacy beneath partisan politics.

Once again, numerous stories focused on the issue of Vice President Dan Quayle's fitness for national office. Journalists fed speculation of a "dump Quayle" movement within the White House, and some reported that he was a substantial enough liability possibly to cost Bush reelection.

THE TURNAROUND

What a difference several months can make to the political fortunes of an incumbent president. George Bush certainly is not alone among modern presidents in that regard. Gerald Ford moved abruptly into the Oval Office with high public and press support merely because he was not Richard Nixon. One month later, the pardon of Nixon plunged Ford's standing and made him an easy target for critical coverage. Jimmy Carter, at a historic low in opinion polls, saw his popularity dramatically rise after the Iran hostage crisis, only to plunge deeply again over the next several months as the crisis persisted. In 1982 and 1983, most analysts dismissed Ronald Reagan as likely to be another in a sequence of failed single-term presidents, only to see him win a landslide reelection in 1984.

Yet for George Bush, the turnaround in his political fortunes seemed the most dramatic, least imaginable. With unprecedented presidential popularity immediately after the Persian Gulf War, leading political observers characterized him as invincible. By 1992, the luster had clearly been stripped from the president's once-shining image as a war hero. To Bush partisans, the turnaround in political fortunes was as though the public had said about the president presiding over victory in war, "thanks, but what have you done for us lately?"

The more charitable explanation was that the public had reacted naturally to a change in circumstances. With the war completed and a recession seemingly getting worse, the public had turned its attention to the domestic sphere—and saw a president who wasn't doing the same.

Presidential Travel Abroad

The president traveled in January to Australia and the Far East amid widespread criticism for ignoring the domestic economy. To reassure the country that he cared about domestic affairs, he explained that the trip was about "jobs, jobs, jobs." It was a no-win situation politically. For couching the trip in domestic economic terms, *Time*'s Strobe Talbott blasted Bush for "pandering" and "diminish[ing] his nation, his office, himself. . . . It's hard to have confidence in a president who so blatantly and abjectly puts his country and the world on notice that the job he is most concerned about is his own."[1]

To make matters worse, press accounts played up the fact that eighteen corporate CEOs—average previous year's salary of $3.1 million—traveled with Bush at taxpayer expense. A good many accounts portrayed that aspect of the trip as a symbol of the weakening U.S. economy: the country's leading businesspeople allegedly groveling for jobs from the Japanese.[2]

The biggest public relations catastrophe for the president occurred when he vomited and then fainted during a state dinner with the Japanese prime

minister in Tokyo. Although film footage of the president becoming suddenly ill—repeatedly shown on network television for several days—
looked disturbing enough, he had merely contracted gastroenteritis. A *Time*
account referred to the scene of the Japanese prime minister cradling Bush
as "an obvious metaphor for the American economy: flat on its back,
seeking succor from a resurgent Japan." Furthermore, Bush's illness "reminded voters that Dan Quayle remains only a heartbeat away from the
Oval Office." The bottom line was, "he should have stayed home."[3]
Newsweek compared the imagery of the event to that of Jimmy Carter nearly
passing out while jogging at Camp David in 1979: "That grisly picture
became a metaphor for a failed presidency."[4]

A *New York Times* editorial labeled Bush's trip "a fiasco." Unfortunately
for the president, few accounts actually focused on the substance of the trip
and what he had accomplished.[5] Buried in an embarrassing *Newsweek*
account of the trip—with a photo sequence of the president fainting—was
the lonely statement that "the president actually accomplished more than
the American press gave him credit for."[6]

The State of the Union

In an effort to create the image of a president ready to concentrate on
domestic concerns, White House strategists put out the word that the
January 28 State of the Union address would be the "defining moment" of
the Bush presidency. Bush opened the address recounting the triumph of
democratic principles throughout much of the world. Then, invoking the
language he had earlier used to express resolve against Iraqi aggression,
Bush said of the economic recession, "this will not stand." The *New York
Times* replied: "This will not fly, would be more like it."

Indeed, the *Times*'s editorial response reflected a common one: that Bush
had failed to offer a bold domestic action plan. The president had proposed
numerous domestic initiatives—including budget cuts, tax incentives, reduction in capital gains tax rate, among others. The *Times* called Bush "not
an anti-recession warrior but a tinkerer."[7] The *Washington Post* agreed that
Bush had "outlined a dressed-up, standstill program of more of the same.
His proposals struck us as being not at all up to the challenges before him."[8]
Even the *Wall Street Journal* complained that "the president's economic
program, as it happens, is too timid for our tastes." The *Journal* wanted more
"dramatic" action from the president—"a unilateral campaign to liberate
the American economy."[9]

Columnists also called for a bold domestic agenda. A. M. Rosenthal
castigated Bush for failing to offer "a coherent plan unified by purpose and
philosophy" rather than "a grab bag of tax proposals."[10] Mary McGrory
wrote that all Bush could offer was tough talk about the economy because
he didn't offer much of a program. She called him "a one-step-at-a-time

man."[11] Richard Cohen criticized the president for merely "tinkering" with domestic problems rather than offering programs that "address structural problems."[12] Television critic Tom Shales said that Bush's speech offered nothing "innovative or bold." The president didn't issue "a call to greatness . . . so much as a call to adequacy."[13] George Will joined the chorus of criticism and mocked the "defining moment" characterization. "The administration is sharply defined as an administration without definition. . . . Americans often wonder what he means. The answer may be that he doesn't mean anything very much. He expresses mere proposals, not serious purposes."[14]

Time, among many others, concluded that Bush's domestic message merely was calculated to help him to win reelection. Furthermore, "the president, as usual, was at his best on foreign policy."[15]

Numerous other columns saw the speech as emblematic of the singular failure of the Bush presidency: no domestic vision. William Raspberry wrote that "nobody who has watched George Bush preside over the catastrophe that is the American economy would accuse him of having an economic policy."[16] David Broder blasted Bush's domestic agenda and said that "the nation deserves better." According to Broder, "a man who is eminently comfortable with the status quo, he cannot bring himself to see or to say that the United States must overhaul fundamental systems that are imposing unacceptable costs on the economy. . . . Bush seems unwilling to confront the need for fundamental reform."[17]

What falling poll numbers and critical coverage did not achieve—getting the president at least to appear to act more aggressive in confronting the recession—many believed would result from the Bush reelection campaign. With an unusual intraparty challenge from a disgruntled movement conservative, Bush apparently did not have the luxury of merely being "presidential," staying above campaign politics.

THE 1992 CAMPAIGN

Coverage of the GOP Primaries

According to a candidate profile in the *Washington Post,* Bush entered the 1992 campaign "an enigmatic and contradictory figure. . . . Despite nearly 30 years in public life . . . Bush remains an elusive figure." Reporter John Yang compared Bush to a character in the Woody Allen film *Zelig*—"the human chameleon who physically adapted himself to those around him." Bush lacked "grand strategies" and was "a reactive person" more than a leader.[18] A *U.S. News* article similarly described Bush as "a political chameleon with no permanent ideological coloration."[19] Another *U.S. News* story characterized Bush's presidency as "remarkably themeless, as if the president preferred dropping in and out of history rather than shaping it to his design."[20] A *Newsweek* profile described Bush as having "no vision to sell to a nation desperate for leadership." Furthermore, "Bush gets the bad notices he deserves: 'tinny,' 'a lapdog,' a 'geek.' "[21]

Bush's image as a man out of touch with the lives of ordinary Americans was bolstered by an erroneous news report in early February that he had marveled at the technology of a supermarket electronic price scanner during a National Grocers Association convention. The *New York Times* published a story about the alleged event, which the newspaper's reporter had picked up from a pool report.[22] In large part because the story dovetailed with an established presidential image, newspapers uncritically reported it. A typical reaction came from the *Washington Post*'s Jonathan Yardley: "The man who runs the United States of America . . . [is] so out of touch with the daily lives of his constituents, he doesn't even know how they go about buying the food that they put on their tables."[23] Although long ago the story has been shown to be erroneous, to this day analyses of the Bush presidency report it as evidence that the president was out of touch with his own constituents' lives.[24]

More critical coverage attended Bush after he handily *won* the New Hampshire primary. Despite easy victory, challenger Pat Buchanan fared "better than expected" in press accounts, resulting in many assessments that Bush's comfortable margin of victory—53 to 37 percent—was nonetheless a repudiation of his presidency. As the *Washington Post* editorialized, Bush "did not do nearly as well as he should have." The primary result confirmed that "Bush has a lot of revising to do."[25] Sources as diverse in viewpoint as the *Wall Street Journal* editorial page and columnist Mary McGrory wrote that New Hampshire voters had sent a "message" to Bush to "do something."[26] Economics columnist Hobart Rowen reasoned that voters were "crying out for a kind of leadership [Bush is] not supplying."[27] David Broder reasoned that Bush had been sent the message that election-year gimmicks could not substitute for "resolute, real-world action." To Broder, Bush had failed once again "to come to grips with" the nation's leading domestic problems.[28] Richard Cohen called Bush the "stand-for-nothing president." Bush was "a president [who] has no message of his own."[29]

What especially disturbed Bush's critics was the appearance that the president had reacted to the New Hampshire primary by reaching far to appease movement conservatives. As a *Newsweek* story opened, "it isn't true, as the critics claim, that George Bush stands for nothing: he seems to stand for whatever Patrick Buchanan wants him to." For trying to outdo Buchanan's conservatism, Bush earned the *New York Times*'s label "President Noodle."[30] The most heavily criticized Bush action was his decision to force the resignation of National Endowment of the Arts Chairman John Frohnmayer. Bush's NEA chairman had drawn the ire of movement conservatives by not supporting their calls for censorship of "obscene" art.

Critics blasted Bush for allegedly taking action against Frohnmayer to appease Buchanan's constituency.[31]

In light of his early campaign performance, journalists began writing of the possible demise of the Bush presidency. Jim Hoagland observed that "Bush the conquering warrior chief of the Persian Gulf has gone in a year to being Bush the out-of-touch, uncaring klutz of New Hampshire."[32] Charles Krauthammer called the Bush presidency "spent. It has not a clue of what it wants to do." Krauthammer assessed that "Bush's tenure will be judged . . . like Gerald Ford's, with a limited agenda that, when completed, lost its reason for being."[33] To Michael Duffy of *Time*, "gone is the commander of Desert Storm, the man who confidently vowed that Saddam Hussein's aggression 'will not stand.'" Bush, he wrote, merely offered "a lackluster three-year domestic record."[34] Over three years in the White House had transformed Bush from the "carefully managed image as a square-shouldered Dudley Do-Right into something closer to the Flim-flam Man."[35]

By mid-March it seemed clear, with Buchanan making only noise as a protest candidate, that Bush would easily be renominated and that the president's likely opponent would be Arkansas governor Bill Clinton. Kenneth T. Walsh characterized the matchup as such: "Which represents the greater danger—Bush's directionless status quo or Clinton's suspect character and amorphous agenda?"[36]

April–June

During the early stages of the general election campaign—the months of spring and early summer during which the certain nominees began to focus on each other—it was becoming clear that most leading journalists strongly preferred Clinton. Although many had reservations about the Democratic candidate, few had anything at all positive to say anymore about Bush. The *Washington Post* ombudsman Richard Harwood found that the editorial writers of most large newspapers believed that Bush did not deserve a second term.[37] Specific arguments included those of Hobart Rowen and the *New York Times*, among many others, that Bush's economic plan either was nonexistent or not viable.[38] *Newsweek*'s Eleanor Clift, a Clinton partisan, echoed the views of many when she asserted that Bush had proved himself merely adept at attack-oriented campaigning. She was hardly alone in revisiting the low-road 1988 campaign and characterizing Bush as a politician who would do almost anything to win.[39] Lacking vision, many commented, Bush's campaign rhetoric therefore lacked substance.[40]

Numerous reports and commentaries at this stage singled out another malady of the Bush presidency: the lack of a message or any sense of policy direction on the home front. Ann McDaniel of *Newsweek* opined that "Reagan and even the 1988 version of Bush ('Read my lips') had a message to sell. And that's where the real problem lies."[41] Kenneth T. Walsh of *U.S. News* commented on the lack of "a sense of direction from the White House." The trouble was that, "without firm ideological moorings or direct experience outside his own Brahmin background, he doesn't know what to make of all the disparate voices he hears."[42]

In the wake of the Los Angeles riots, numerous reports criticized the president for not immediately traveling to the troubled city to make a symbolic display of federal commitment to resolving inner-city problems. Once again, the apparent lack of a bold presidential response led many, including Mary McGrory, to lambaste Bush for being "out of step" with the nation's problems. In fact, McGrory said that former baseball commissioner Peter Ueberroth, not Bush, was the ideal Republican "role model" for establishing a program to rebuild the city. "Bush prefers not to talk about Los Angeles at all. Ueberroth talks about it like a liberal Democrat."[43]

Perhaps most devastating to Bush was a June 29 *Time* report entitled "The Incredible Shrinking President." That report pictured a serious-looking Vice President Quayle speaking behind a podium with a miniaturized Bush sitting on Quayle's shoulder and grinning. According to Michael Duffy, the president's political stature was so low that "world peace and a cure for the common cold might not revive him." It was Quayle—with his core conservative views and frequent attacks on the "cultural elite"—whose focused message "remind[ed] voters how few convictions Bush has." Indeed, "Bush's message is so muted and confused that Quayle threatens to eclipse the president."[44]

July–August

Conservative columnist Paul A. Gigot took on the issue of whether the unpopular vice president was a major impediment to Bush's reelection prospects. "Voters aren't waiting for a vice president to leave the ticket. They're waiting for a president to lead the country."[45] A. M. Rosenthal turned the tables and asked, "should Bush run?" He concluded that the president should volunteer to exit with respect rather than wait to be fired. "At home, his first term has sunk the country in depression—depression of the soul—not sure which will come first, the factory closing slip or the next urban riot."[46]

Nonetheless, many columnists continued to turn up the heat on the "dump Quayle" movement. George F. Will listed "five things [Bush] could do" to revive a faltering campaign. One of them was to replace Quayle with a person of stature, such as Colin Powell.[47] Quayle offered to leave the ticket, and Bush refused.

Most of the press criticism of the Bush campaign ultimately focused on the president. According to most of the reporters, the campaign failures were the result of the failures of the Bush presidency. In July alone, Will penned three columns on Bush's shortcomings: (1) "Clinton Can Beat Bush" criticized the "intellectual bankruptcy of Bush-style Republicanism"; (2) "Bush's Muddy Message" implored the president to take some action "just to show he has a pulse"; and (3) "A Figure of Genuine Pathos" blasted Bush's "incoherence that afflicts a public persona operating without a public philosophy."[48]

Jim Hoagland saw the GOP campaign unhinging from "Bush's record of economic failure."[49] Others blamed Bush for a "lack of passion and priority" (Meg Greenfield), the lack of "urgent and bolder" economic programs (David Gergen), the lack of a forward thinking message or program (Kenneth T. Walsh), the lack of a record to advertise which led him to engage in "slash and burn" and "despicable" negative campaigning (Joe Klein, Michael Kinsley).[50]

To say that the press coverage of Bush's presidency and campaign had turned decidedly negative by midsummer does not convey strongly enough the extent of the criticism. The Bush campaign ultimately perceived itself as fighting the reelection battle on two fronts: against the Democrats and against the national media.

The Bush campaign tried a number of strategies to bolster the administration's image. For example, the campaign promoted Bush's domestic record with a detailed list of accomplishments. The effort went generally unrecognized. Just prior to the mid-August GOP nominating convention in Houston, Bush appointed Secretary of State James A. Baker III as the campaign manager. Given Baker's campaign experience, the effort was supposed to signal Bush's intention to run a much smoother, more energetic campaign. Instead, commentaries criticized the move as putting campaign politics above foreign affairs, and some suggested that no campaign whiz could change Bush's fundamental problems: a poor economy and no agenda to address it.[51]

Opinion polls at the time showed that the public was disgruntled with the nation's political leadership and desired change. The Bush campaign response was to try to recast the status quo president as an agent of fundamental change. A good many commentaries maintained that all campaign efforts to recast Bush's image would fail because, as *U.S. News and World Report* explained, "the president is a fully formed character, steeped in the genteel ways of the old-fashioned Washington establishment. There is little chance he can break the capital's shackles." The lengthy story by Kenneth T. Walsh, "Prisoner of Washington," offers an excellent summary of the major criticisms of Bush. For example:

He appears to be a prisoner of his patrician commitment to rule by a governing elite, guided by common sense rather than a spirit of innovation or a clear ideology. . . . Bush has yet to find a unifying philosophy. . . . Bush recoils from steps that can serve a chief executive well—confronting adversaries to get his way and going over their heads to appeal to some national purpose. . . . He has no overarching worldview of

his own.... [Bush possesses] character traits that dampen his capacity to lead boldly
... [especially] his scant interest in ideas and his unease at leading showy crusades.
... He will never be a political outsider and he can never credibly argue that he is
an agent of fundamental change.[52]

Joe Klein and Ann McDaniel traced Bush's likely downfall to "the hubris
and passivity that attended his victory in the gulf war." After the war, Bush
could have launched a major domestic offensive. "But Bush chose to do
nothing of substance and his inaction remains a puzzlement."[53] According
to Howard Fineman and McDaniel, lacking vision and a positive message,
Bush began "using time-tested slime-and-distance tactics." To have any
chance at all to win, "a lifelong accommodator, compromiser, fixer of the
day's problems, Bush will finally have to tell the nation what moves him
and what kind of America he envisions."[54]

According to many, even without a coherent message Bush was determined, as he put it, "to do what I have to do to be reelected." To Anthony
Lewis, that meant that the president was not above, for example, ordering
the bombing of Iraq merely to gain political favor among voters.[55] A more
substantiated charge was leveled by Michael Kinsley, who accused the
president—who had said that Bill Clinton had raised taxes in Arkansas 128
times—of purposefully distorting his opponent's gubernatorial record.
Kinsley documented the absurdity of Bush's claim so effectively that numerous other commentaries cited the columnist's evidence as proof positive that the GOP campaign engaged in distortions.[56]

The Republican Party convened in Houston on August 17 for its nominating convention. The first evening highlighted former president Ronald
Reagan's address. Yet the controversial decision to allow defeated candidate Patrick Buchanan to address the convention that same evening ruined
chances for a positive display of the party. Though the Bush camp allowed
the former candidate to speak only in return for an endorsement, it made
the costly mistake of not clearing Buchanan's speech in advance.

Because of some longer than anticipated speeches, Buchanan's speech
was during prime time, Reagan's later. Buchanan declared the country in
the throes of a "cultural war," and the excessive tone of his rhetoric clearly
offended many more moderate and independent voters than it mobilized
disgruntled far-right voters for Bush.

Many commentaries panned the convention as a "family values fest"
characterized by attacks on the GOP opponents' allegedly less wholesome
lifestyles. Speeches by the Reverend Pat Robertson, Marilyn Quayle, Dan
Quayle, and Barbara Bush were singled out as divisive and sometimes
mean-spirited. George F. Will lambasted the "thick soup of values blather"
and "unpleasant" rhetoric of the convention. He singled out speeches by
Robertson, Mrs. Quayle, and Mrs. Bush as particularly offensive. The
Republicans, he wrote, had "turn[ed] political disagreement into moral

assault."[57] Fineman and McDaniel characterized the convention as "a four-day festival of fear and social antagonism" filled with hate-mongering attacks on homosexuals, feminists, trial lawyers, the media, and, especially, Hillary Clinton.[58] Molly Ivins called the convention "sour, mean and dull."[59] Editorials and commentaries in the *New York Times, Washington Post*, and elsewhere joined the strong criticism of the convention rhetoric.[60]

Richard Harwood considered whether the severely negative media reaction to the "family values fest" reflected the cultural/social values of the journalists. He conceded that such differences in perspective had to be acknowledged in any analysis of the media's reaction to the GOP convention. Major media corporations reflect urban, largely Democratic, values. Many in the media are "in the forefront of the feminist and gay movements."[61] Conservative columnist James J. Kilpatrick more bluntly lambasted the "media dirge" during the convention and predicted that the public revulsion toward biased coverage would help Bush to win reelection.[62] GOP delegates were more blunt yet. Many carried posters or wore shirts headlining "Stop the Liberal/Media Lynch Mob." The president said many times during the campaign that his favorite bumper sticker read ANNOY THE MEDIA—REELECT BUSH.

The family values fest had perhaps one political benefit for the GOP campaign: it would help to mobilize movement conservatives while perhaps giving Bush a chance to appear moderate by contrast. If the convention could both demonize the opposition and make Bush appear kinder and gentler, strategists suggested, the GOP would get a substantial postconvention boost.

It was not to be. Although some, including David Broder, thought that Bush had made a decent nomination speech, many more characterized the address as too reflective of the overall regrettable tone of the convention.[63]

For example, Ivins described Bush's leadership vision in the speech as "Congress is awful and the other guy is a louse."[64] Charles Paul Freund called the address "a long, dull blame-casting acceptance speech."[65] Tom Shales disliked Bush's heavy-handed attacks on Clinton and the Democrats.[66] Anthony Lewis more bluntly called these partisan jabs "lies," George Will lambasted the president's "abundance of insincerity," and the *Washington Post* decried how Bush had "bent the truth about the future and the past."[67]

By late August the tone of the press coverage of Bush's candidacy had been firmly established. Efforts to recast Bush's image or revitalize his candidacy during the convention were treated derisively. Especially mocked were Bush's efforts, like those of many underdog candidates, to portray himself as a modern-day Harry Truman—an embattled incumbent on the verge of a great political comeback. Albert R. Hunt retorted that "'give 'em hell Poppy' just ain't 'give 'em hell Harry.'" For one thing, Truman had "a clear message" and an agenda.[68] Journalists strongly derided Bush when he criticized the Democratic platform for not including the word "God," and they characterized his conviction to get serious about dealing with the economy in a second term as either disingenuous or, based on the first-term record, not credible.[69]

September–November

In September, numerous commentaries revisited the controversial GOP convention and continued to lambaste its "mean-spirited" and "divisive" rhetoric. Among the other characterizations were "pretty nasty" (*Washington Post*), "meanness and emptiness of . . . rhetoric" (David Broder), "intolerance" (Charles Krauthammer), "overheated . . . rhetoric" (Michael Duffy), "bigotry" and "intolerance" (Richard Cohen), "strident . . . message" (Ann McDaniel and Howard Fineman).[70]

Ultimately, these and other commentaries placed blame for such rhetoric on Bush. And many of the journalists perceived the tone of Bush's own comments during the campaign to be not much better than the convention rhetoric. Cohen summed up concisely the overwhelming press consensus of Bush's campaign. "He has no program to advance, nothing to say except the other fellow is no good."[71] Steven V. Roberts maintained that a Bush victory would mean that voters decided the president was inadequate but Clinton was worse. "Bush cannot win a contest based on his performance."[72] Numerous journalists implored the president to tone down the campaign rhetoric and offer voters a positive message.[73]

During the final month of the campaign, Bush's coverage was more negative than at any other period. Negative coverage centered on the following themes: Bush carried out a smear campaign against his opponents; his character-related attacks on Clinton lacked credibility because of his own flaws, especially regarding his policy reversals and alleged role in the Iran-contra scandal; his campaign offered no program for a second term, no leadership vision.

First, the charge of negative campaigning. Bush indeed focused his message on Clinton's alleged character flaws. In particular, Bush lambasted his opponent's efforts as a young man to avoid military service and allegations that Clinton had organized anti-American demonstrations in London and Moscow in 1969. Anna Quindlen called Bush's attacks a new lowpoint in the history of campaign politics.[74] Richard Cohen charged that Bush had "turned an odious campaign tactic into farce and his own reputation into mud."[75] Dan Balz, Mary McGrory, the *Washington Post*, and numerous others came to Clinton's defense and blasted the president's campaign tactics.[76] Joe Klein characterized Bush's attacks as "petty," "vicious," an "anti-Clinton sleazathon," full of "ham-handed Red baiting."

It may seem harsh to argue that George Bush has debased presidential discourse in ways that would have been unimaginable little more than a decade ago—but so be it. He has. Never before has a candidate for president been so directly, *personally*, mean-spirited and derogatory toward his opponents, so willing to indulge in demagogic innuendo.[77]

Second, journalists raised questions about Bush's own flaws. They argued that Bush distorted his opponents' records (Anthony Lewis, Michael Kinsley), that he changed policy positions out of political convenience and broke campaign promises (Richard Cohen, Molly Ivins, Michael Kramer, *Washington Post*), and that he engaged in distasteful name-calling—Albert Gore, Jr., was "ozone man," Clinton and Gore "bozos"—and had debased the office of the presidency (Lewis).[78] The strongest rejoinder came from Lewis. "More than any incumbent president in memory he has been a candidate without shame. Lies, hate, vulgarity: Nothing has been too shameful for George Bush."[79]

Once the president weighed in with attacks on Clinton's veracity, journalists revisited the role that Bush may have played while vice president in the Iran-contra scandal. To all questions about his alleged knowledge of the arms-for-hostages deal, Bush claimed to have been "out of the loop" in the decision-making process and retorted that he had tirelessly already answered all queries about the controversy. Nonetheless, many questioned Bush's veracity. Richard Cohen, Leslie Gelb, Anthony Lewis, and the *New York Times*, among others, characterized Bush's statements on the controversy as "lies," "Nixonesque," "the rot of corruption."[80]

Third, journalists continued to describe Bush as having offered no substantive program or leadership vision. According to William Raspberry, Bush "has offered no vision of where he wants to take America."[81] Richard Cohen maintained that Bush "cannot articulate why he should get another term in the White House. He cannot for the life of him spell out an agenda for the next four years that makes the slightest sense."[82] The *Washington Post* editorialized that "the last two years [of the Bush presidency] were a blank because he ran out of serious goals and relevant ideas; he is still without them."[83] To the *New York Times*, "lacking leadership [Bush's] capacity to govern has collapsed."[84] *U.S. News and World Report* concluded that "Bush will never change his stripes" and that his presidency was "anchorless."[85] He failed to offer the country "a positive national message."[86]

Even in his reputed area of expertise—foreign affairs—Bush fared poorly in a good many accounts. For the most part, much to Bush's dismay, campaign coverage gave little heed to the international arena—a fact lamented in one column by David Broder.[87] The relatively few such accounts failed to give any boost to the president. Both Stephen Rosenfeld and the *New York Times*, to cite just two examples, argued that it was Clinton, not Bush, who articulated a more forward-looking foreign policy agenda for the post–cold war world.[88]

And the president earned the scorn of many when, in the heat of the last days of the campaign, he called Clinton and Gore "two bozos" who knew less about foreign policy than Millie, the Bush family dog. One column measured Bush's foreign policy record "by his own bozo standard" and found him to be the only real clown in the race.[89]

Bush's campaign held out the hope that the president would best his rivals Clinton and Ross Perot in the three scheduled debates. According to the press corps, Clinton handily won the first two debates, and Bush's relatively strong performance in the final debate was too late to revive his candidacy. Commentaries suggested that Bush's chances may have ended with a listless performance in the second debate held in Richmond, Virginia. In fairness, the talk-show format suited Clinton's skills more than Bush's, but when the president on several occasions glanced at his watch, the appearance was that he knew that his presidency was finished and just wanted to get the ordeal over with. *Time* concluded that "the president looks and sounds like a loser." Furthermore, "the candidate is physically present at the debates but is already mentally off at the Bush Library in Texas or on the links in Kennebunkport."[90]

Clinton handily won the election with 370 electoral votes (43 percent of the popular vote) to Bush's 168 electors (and 38 percent of the vote). Perot pulled 19 percent of the popular vote, but no electors. The *Washington Post* celebrated that Bush's "uncommonly personal and mean-spirited" campaign "didn't work."[91] Michael Kinsley gloated "I FEEL GREAT!" Celebrating the election of "our man," Bill Clinton, Kinsley called the Democratic win "sweet revenge on George Bush for the loathsome, dishonest and empty campaign that won him the White House in 1988. . . . This election has restored my faith in my fellow citizens."[92] Charles Krauthammer declared Bush's campaign "a failure of character" and the election result a rejection of the man, not of a governing philosophy.[93] David Broder attributed the incumbent's defeat to a campaign that demonized Clinton rather than offered a second-term program.[94]

Were the media unfair to Bush in the 1992 campaign? Content analyses of the coverage suggest that Clinton clearly got the best from the media. The *Washington Post* ombudsman reviewed her paper's coverage in the final seventy-three days of the campaign. "If the *Post* is an example, news coverage at the end of the campaign was lopsided—very lopsided." Joann Byrd found that the pictorial depictions of the candidates in the *Post* also overwhelmingly favored Clinton.[95]

William A. Henry III of *Time* took on the media bias controversy. Interviewing reporters who covered the campaign, he found very few willing to speak on the record. Yet "it is widely admitted in private that many journalists covering Bill Clinton feel generational affinity and unusual warmth toward him—and that much of the White House press corps disdains President Bush and all his works." He quoted James Gertenzang of the *Los Angeles Times* and an anonymous *Washington Post* reporter.

Gertenzang: Reporters feel condescension and contempt for Bush. There really is that attitude. They're openly derisive.

Post reporter: God, I hope Bush doesn't get reelected. It'll be so boring: no fresh ideas, the same old people running the show and more Capitol Hill gridlock. A Clinton administration would be a much better story.[96]

Frequent Bush critic, David Gergen agreed that "the press coverage was tilted against Bush. . . . [T]he piling on by many in the press went far beyond appropriate bounds." Furthermore,

many in the press simply tired of Bush, wanted a fresh story and down deep shared the same disappointments in Bush that voters had expressed. Also, in age and outlook, many in the press are much closer to Clinton than to Bush. Whatever the reason, the press leaned toward the Democratic challenger.[97]

To this day, the anger felt by Bush supporters toward the media runs very deep. In my interviews with Bush White House communications advisers, several spoke at length about what they considered the unfairness of the campaign coverage. Some cited it as the leading factor in Bush's loss; others said it was one of the most crucial factors.

There is no doubt that the campaign coverage tilted toward Clinton. But the quality of that coverage must be considered within the framework of a miserably run incumbent campaign and a relatively smooth Clinton–Gore general election campaign. Furthermore, the negative campaign coverage directed toward Bush must be considered within the framework of his administration's policy agenda in 1992—and the press's response to Bush's initiatives.

THE DOMESTIC POLICY AGENDA

As had been the case throughout the first three years of his term, press coverage in 1992 emphasized what some called Bush's "skimpy domestic agenda" and "the thinness of his domestic program."[98] A good many accounts portrayed Bush as lacking conviction on domestic policy issues— that, according to the *Washington Post*, "on domestic issues what he mainly does is gauge the wind."[99] E. J. Dionne, Jr., maintained that Bush simply did not like to spend time on domestic issues. Therefore, "when Bush runs through the catalogue of his domestic programs, he does it with all the excitement and thematic coherence of someone reviewing a hardware-store shopping list for a tile repair job."[100]

The combination of a staggering domestic economy and appearance of presidential inaction contributed more than anything to the critical press.

Some referred to Bush's proposed program to revitalize the economy—
capital gains tax cut, middle class income tax cut, housing vouchers—as
inadequate to address the severity of the recession.[101] Some mocked Bush's
insistence that the economy wasn't as bad as some had portrayed it.[102]
Others said that Bush—given his privileged upbringing—was too out of
touch with the problems of middle-class America to have any idea of what
to do about the recession.[103]

Bush set off a firestorm of press criticism in March when he declared in
an interview that his decision to sign the 1990 deficit reduction package was
a mistake. For Bush, what may have been an attempt to mollify conservatives ended up reviving his image as lacking core convictions on domestic
issues. The *New York Times* called Bush "President Noodle" and said that he
suffered "an appalling lack of conviction." The *Times* believed that the
budget deal was a good one and, like many opinion leaders, argued that
Bush's mistake was in making a "no-new-taxes" pledge, not in breaking
it.[104] A *Times* profile of the "Bush record" reported that the term "flip-flop"
had become a media "staple" in referring to the president's economic
policies.[105] Bush was clearly in a no-win situation of his own making
because of the no-new-taxes pledge: when he refused to raise taxes, many
opinion leaders denounced his rigidity in light of competing economic
needs, such as budget reduction. When he compromised with Congress on
tax issues, opinion leaders charged him with hypocrisy.[106]

Largely in response to criticism of him as lacking a plan to deal with the
staggering economy, the president delivered what his administration billed
as his major economic policy address on September 10 before the Economic
Club of Detroit. In the address, Bush articulated long-range goals for
economic revitalization. He proposed to expand free trade agreements to
open new markets for U.S. goods and to support health care and educational "choice" as well as governmental and legal reform. Some commentators viewed that speech as substantive, far-reaching, and even somewhat
thematic. David Broder and Paul Gigot both saw the potential for the
emergence of a Bush domestic vision, but only if the president followed
through with action.[107] Yet, as Gigot pointed out, many more in the press
critically responded that the speech contained nothing "new"—defined as
large-scale, expensive policy initiatives.[108] For example, Michael Kramer
called the speech "a gussied-up rehash of old ideas."[109] The *Washington Post*
agreed that "this was just the same old stuff, better phrased than in the past,
but no more persuasive or plausible as a prescription for economic revitalization."[110] *U.S. News* maintained that the speech "was really a political
document designed" to show that Bush really did have a domestic
agenda.[111]

Journalists criticized the president's stewardship in other policy areas as
well. They maintained that Bush had failed to propose the kind of broad-
sweeping environmental program to justify his desire to be known as the

"environmental president." His reluctance to attend an international conference in Rio de Janeiro on the environment and mocking of Al Gore as the "ozone man" exacerbated the criticism.[112] Journalists also largely dismissed Bush's claim to be the "education president" because he had, according to a *New York Times* profile, "few tangible accomplishments" in that area.[113] Many criticized the president for allegedly responding too slowly to relieve victims of an August hurricane disaster in Florida.[114]

The most severe criticism of the president's response time to a crisis occurred in May, after riots broke out in Los Angeles. The unexpected acquittal of white police officers of criminal charges of brutality against an African-American arrestee fueled the worst urban unrest the nation had seen in over two decades. If nothing else, all agreed that symbolically the president had to demonstrate his concern and commitment to address the crisis.

Although some cynically suggested that the Bush White House would enjoy exploiting the crisis for political gain, most criticized the president for not traveling immediately to Los Angeles to demonstrate his concern and for not using the crisis as a vehicle to promote an aggressive urban program.[115] Indeed, the president made a televised address on the crisis and traveled to Los Angeles, although a full week after the riots had begun. Once again, many argued that Bush's personal background did not make it possible for him to empathize with the problems of inner-city residents and that he was too out of touch and unfamiliar with such problems to offer solutions.[116]

THE FOREIGN POLICY AGENDA

If not recognized for his domestic policy record, Bush could certainly claim to have been the "foreign policy president." But in an election year, Bush confronted two major problems in promoting his accomplishments.

First, voters cared more about presidential leadership of the domestic economy. With the economy in the doldrums during the election year, polls evidenced a lack of public interest in Bush's accomplishments abroad. Thirteen months after the Persian Gulf victory, at a March Wholesale Grocers' convention, Bush's appearance was preceded by a slick video portrayal of the Persian Gulf triumph. Nobody applauded.

Second, press coverage of Bush's foreign policy acumen had entered a revisionist phase. As we shall see, press accounts called into question Bush's reputation for foreign policy acumen, and many wondered whether the president also lacked vision internationally.

No press coverage was so devastating as that which questioned whether the Persian Gulf War had actually been avoidable. Led by the scandal-conscious Bush critic William Safire, the press dubbed Bush's pre–Persian Gulf War actions toward Saddam Hussein "Iraqgate."

Rather than search for something new or "newsworthy" by reinterpreting earlier events, journalists used new evidence—some in the form of previously classified government documents—to question whether the president had once aided Hussein's military buildup. According to many press accounts, the president had provided Iraq with large grain subsidies that ultimately were used for a military buildup and nuclear weapons development. Some commentators merely accused Bush of having erred in his previous prewar judgment of the Iraqi government—a point that even the administration conceded.[117] Indeed, the president had tried to engage the Iraqi leader in a positive dialogue and offered aid and other inducements to try to create a peaceful relationship. Although the administration admitted to mistakes in pursuing a diplomatic course, Bush strongly denied accusations that he either acted improperly or unwittingly created the conditions that led to the Persian Gulf War.[118]

The most devastating accounts accused Bush of having illegally circumvented Congress, withheld information from Congress and the public, engaged in a cover-up of wrongdoing, obstructed justice, and made fraudulent use of public funds. Jim Hoagland called the administration's prewar actions "shameful" while other leading columnists and editorialists also leveled accusations of high-level wrongdoing.[119]

Furthermore, as Bush's reelection campaign was faltering, press accounts reported what a New York Times profile called the "dark possibility that no one in the White House wants to contemplate: That President Hussein may hold on to his job longer than President Bush."[120] Such accounts reminded voters that the end of the war did not result in a "conclusive peace," that Bush had ultimately failed to topple Saddam Hussein and annihilate Iraq's military capability, and that the Kurdish people continued to suffer at the hands of Iraqi troops.[121]

Throughout the year, press coverage of Bush's foreign policy record largely tracked consistently with that of his domestic policy record. That is, various reports and commentaries characterized Bush's policies as evidencing a "lack of vision," lack of an "overarching strategy," "reactive," "no leadership," and "feckless." No longer did the press report that there were two George Bushes: one in domestic affairs, the other in foreign affairs.

Certainly the wearing off of the post–Persian Gulf War afterglow had much to do with the widespread press consensus that Bush's leadership difficulties extended into the international realm. But there clearly was much more to it than that. Journalists assessed Bush's foreign policy leadership against the standard of what a New York Times profile called "a creative, forward-looking leader."[122] According to many accounts, Bush's cautious, "prudent" foreign policy approach better suited the cold war era, not the post–cold war years.[123] According to Leslie Gelb, Bush was "much more attuned to the passing era of balance-of-power politics than to the coming world where policies need to transcend national boundaries and perspectives."[124]

What evidence did journalists provide for their harsh assessments in 1992? Some maintained that Bush had passively watched communism crumble and then took the credit for major events that just happened to have coincided with his tenure as president.[125] Many pointed to what they considered his overtly cautious, slow response to Democratic movements in the Baltic region.[126] Commentators blasted the president for arranging a private meeting with the Chinese prime minister and for not taking a "tougher presidential stand" against human rights abuses by the Chinese government.[127] Some went so far as to suggest that Bush had an affinity for dictators over democratic movements: consider, they said, his tardiness in embracing Boris Yeltsin as the new Russian leader, his slow response to aiding Russian democratization, as well as his policies toward China.[128] A. M. Rosenthal wrote,

[Bush] has never really shown he understands the strength of America's greatest asset: political democracy. . . . Bush protects a Chinese tyranny that gave us the Khmer Rouge. He appeases Middle Eastern dictatorships that live by war against neighbors or their own people. He seems in mourning for the Communist Soviet Kremlin of the Gorbachev era.[129]

Not all reviews of Bush's foreign policy were so negative in this election year. Although journalists frequently characterized Bush as willing to do anything to win reelection, they praised his politically risky stand against Israeli reluctance to give up occupied West Bank territories in exchange for Arab recognition. Bush withheld a $10 billion loan guarantee to Israel until its government embraced the land-for-peace plan. Although reviled by the U.S. pro-Israel lobby for this stand, Bush didn't budge until a new Labor-led Israeli government embraced land-for-peace. Some called Bush's actions politically courageous and one of his biggest foreign policy successes.[130]

Throughout the year, Bush negotiated with Boris Yeltsin to reduce U.S. and Russian nuclear arsenals. Announcements of substantial cutbacks in January and again in June resulted in favorable commentary on Bush's actions, although some suggested that it was Yeltsin who demonstrated the boldest initiative and resolve in the discussions.[131] The "truly historic" post-election SALT II agreement to dramatically reduce both nations' nuclear arsenals was, according to the *New York Times*, "a fine way for President Bush to close out his term, and the cold war era." The agreement ensured the administration's "place in history."[132]

Many were less certain of how Bush's response to the Serbian slaughter of Bosnians in the former Yugoslavia would be viewed in history. Although some maintained that U.S. leadership could not resolve the bloody civil war in the former Yugoslavia, others, led by columnist Anthony Lewis, denounced the president's reluctance to intervene militarily as an egregious moral failure.[133]

Journalists offered a mixed assessment as well to the president's efforts to aid hunger relief in Somalia. Most praised his decision to send U.S. troops to aid the United Nations rescue operation, although some suggested that Bush should have made a clear statement of his objectives in sending the troops and perhaps even a long-term commitment to resolve the crisis.[134]

The *New York Times* highly praised Bush's postelection foreign policy leadership. In the closing weeks of his presidency, Bush committed troops to Somalia, demonstrated greater commitment to combat Serbian aggression against Bosnians, signed the START treaty with Russia, and concluded negotiations on NAFTA with Canada and Mexico. According to the *Times*, "given the breadth of Mr. Bush's foreign policy achievements—in slashing nuclear weapons, promoting democracy, punishing aggressors, combating famine and promoting freer trade—he has much to talk about."[135]

CONCLUSION: THE BUSH LEGACY

The *Times*'s favorable retrospective of Bush's foreign policy accomplishments was reminiscent of the "two George Bushes" assessments. Indeed, during the presidential transition period journalists speculated about how history would treat the Bush presidency. The answer: a mixed record—competent in foreign affairs, devoid of a domestic policy agenda. The *New York Times*, for example, labeled Bush "an incomplete president." He exercised foreign policy leadership "cleverly and energetically. But on the home front he was just the reverse, clumsy and irresolute. As the cold war receded, his domestic agenda was exposed as little more than a list of talking points." To the *Times*, Bush had engineered some real accomplishments in his first two years in office, but he then slipped into passivity, pandered to the ideological right and lost his "sense of direction."[136]

The *Wall Street Journal* too judged Bush's domestic agenda as directionless.

The campaign was incoherent because economic policy was incoherent. Was renouncing the tax pledge a mistake, or making the tax pledge a mistake? Were the Reagan years to be embraced or blamed? . . . Mr. Bush was never able to make up his mind. . . . The end result was the opposite of presidential bearing, an image of confusion and indecision.[137]

To David Gergen "there was a strange disconnect between [Bush's] preoccupation with crises overseas and his airy detachment from the quiet crises gripping Americans here at home." In foreign affairs, during an era of remarkable change abroad, Bush was "exactly the right man at the right place." In domestic affairs "the [Bush] White House slept."[138]

Time reported that "foreign policy brought Bush his greatest success" and if he "had devoted to domestic issues a fraction of the energy and initiative he ha[d] lavished on foreign policy" the president may have been rewarded with a second term.[139] *Newsweek* added that "diplomatic crisis management was always [Bush's] strong suit."[140]

U.S. *News*'s Kenneth T. Walsh maintained that Bush's legacy was that of a "transition presidency." Bush was a "caretaker" who "left virtually no ideological or political footprints." Furthermore,

His presidency was defined by what it was *not*—not aggressive, not imaginative, not particularly memorable. No style of leadership or governing slogan bears Bush's name, no comprehensive agenda bears his imprimatur, such as Reaganomics, the New Frontier or the New Deal. . . . And if Bush did not remake the presidency, he felt no need to try. . . . He marginalized the presidency. . . . [Bush] failed to develop any path-breaking new initiatives.

According to Walsh, Bush showed leadership acumen in the Middle East peace process, cultivating world leaders to support U.S. goals and interests—which paid off in the Persian Gulf War—but the president's "modest domestic achievements" did not match his failures.[141]

David Broder examined the Bush presidency in the context of the Reagan–Bush era. Broder positively assessed the GOP presidencies for having supported democratic movements abroad and for their role in the dramatic changes in Eastern Europe and the former Soviet Union. But in the domestic realm, "no such triumph can be claimed" given White House failures in such areas as government spending, social policy, and inner-city problems.[142] Ann McDaniel wrote that "Bush was defeated by his failure to govern."[143] William Safire added that with Bush at the helm, the Reagan–Bush era had "lost its sense of direction."[144] Michael Kinsley believed that "Bush will be remembered as a failed president"—one whose image the Democrats could run against for years, the way in which Republicans campaigned for years against the image of Jimmy Carter.[145] George F. Will attributed Bush's electoral rejection to a presidency that, unlike Reagan's, lacked conviction and passion.[146]

Not all of the early retrospectives of the Bush years were so negative. The *New York Times* praised the president's "thousand points of light" program which honored volunteers and encouraged civic-mindedness.[147] Ann McDaniel praised Bush for having been "true to his ideal of public service."[148] Hugh Sidey concluded that Bush had a more substantive record of accomplishment than the administration was able to communicate.[149] The *Washington Post* somewhat surprisingly bolstered that view when it editorialized that even in domestic affairs, "in his largely forgotten first two years, he did better than his current reputation allows." To be sure, when the economy faltered and the public demanded action, Bush "never found all that much wrong with the state of the union [and] produced a cautious and limited presidency." But Bush did achieve real policy progress in some domestic areas—clean air, civil rights for the disabled—and he managed foreign affairs "with skill."[150] Many of Bush's achievements "were substantial and real."[151]

After four years, journalists assessed the Bush presidency as a set of paradoxes: Bush had a good foreign policy record and a poor domestic one; he projected strength abroad and indifference at home; he was at times decent, honest, magnanimous and at others mean-spirited, partisan, and shrill; he could claim some real domestic accomplishments, but his overall record was disappointing; he was a "foreign policy president" who was at times limited in vision by a cold war mentality.

To the leading press corps, Bush's record was mixed: worthy of note for certain accomplishments, but overall a limited, status quo presidency.[152] It was not the kind of presidential record that dovetailed with journalistic expectations for bold, visionary leadership.

NOTES

1. Strobe Talbott, "The Low Point of the Bush Presidency," *Time*, January 13, 1992, p. 29.

2. See Ann McDaniel, "A Case of the Political Flu," *Newsweek*, January 20, 1992, p. 31.

3. Michael Duffy, "Mission Impossible," *Time*, January 20, 1992, p. 14.

4. McDaniel, p. 30.

5. "Lost in Tokyo," *New York Times*, January 10, 1992, p. A26. Two reports focused on the substance of the trip: Bill Powell, "The Good News in Bush's Trip," *Newsweek*, January 20, 1992, p. 34; Robert L. Bartley, "Asia Trip May Yet Win a New Verdict: Successful Debacle," *Wall Street Journal*, January 14, 1992, p. A14.

6. McDaniel, p. 31.

7. "The Tinkerer: Mr. Bush's New War and Paper Sword," *New York Times*, January 30, 1992, p. A20.

8. "The State of the Union," *Washington Post*, January 29, 1992, p. A20.

9. "Will George Do It?" *Wall Street Journal*, January 30, 1992, p. A12.

10. A. M. Rosenthal, "The Best in Him," *New York Times*, January 31, 1992, p. A27.

11. Mary McGrory, "Bush's Muscular Message," *Washington Post*, January 30, 1992, p. A2.

12. Richard Cohen, "Government and the Family (1)," *Washington Post*, January 30, 1992, p. A23.

13. Tom Shales, "The Main Event: Bush vs. Recession," *Washington Post*, January 29, 1992, pp. B1, B8.

14. George F. Will, "The President's Own Worst Enemy," *Washington Post*, January 30, 1992, p. A23.

15. Michael Duffy, "Deficits Don't Matter; Votes Sure Do," *Time*, February 10, 1992, p. 25. See also Tom Morganthau, "Decoding Bush," *Newsweek*, February 10, 1992, p. 23; and Evan Thomas, "What Bush Should Say," *Newsweek*, January 13,

1992, pp. 20–21. The latter suggested bold programs—again the measure of the president's performance—but concluded that the administration considered them too politically risky.

16. William Raspberry, "What Is the President Waiting For?," *Washington Post*, January 17, 1992, p. A21.

17. David S. Broder, "The Costs of Opportunism," *Washington Post*, February 2, 1992, p. C7.

18. John E. Yang, "An Enigmatic President Is a Study in Contrasts," *Washington Post*, February 12, 1992, p. A19. A *Post* editorial also called Bush "reactive" and described his domestic agenda as "h[is] likes and wants to keep things pretty much as they are." See "Message Control," *Washington Post*, January 19, 1992, p. C6.

19. Kenneth T. Walsh and David Gergen, "Skidding and Stalling," *U.S. News and World Report*, January 27, 1992, pp. 31–32.

20. Kenneth T. Walsh and David Gergen, "Blowin' in the Wind," *U.S. News and World Report*, February 10, 1992, p. 24.

21. Howard Fineman, "Bush's Bad Dream," *Newsweek*, January 27, 1992, p. 16.

22. Andrew Rosenthal, "Bush Encounters the Supermarket, Amazed," *New York Times*, February 5, 1992, pp. A1, A19.

23. Jonathan Yardley, "President Bush, Checkout-challenged," *Washington Post*, February 10, 1992, p. B2.

24. See, for example, Betty Glad, "How George Bush Lost the Election," in Stanley A. Renshon, ed., *The Clinton Presidency: Campaigning, Governing, and the Psychology of Leadership* (Boulder, Co.: Westview Press, 1995), p. 22.

25. "The New Hampshire Vote," *Washington Post*, February 20, 1992, p. A24.

26. Mary McGrory, "Don't Take Us for Granite," *Washington Post*, February 20, 1992, p. A2; "Now Do Something," *Wall Street Journal*, February 20, 1992, p. A14.

27. Hobart Rowen, "Primaries Offer Economic Primer," *Washington Post*, February 23, 1992, p. H1.

28. David S. Broder, "Winners and Losers," *Washington Post*, February 20, 1992, p. A25.

29. Richard Cohen, "Conviction Candidates," *Washington Post*, February 20, 1992, p. A25. See also George F. Will, "What Happened to Bush?" *Washington Post*, February 20, 1992, p. A25.

30. Ann McDaniel, "Is Buchanan Running the Country?" *Newsweek*, March 16, 1992, p. 29. *New York Times* editorial quoted in same.

31. Anthony Lewis, "The Road Not Taken," *New York Times*, March 8, 1992, sec. 4, p. 15; McDaniel, "Is Buchanan Running the Country?"; "Mr. Bush's Artless Surrender," *New York Times*, February 26, 1992, p. A20. Among the many other commentaries blasting Bush's alleged pandering to the far right were Richard Cohen, "Heart of GOP Darkness," *Washington Post*, March 3, 1992, p. A17; Hobart Rowen, "In IMF Fund Battle, Bush Reads Buchanan's Lips," *Washington Post*, March 8, 1992, p. H1; "Who Speaks for the President?" *New York Times*, March 13, 1992, p. A30; George F. Will, "Vacuum vs. Resentment," *Newsweek*, March 9, 1992, p. 74.

32. Jim Hoagland, "Let Bush Be Bush," *Washington Post*, February 25, 1992, p. A17.

33. Charles Krauthammer, "Bush's Spent Presidency," *Washington Post*, March 6, 1992, p. A23.

34. Michael Duffy, "Why Is This Man Smiling?" *Time*, March 16, 1992, pp. 21–22.

35. Michael Duffy, "Is Bush Getting a Free Ride?" *Time*, April 27, 1992, p. 35.

36. Kenneth T. Walsh, "Face-off: Bush vs. Clinton," *U.S. News and World Report*, March 30, 1992, p. 36.

37. Richard Harwood, "To Choose a President," *Washington Post*, May 3, 1992, p. C6.

38. "Now, Where's Their Beef?" *New York Times*, June 23, 1992, p. A20; Hobart Rowen, "Bill Clinton's Economic Plan: The Right Road," *Washington Post*, June 28, 1992, p. H1.

39. Eleanor Clift, "Perot vs. Bush: Campaign or Vendetta?" *Newsweek*, June 15, 1992, pp. 26–27.

40. Jonathan Alter, "Why Bush Will Get Zapped," *Newsweek*, April 27, 1992, p. 30; Kenneth T. Walsh et.al., "Time for a Makeover," *U.S. News and World Report*, April 20, 1992, pp. 28–31.

41. Ann McDaniel, "Bush: The White House Blame Game," *Newsweek*, June 22, 1992, pp. 33–34.

42. Kenneth T. Walsh, "Bush's Secret Pals Network," *U.S. News and World Report*, June 15, 1992, pp. 30–31.

43. Mary McGrory, "Ueberroth, a GOP Role Model," *Washington Post*, June 9, 1992, p. A2.

44. Michael Duffy, "The Incredible Shrinking President," *Time*, June 29, 1992, pp. 50–51.

45. Paul A. Gigot, "It's the Boss, Not His Veep, Who's the Problem," *Wall Street Journal*, July 24, 1992, p. A10.

46. A. M. Rosenthal, "Should Bush Run?" *New York Times*, July 31, 1992, p. A27.

47. George F. Will, "Bush's Muddy Message," *Washington Post*, July 23, 1992, p. A31.

48. George F. Will, "Clinton Can Beat Bush," *Washington Post*, July 12, 1992, p. C7; Will, "Bush's Muddy Message," *Washington Post*, July 23, 1992, p. A31; Will, "A Figure of Genuine Pathos," *Washington Post*, July 29, 1992, p. A23.

49. Jim Hoagland, "Cloud over the President," *Washington Post*, July 9, 1992, p. A23. See also John Liscio, "Bush's Last Stand," *U.S. News and World Report*, July 13, 1992, pp. 49–50.

50. Meg Greenfield, "Bush's Problem," *Washington Post*, July 27, 1992, p. A17; David Gergen, "The Choices before Bush," *U.S. News and World Report*, July 20, 1992, p. 39; Kenneth T. Walsh, "The Growing Panic in the Bush Camp," *U.S. News and World Report*, July 27, 1992, p. 32; Joe Klein, "Bush: Back in Tension City," *Newsweek*, July 20, 1992, p. 44; Michael Kinsley, "Hoist by his Own Perot," *Washington Post*, July 9, 1992, p. A23.

51. See David S. Broder, "Baker's Move: Good for the Campaign, but What about the Country?" *Washington Post*, August 14, 1992, p. A23; "Mr. Baker Back from State," *Washington Post*, August 14, 1992, p. A22. Bush boasted that Baker would help "develop an agenda for the second term." Mary McGrory retorted that that was "something they both might have thought of several years ago." See "Can

You Find George?" *Washington Post*, August 16, 1992, p. C5. A similar argument appeared in the editorial "Chief of Staff Baker," *Wall Street Journal*, August 14, 1992, p. A10.

52. Kenneth T. Walsh, "Prisoner of Washington," *U.S. News and World Report*, August 24, 1992, pp. 22–26.

53. Joe Klein and Ann McDaniel, "What Went Wrong?" *Newsweek*, August 24, 1992, p. 22. See also Dan Goodgame, "What's Wrong with Bush?" *Time*, August 10, 1992, pp. 25–27.

54. Howard Fineman and Ann McDaniel, "Bush: Back to Basics," *Newsweek*, August 17, 1992, pp. 28–30.

55. Anthony Lewis, "The Vicar of Bray," *New York Times*, August 17, 1992, p. A19.

56. Michael Kinsley, "Anatomy of a Smear: How Many Times Did Clinton and Bush Raise Taxes?" *Washington Post*, August 11, 1992, p. A17; Kinsley, "128 Skidoo: A Phony Number and George Bush's Bottomless Cynicism," *Washington Post*, September 3, 1992, p. A23; "The Actual Clinton Tax Record," *Washington Post*, September 3, 1992, p. A22. To cite just one example, the Bush campaign counted as a Clinton tax increase a one-dollar fee imposed on convicted criminals to partially cover court costs.

57. George F. Will, "This Thick Soup of Values-Blather," *Washington Post*, August 23, 1992, p. C7.

58. Howard Fineman and Ann McDaniel, "Bush: What Bounce?" *Newsweek*, August 31, 1992, p. 28.

59. Molly Ivins, "A Feast of Hate and Fear," *Newsweek*, August 31, 1992, p. 32.

60. See, for example, Dan Balz and Jonathan Freedland, "Bush Nominated for 'Fight of Our Life': Values Night Looks like Family Feud," *Washington Post*, August 20, 1992, p. A1; Jonathan Yardley, "Giving Family Values the Freudian Slip," *Washington Post*, August 24, 1992, p. B2; "Houston's Two Conventions," *New York Times*, August 23, 1992, sec. 4, p. 14; "Truly Slick," *Washington Post*, August 19, 1992, p. A18.

61. Richard Harwood, "Along the Cultural Divide," *Washington Post*, August 21, 1992, p. A25.

62. James J. Kilpatrick, "He Can Win—Despite the Media Dirge," *Washington Post*, August 23, 1992, p. C7.

63. David S. Broder, "Late, but Not a Bad Start," *Washington Post*, August 23, 1992, p. C7. Although Broder liked the speech, he wrote that "it [did] not exist in a vacuum" and then discussed the political troubles caused by Bush's "feckless leadership." See also Mary McGrory, "Houston: Pandering and Pandemonium," *Washington Post*, August 23, 1992, pp. C1, C2. She praised Bush's "dignity" and lack of pandering in the speech but derided the failure to offer new programs and "a blueprint for better times." See also Dan Balz, "Bush Was Primed, But Speech Leaves Many Questions," *Washington Post*, August 21, 1992, pp. A1, A29.

64. Molly Ivins, "A Feast of Hate and Fear," p. 32.

65. Charles Paul Freund, "Bush Comes to Shove," *Washington Post*, August 23, 1992, p. C5.

66. Tom Shales, "Bush, Knocking 'Em Senseless," *Washington Post*, August 21, 1992, p. B1.

67. Anthony Lewis, "The Price of Lies," *New York Times*, August 24, 1992, p. A15; George F. Will, "This Thick Soup of Values Blather"; "Reelection Bait," *Washington Post*, August 23, 1992, p. C6.

68. Albert R. Hunt, "Truman and Bush—No Comparison," *Wall Street Journal*, August 18, 1992, p. A16. See also Jonathan Alter, "Truman and the Man in the Mirror," *Newsweek*, September 21, 1992, p. 50; Hugh Sidey, "Just Wild about Harry," *Time*, September 14, 1992, p. 40.

69. On "God" reference see "Mr. Bush Crossing the Line," *New York Times*, August 26, 1992, p. A20. On Bush's failed domestic record see Donald Baer, "The Race," *U.S. News and World Report*, August 31/September 7, 1992, pp. 34–40; David S. Broder, "Window Dressing," *Washington Post*, August 18, 1992, p. A13; Molly Ivins, " . . . Not Your Normal Smear," *Washington Post*, August 26, 1992, p. A23; Michael Kinsley, "The Case for Bush," *Washington Post*, August 20, 1992, p. A19; George F. Will, "Serious People Flinch," *Washington Post*, August 26, 1992, p. A23. Will slammed "the intellectual slum that is the Bush campaign, with its riffraff of liars and aspiring ayatollahs."

70. "What Family Values?" *Washington Post*, September 10, 1992, p. A28; David S. Broder, "In Comes Baker, Out Go the Issues," *Washington Post*, September 8, 1992, p. A21; Charles Krauthammer, "The Issue-thin Campaign," *Washington Post*, September 11, 1992, p. A23; Michael Duffy, "No Miracles Yet," *Time*, September 21, 1992, p. 23; Richard Cohen, "The Great Whiner," *Washington Post*, September 10, 1992, p. A29; Ann McDaniel and Howard Fineman, "Down to Business," *Newsweek*, September 21, 1992, p. 39.

71. Richard Cohen, "The Great Whiner."

72. Steven V. Roberts, "How Bush Could Win It All," *U.S. News and World Report*, September 28, 1992, p. 40.

73. See Leslie H. Gelb, "Mr. Bush, Statesman . . . " *Washington Post*, September 24, 1992, p. A29; Molly Ivins, "On the Ballot, Continued Recession," *Washington Post*, September 30, 1992, p. A23; Anthony Lewis, "The Two Faces of George," *New York Times*, September 21, 1992, p. A17; Anthony Lewis, "Weakness at the Top," *New York Times*, September 7, 1992, p. A19; "Straight Talk about the Draft," *New York Times*, September 23, 1992, p. A26.

74. Anna Quindlen, "Rumor Has It," *New York Times*, October 11, 1992, sec. 4, p. 17.

75. Richard Cohen, "Accusations beyond Parody," *Washington Post*, October 9, 1992, p. A27; Cohen, "A Chilling Disdain for Truth," *Washington Post*, October 6, 1992, p. A21.

76. Dan Balz, "Character Issue Cuts Both Ways," *Washington Post*, October 9, 1992, p. A1; Mary McGrory, "Bush's Thing about Oxford," *Washington Post*, October 1, 1992, p. A2; "Anything to Win," *Washington Post*, October 9, 1992, p. A26.

77. Joe Klein, "Bush's Desperate Game," *Newsweek*, October 19, 1992, p. 26. See also Michael Kramer, "It's Clinton's to Lose," *Time*, October 19, 1992, p. 30.

78. Anthony Lewis, "Foul Words and False," *New York Times*, November 2, 1992, p. A19; Michael Kinsley, "Stay Mad," *Washington Post*, October 29, 1992, p. A31; Richard Cohen, "Contrived Political 'Character,'" *Washington Post*, November 1, 1992, p. C7; Molly Ivins, "Whose Character?" *Washington Post*, October 23, 1992, p. A21; Michael Kramer, "The Truth about Bush's Hypocrisy," *Time*, October

5, 1992, p. 44; "The Character Issue," *Washington Post*, October 15, 1992, p. A30; "Character (Cont'd)," *Washington Post*, October 25, 1992, p. C6.

79. Anthony Lewis, "Foul Words and False."

80. Richard Cohen, "What Did Bush Know?" *Washington Post*, September 22, 1992, p. A21; Leslie Gelb, "If All Is Character," *New York Times*, October 11, 1992, sec. 4, p. 17; "Mr. Bush Had to Know," *New York Times*, October 5, 1992, p. A20; "What the President Knew," *New York Times*, October 19, 1992, p. A16. Lewis penned five columns on the topic: "The Cover-up Crumbles," *New York Times*, October 5, 1992, p. A21; "Foul Words and False"; "Living With Lies," *New York Times*, October 30, 1992, p. A31; "Loop the Loop," *New York Times*, October 6, 1992, p. A31.

81. William Raspberry, "Bush: Out of Luck," *Washington Post*, October 5, 1992, p. A19.

82. Richard Cohen, "Unhappy Warrior," *Washington Post*, October 29, 1992, p. A31.

83. "At Stake on Tuesday," *Washington Post*, November 1, 1992, p. C6.

84. "George Bush's Failure, Bill Clinton's Promise," *New York Times*, October 25, 1992, sec. 4, p. 14.

85. Matthew Cooper, Kenneth T. Walsh, Jerry Buckley, "Now, It's Down to the Wire," *U.S. News and World Report*, November 2, 1992, pp. 28–31.

86. Kenneth T. Walsh, "Warning to Voters: The Worst Is Yet to Be," *U.S. News and World Report*, October 25, 1992, p. 17.

87. David S. Broder, "Let's Hear It for Foreign Policy," *Washington Post*, October 7, 1992, p. A25.

88. Stephen S. Rosenfeld, "Beating Bush at His Own Game," *Washington Post*, October 9, 1992, p. A27; "The Cold War: Get Over It," *New York Times*, October 22, 1992, p. A26.

89. Leslie H. Gelb, "George, Bill and Millie," *New York Times*, November 1, 1992, sec. 4, p. 17.

90. Margaret Carlson, "While the Getting's Good," *Time*, October 26, 1992, p. 28. Among the debate assessments were Richard Cohen, "Throw in the Towel," *Washington Post*, October 21, 1992, p. A19; Jim Hoagland, "Bush's Place in History," *Washington Post*, October 17, 1992, p. A23; William Safire, "Clinton Doesn't Lose," *New York Times*, October 12, 1992, p. A19; "The First Debate Leaves Clinton in Front," *Time*, October 19, 1992, p. 18.

91. "The Presidency . . . " *Washington Post*, November 5, 1992, p. A22.

92. Michael Kinsley, "Vindication," *Washington Post*, November 5, 1992, p. A23.

93. Charles Krauthammer, "Modest Election, Personal Defeat," *Washington Post*, November 7, 1992, p. A21.

94. David S. Broder, "Losers and Winners," *Washington Post*, November 5, 1992, p. A23.

95. Joann Byrd, "73 Days of Tilt," *Washington Post*, November 8, 1992, p. C6.

96. William A. Henry III, "Are the Media Too Liberal?" *Time*, October 19, 1992, pp. 46–47.

97. David Gergen, "Was the Press Unfair to Bush?" *U.S. News and World Report*, November 9, 1992, p. 100.

98. "Borrow-and-Spend Republicans," *Washington Post*, August 26, 1992, p. A22; David S. Broder, "Warnings That Bush Didn't Heed," *Washington Post*, July 8, 1992, p. A29.

99. "The Other Character Question," *Washington Post*, April 19, 1992, p. C6. See also, for example, Michael Kramer, "Searching in Vain for the True Bush," *Time*, March 9, 1992, p. 26.

100. E. J. Dionne, Jr., "Guess Who Lost Bush's Agenda," *Washington Post*, August 2, 1992, pp. C1, C3.

101. "Mr. Bush's Action List," *Washington Post*, September 11, 1992, p. A22; David E. Rosenbaum, "On the Economy, Bush Followed Reagan's Lead, Not His Success," *New York Times*, June 29, 1992, pp. A1, A10; Hobart Rowen, "Bush's Recovery Plan a Right-wing Sop," *Washington Post*, February 9, 1992, p. H1.

102. See, for example, Hobart Rowen, "A Likely Story about the Economy," *Washington Post*, June 11, 1992, p. A27.

103. See, for example, Anthony Lewis, "The Two Nations," *New York Times*, February 13, 1992, p. A27.

104. "President Noodle," *New York Times*, March 5, 1992, p. A26. See also "Flip, Flop . . . Flip?" *Washington Post*, March 5, 1992, p. A20.

105. David E. Rosenbaum, "On the Economy, Bush Followed Reagan's Lead, Not His Success."

106. See, for example, "13 New Taxes," *Washington Post*, October 26, 1992, p. A20.

107. David S. Broder, "With Two Economic Plans, We Have a Choice," *Washington Post*, September 16, 1992, p. A21; Paul A. Gigot, "Baker Bids to Give Bush Economic Vision," *Wall Street Journal*, September 11, 1992, p. A18.

108. Gigot, "Baker Bids to Give Bush Economic Vision."

109. Michael Kramer, "Bush as Mr. Scrooge," *Time*, September 28, 1992, p. 46.

110. "Mr. Bush's Action List," *Washington Post*, September 11, 1992, p. A22.

111. Kenneth T. Walsh, "The A Team's Sales Drive," *U.S. News and World Report*, September 21, 1992, p. 30.

112. See, for example, "The Courage to Bend in Rio," *New York Times*, June 12, 1992, p. A24; "Don't Blame the Owl," *New York Times*, September 21, 1992, p. A16; "Icy Words on Global Warming," *New York Times*, March 30, 1992, p. A16; "On Global Warming: Why So Chilly?" *New York Times*, May 24, 1992, sec. 4, p. 10; "The 'Environmental President' . . . " *Washington Post*, June 7, 1992, p. C6; "Mr. Bush's Political Environment," *New York Times*, May 19, 1992, p. A22; "The Rest of the World Had a Great Time," *Time*, June 22, 1992, p. 24; Sharon Begley, "The Grinch of Rio," *Newsweek*, June 15, 1992, pp. 30–32.

113. Susan Chira, "Long Fight for Local Support Hampers Bush on Education," *New York Times*, June 30, 1992, p. A1.

114. See, for example, "Mr. Bush Inherits the Wind," *New York Times*, September 2, 1992, p. A18.

115. On Bush's political machinations see Michael Kramer, "Two Ways to Play the Politics of Race," *Time*, May 18, 1992, pp. 35–36; Kenneth T. Walsh, "All Dressed Up and No Place to Go," *U.S. News and World Report*, May 18, 1992, pp. 10–11. On poor presidential response time see David S. Broder, "Now the 'Character Question' Has Been Written in Fire," *Washington Post*, May 5, 1992, p. A25; Mary McGrory, "Bush's No-show on Los Angeles," *Washington Post*, May 5, 1992,

p. A2. On Bush's lack of an urban program see "An Urban Policy?" *Washington Post*, May 10, 1992, p. C6; "Los Angeles and Beyond," *Washington Post*, May 3, 1992, p. C6; "Response to Los Angeles (Cont'd)," *Washington Post*, May 6, 1992, p. A28; Kramer, "Two Ways to Play the Politics of Race"; Walsh, "All Dressed Up and No Place to Go."

116. On being out of touch see Rowland Evans and Robert Novak, "Operation Domestic Storm," *Washington Post*, May 13, 1992, p. A23; Michael Kramer, "What Can Be Done?" *Time*, May 11, 1992, p. 41; Anthony Lewis, "Only Connect," *New York Times*, May 10, 1992, sec. 4, p. 17; William Raspberry, "When People Feel They Don't Matter," *Washington Post*, May 4, 1992, p. A23.

117. See Leslie Gelb, "Bush's Iraqi Blunder," *New York Times*, May 4, 1992, p. A17; Leslie H. Gelb, "Cuddling Saddam," *New York Times*, July 9, 1992, p. A21; Richard Lacayo, "Did Bush Create This Monster?" *Time*, June 8, 1992, pp. 41–42; Elaine Sciolino and Michael Wines, "Bush's Greatest Glory Fades as Questions on Iraq Persist," *New York Times*, June 27, 1992, pp. 1, 8; "Mr. Bush's War," *Washington Post*, October 10, 1992, p. A26.

118. A. M. Rosenthal, "Call in the D.A.," *New York Times*, October 23, 1992, p. A33.

119. Jim Hoagland, "Blowing Smoke," *Washington Post*, May 26, 1992, p. A17. See also Jim Hoagland, "Engulfed," *Washington Post*, October 11, 1992, p. C7; Stephen J. Hedges, "The Growing Saga of Bush and Iraqgate," *U.S. News and World Report*, June 1, 1992, p. 33; William Safire, "Bush's Scandal," *New York Times*, October 1, 1992, p. A25; William Safire, "Not in the System," *New York Times*, June 25, 1992, p. A31; William Safire, "Crimes of Iraqgate," *New York Times*, May 18, 1992, p. A17; "How to Deter Devious Foreign Policy," *New York Times*, October 6, 1992, p. A22; "Plenty of Smoke about Iraq," *New York Times*, June 23, 1992, p. A20; "Who Got Stung? Not Iraq," *New York Times*, November 14, 1992, p. A18; "The Tilt to Iraq," *New York Times*, May 26, 1992, p. A16.

120. Sciolino and Wines, p. 8.

121. No "conclusive peace" from "Iraq: Hanging Tough Isn't Enough," *New York Times*, January 7, 1993, p. A22. See also Jim Hoagland, "Just like Hannibal," *Washington Post*, September 1, 1992, p. A17; Jim Hoagland, "Our Conscience and the Kurds," *Washington Post*, March 10, 1992, p. A17; A. M. Rosenthal, "The Absent Americans," *New York Times*, May 15, 1992, p. A29; Sciolino and Wines, p. 8.

122. Andrew Rosenthal and Joel Brinkley, "Bush in a World Remade: Will the Old Compass Do?" *New York Times*, June 25, 1992, p. A25.

123. See, for example, Ibid., pp. A1, A25; Leslie Gelb, "No More Hawks and Doves," *New York Times*, October 8, 1992, p. A35; David Ignatius, "After the Wars: The Lonely Superpower," *Washington Post*, June 28, 1992, pp. C1, C2.

124. Leslie H. Gelb, "Bush Report Card," *New York Times*, March 27, 1992, p. A35.

125. See, for example, Richard Cohen, "Hollow War Cry," *Washington Post*, April 30, 1992, p. A23; Meg Greenfield, "Who Gets Credit?" *Washington Post*, August 24, 1992, p. A17.

126. See, for example, Gelb, "Bush Report Card"; Ignatius, "After the Wars: The Lonely Superpower," pp. C1, C2; Anthony Lewis, "Triumph and Tragedy," *New York Times*, September 28, 1992, p. A15; A. M. Rosenthal, "10 Choices, 10

Errors," *New York Times*, January 10, 1992, p. A27; "But Stop Magnifying Threats," *New York Times*, April 2, 1992, p. A22.

127. Anthony Lewis, "Chinese Promises," *New York Times*, June 11, 1992, p. A23; A. M. Rosenthal, "Prisoners of China," *New York Times*, February 4, 1992, p. A21; A. M. Rosenthal, "Toys or Torture," *New York Times*, December 18, 1992, p. A39; William Safire, "Needed: A China Policy," *New York Times*, September 14, 1992, p. A19; "Mr. Bush Meets Mr. Li," *Washington Post*, January 31, 1992, p. A18; "Still Tiptoeing," *Washington Post*, March 4, 1992, p. A22; "One-fisted Strength on China," *New York Times*, August 29, 1992, p. A18.

128. Gelb, "Bush Report Card"; Jim Hoagland, "Bush and the Gorbachev–Yeltsin Feud," *Washington Post*, June 9, 1992, p. A15; Rosenthal, "10 Choices, 10 Errors"; Safire, "Needed: A China Policy" and "When to Use Force," *New York Times*, January 7, 1992, p. A23; "Aid for Russian Democracy," *Washington Post*, March 23, 1992, p. A14; "Foreign, to the Democrats," *New York Times*, March 15, 1992, sec. 4, p. 16; "The Need to Lead, for Russia," *New York Times*, March 11, 1992, p. A22.

129. A. M. Rosenthal, "Who Lost Mr. Bush?" *New York Times*, March 24, 1992, p. A21.

130. Ignatius, "After the Wars"; Michael Kramer, "Bush's Reward for Courage," *Time*, August 3, 1992, p. 44.

131. Rowland Evans and Robert Novak, "Yeltsin's Sweet Summit," *Washington Post*, June 19, 1992, p. A27; Thomas L. Friedman, "Bush's Roles on World Stage: Triumphs, but Troubles Too," *New York Times*, June 26, 1992, pp. A1, A12; Stephen S. Rosenthal, "Nuclear Forces in the Future," *Washington Post*, June 19, 1992, p. A27; Rosenthal and Brinkley, "Bush in a World Remade: Will the Old Compass Do?" pp. A1, A25; "Taming the Nuclear Menace," *Washington Post*, January 30, 1992, p. A22; "Truth and Consequences," *Wall Street Journal*, June 17, 1992, p. A16.

132. "A Farewell to MIRV's," *New York Times*, December 30, 1992, p. A14.

133. Anthony Lewis, "Death at Bush's Door," *New York Times*, October 9, 1992, p. A33; Lewis, "New Year Resolution," *New York Times*, January 1, 1993, p. A27; Lewis, "Nodding to Bullies," *New York Times*, August 28, 1992, p. A25; Lewis, "Weakness and Shame," *New York Times*, June 14, 1992, sec. 4, p. 19; Lewis, "Yesterday's Man," *New York Times*, August 3, 1992, p. A19. See also "At Least: Slow the Slaughter," *New York Times*, October 4, 1992, sec. 4, p. 16.

134. Paul A. Gigot, "Peace in Somalia May Require New Colonialism," *Wall Street Journal*, December 4, 1992, p. A8; Anthony Lewis, "Closing Our Eyes?" *New York Times*, November 27, 1992, p. A33; "Do It Right in Somalia," *New York Times*, December 1, 1992, p. A24; "From Start to Finish," *New York Times*, December 31, 1992, p. A24; "Intervention in Somalia," *New York Times*, December 4, 1992, p. A30; "What's the Goal in Somalia?" *New York Times*, December 5, 1992, p. A18.

135. "From Start to Finish."

136. "An Incomplete President," *New York Times*, November 8, 1992, sec. 4, p. 16.

137. "The Economy Stupid," *Wall Street Journal*, November 6, 1992, p. A14.

138. David Gergen, "A Farewell to Mr. Bush," *U.S. News and World Report*, January 25, 1993.

139. J.F.O. McAllister, Bruce van Voorst, and Yuri Zarakhovich, "Out with a Bang," *Time*, January 11, 1993, pp. 18, 19.

140. Russell Watson, "A Farewell Tour," *Newsweek*, January 11, 1993, p. 16.

141. Kenneth T. Walsh, "Caretaker: From Here to Uncertainty," *U.S. News and World Report*, November 16, 1992, pp. 82, 84–85.

142. David S. Broder, "12 Pretty Good Years for the GOP," *Washington Post*, January 17, 1993, p. C7.

143. Ann McDaniel, "Bush: The Fingers of Blame," *Newsweek*, November 16, 1992, p. 44.

144. William Safire, "Losers, Not Weepers," *New York Times*, November 5, 1992, p. A35.

145. Michael Kinsley, "Vindication," *Washington Post*, November 5, 1992, p. A23.

146. George F. Will, "A Continental Shrug," *Washington Post*, November 5, 1992, p. A23.

147. "976 Points of Light and Counting," *New York Times*, December 8, 1992, p. A24.

148. Ann McDaniel, "Exit on the High Road," *Newsweek*, November/December 1992, p. 12.

149. Hugh Sidey, "Tidings of Sadness and Loss," *Time*, November 30, 1992, p. 38.

150. " . . . Summing Up Mr. Bush," *Washington Post*, January 20, 1993, p. A20.

151. "The Next Presidency . . . " *Washington Post*, January 20, 1993, p. A20.

152. See Michael Duffy and Dan Goodgame, *Marching in Place: The Status Quo Presidency of George Bush* (New York: Simon and Schuster, 1992).

7

The Public Presidency of George Bush

George Bush became president after the conclusion of perhaps the most public relations–driven presidency in U.S. history. Bush suffered the dual problem of having to establish his own identity while others contrasted his public presidency to that of his predecessor.

Although many expected Bush to follow the Reagan model of public leadership, it is clear that the Bush White House developed its own distinct strategies. To understand the Bush approach, I interviewed a number of White House staff who worked on Bush's press relations, communications strategy, and speechwriting. I conducted the following interviews from July 8, 1994, to April 28, 1995:

David Demarest, director of White House Office of Communications, July 8, 1994.

Marlin Fitzwater, press secretary, July 9, 1994.

Mary Kate Cary, senior writer for communications and speechwriter, April 19, 1995.

Andrew Furgeson, speechwriter, April 21, 1995.

Curt Smith, speechwriter, April 21, 1995.

Tony Snow, director of speechwriting and deputy assistant to the president for media affairs, April 24, 1995.

Dan McGroarty, deputy director of speechwriting, April 28, 1995.

In what follows, I describe and analyze the three major components of Bush's public presidency: (1) the press office; (2) the White House Office of Communications; (3) the speechwriting office. I then examine the perspec-

tives of Bush's communications advisers on the White House's press relations strategies and successes.

THE PUBLIC PRESIDENCY

The Press Office

The primary role of the press office is to respond to the daily needs of the
White House press corps—to present the administration point of view to
reporters and to answer their many queries about administration activities.
The press office issues media credentials, prepares the president's daily
news summary, and conducts regular press briefings. The head of that office
is the press secretary.

Marlin Fitzwater served as the press secretary to President Bush for all
four years. Although the press office generally is not responsible for planning a long-range White House communications strategy, for each administration that division employs its own approach to press relations. In the
Reagan White House, for example, critics charged the press office with
engaging in media manipulation. Indeed, press spokesperson Larry
Speakes so boldly kept a sign on his desk that asserted: "You don't tell us
how to stage the news and we won't tell you how to cover it." Speakes even
confessed at one point to having made up presidential quotations to fill the
void at times when Reagan had said nothing.

Bush asked Fitzwater in November 1988 to serve as the presidential press
secretary. Fitzwater accepted and wrote a memorandum to the president-
elect suggesting the elements of a White House press strategy. As Fitzwater
explained, "the idea was to grant maximum exposure to the press" and to
approach press relations very differently from the Reagan presidency.

Fitzwater emphasized that in no way did Bush try to denigrate Reagan
by adopting a different press relations strategy. The purpose instead was to
develop a strategy that best suited George Bush's own style, strengths, and
preferences.

Fitzwater had a good deal of experience learning the approach that
would best suit Bush. He had served as Vice President Bush's press secretary during most of the Reagan years (he became the presidential spokesperson in 1987). In 1985, Fitzwater and Bush agreed on an arrangement
under which the vice president would grant a number of one-on-one
interviews with leading reporters and columnists. Based on the assumption
that Bush would run for president in 1988 and win, this strategy would
enable him to establish a good rapport with the journalists that would pay
off once he became president. In 1985 and 1986 Bush participated in about
seventy-five such one-on-one interviews. Fitzwater recalled that

He paid a price for that. Of the 75 interviews, almost every one resulted in a bad
story. Almost everyone wrote that he was loyal to a fault to Ronald Reagan, had no

ideas of his own, and was a generally weak Vice President. In some way, each story was critical.

Fitzwater said that he told Bush to keep doing the interviews, despite the negative coverage. The press secretary believed that the long-term relationships were more important than some stories written in the mid-1980s that soon would be forgotten.

In his November 1988 memorandum, Fitzwater recommended that the president-elect make use of these relationships with the journalists by granting a great deal of access to the press. "I knew that Bush was good at it one-on-one. He knew the media and he tended to practice a personal brand of leadership anyway."

The press secretary also recommended giving up the elaborate White House East Room press conferences in favor of less formal afternoon conversations with reporters in the White House briefing room. This approach had three advantages: (1) it afforded more effective communications with reporters that would give the president better quality feedback; (2) it provided an opportunity to showcase Bush's command of process and policies; (3) it contrasted Bush and Reagan in a stylistic and substantive sense.

Fitzwater felt that this strategy worked well for Bush—at least for the first three years of the term. Bush maintained a good rapport with the journalists and although "they were critical of him, there was never really a bitter edge to it at all."

Bush gave 280 press conferences during his four years in office, far more than Reagan had given during either term in office. That showcased Bush's policy of openness with the press, again in contrast to the Reagan White House.

In part, because of reporters' sensitivity to media manipulation after eight years of the Reagan presidency, Bush gave less emphasis than his predecessor to public relations stunts. There were some such events as the president declaring his dislike of broccoli followed by the Broccoli Manufacturers of America dumping a semi-truck full of their product on the lawn of the south end of the White House. For the most part, Bush's strategy was to show that he was open to reporters' questions, knowledgeable of issues, and not enamored of P.R. gimmickry.

Several of Bush's communications advisers said that the president's openness toward the press and friendly relations with reporters had failed to earn him any positive coverage. Although, as Fitzwater said, there was not a "bitter edge" to the relationship between Bush and the press, reporters were critical of the president's leadership nonetheless. Speechwriter Curt Smith noted that it disturbed Bush greatly that White House efforts to do what the press wanted didn't help much to improve press coverage. Smith stated that Bush operated with a "code of honor"—treat people decently, and they will behave the same in return. Unfortunately for Bush, Smith explained, reporters work with a different code: cover politicians critically, regardless of personal treatment from them.

Communications director David Demarest said that reporters "genuinely liked" Bush as a person. "Did it mean that they cut him a break during the campaign? Not in the least. They were damn tough on us."

During the early stages of Bill Clinton's presidency, many reporters complained strongly about the unfriendly, almost hostile treatment they received from the White House press office. Clinton White House staff told some reporters, in effect, "look how nice George Bush treated you and look where it got him."

Fitzwater recalled the difficulty that Bush sometimes had accepting how journalists did their jobs.

Politicians oftentimes have trouble understanding that reporters are different. They're not politicians. The rules for them are different. The rules for journalists are completely their own. Nothing else applies.

For example, if you do a favor for a congressman, you expect a favor in return. If you do a favor for a reporter, don't ever expect a favor in return. President Bush had that difficulty because he saw reporters in a personal light. . . . He put a lot of emphasis on personal relationships.

I remember one case where a reporter wrote a very negative story about the president. Bush was surprised. "Why did he do that?" he said. "We had him over to the house, we had such a nice conversation, he came out for the hot dog fry."

Dealing with reporters is like giving gifts to relatives. You do it because it's the right thing to do, not because you think you'll get something out of it.

White House Office of Communications (WHOC)

The White House Office of Communications serves different functions than those of the press office. The WHOC serves the needs of regional media; it coordinates information coming out of the executive branch; and, as John Anthony Maltese has illustrated, it engages in long-term strategies to help convey to the public the White House "spin" on events. Under the Bush administration, Maltese explains, "the Office of Communications and its director shrank into relative anonymity."[1]

David Demarest served as Bush's director of communications from January 1989 until June 1992. Margaret Tutwiler ran the WHOC during the crucial months of the reelection campaign.

In the Bush administration, the WHOC's functions included speechwriting, media relations, interest group outreach, and intergovernmental communications. At its peak, the WHOC had sixty-two staffers. Among the subunits were *public liaison*, which was responsible for relations between the White House and all interest groups; the *public affairs group*, which coordinated policy messages across cabinet agencies; the *intergovernmental affairs* unit, which served as the liaison between the White House and governors, mayors, state legislators, and county officials; and *speechwriting* (discussed below).

The Bush WHOC operated very differently from that office in the Reagan administration. According to Demarest,

The Reagan White House worked at establishing a "line of the day" and all operations were held hostage to the phrase of the day that the White House wanted that evening on the news. . . . Generally, the press resented that, considered it manipulative.

Demarest said that he wanted the WHOC to operate very differently from Reagan's, in part because many journalists had become tired of the Reagan-era practices and in part because he felt that such heavy-handed tactics were degrading to both the White House and the press corps. Demarest said that that doesn't mean that the Bush White House ignored the need "to emphasize certain themes . . . to advance our goals." Rather,

We felt that having a more open, two-way relationship with the press made better sense. We tried to normalize that relationship, make it more businesslike and to place the onus on the press to decide what it was going to cover as the most important message or theme of the day.

The WHOC would advertise key events or presidential actions but did not limit media contact and visibility to those activities. The bizarre result was that journalists criticized the Bush White House for not being as skillful as Reagan's at controlling the message and manipulating journalists. *Washington Post* editor David Ignatius observed that his colleagues actually complained about Bush's practices of openness, accessibility, minimizing P.R. gimmickry, and avoiding what Reagan's people called "manipulation by inundation."[2]

Demarest acknowledged that there was "a good deal of tension in the White House over this strategy." Some in the White House argued that the administration needed to do a better job to "get the message out." Demarest disagreed.

To me, there was always more than one issue that warranted presidential participation. And I wasn't willing to determine, if two important issues were being dealt with at a particular time, that we had to close the press off from one meeting so it could only cover another. That probably cost the president some of the appearance of focus because most of the media want things to be simplified. We were reluctant to do that.

We were not afraid of access or criticism. We decided to have an open relationship with the press. . . . David Gergen spent half of his day spinning the networks. I never did that . . . I was much more comfortable having the president's words taken at face value. For me, or anyone else, to presume to tell people what the president *really* meant, struck me as arrogant.

Much of the impetus for this approach, of course, came from the president who, according to Demarest, "did not like to be stage-managed." Bush didn't worry a great deal about press coverage or improving his public relations because for almost the first three years of the term he was popular. Once the president's popularity slide began in late 1991, panic set in at the White House. Many began to blame the lack of focus and the failure to communicate a message. Several of the speechwriters assessed that the Bush White House had gone so far to prove that it wasn't at all like the Reagan White House that Bush had failed to do such fundamental things as simplify a message to build public support for policies. In a scathing book on the Bush White House, the assistant to the president for domestic policy, Charles Kolb, agreed. He argued that the White House Office of Communications under Demarest had failed to link presidential rhetoric with the administration policy agenda. By downplaying rhetoric and communications strategy, Kolb concluded, the White House undermined its own agenda.[3]

Demarest maintained that in the end, press strategy did not determine the nature of Bush's coverage. He attributed the undoing of the Bush presidency more to policy and the economy than to press strategy.

Speechwriting Division

This division was a part of the White House Office of Communications. During his term, Bush had anywhere from four to seven speechwriters at any one time. For most of his presidency there were five speechwriters. Several of the speechwriters pointed out that Bush gave approximately twice as many speeches per year in office as Reagan had, although with a substantially smaller speechwriting division.

The original structure of the division included five writers—Curt Smith, Dan McGroarty, Ed McNally, Mark Lang, and Mark Davis—and a head of speechwriting, Chriss Winston. The head of the division actually was not herself a regular writer, but a general editor who played the broker position among the many people in the administration who tried to influence speeches.

Several months into the administration the White House expanded the speechwriting division. Mary Kate Cary, who had been promoted from senior writer for communications to speechwriter, described the speechwriting process as "very messy." According to her and several other writers, the head of the division gave the speechwriting assignments. Researchers collected materials relevant to the topic for the writer, who would then draft a speech and send it to the division head for editing. At that time the researchers did the fact-checking while the fourteen assistants to the president and relevant cabinet members received copies of the speech draft. Each of those persons had an opportunity to edit the speech and send comments to the division head—but not the writer—who acted as the broker. The division head did the final editing and sent the speech to Bush, who frequently did additional editing of his own.

Each speechwriter was somewhat critical of the process. Some said that having a regular speechwriter as the division head would have been preferable because that person could have better defended what the writers were doing. Some maintained that the editing process meant that many factions had to be accommodated in speeches—and that made it difficult to achieve broadly thematic addresses. Andrew Furgeson joined the administration as a speechwriter in January 1992. He recalled that

There were thousands of chefs. It was frustrating to someone like me who came from journalism and was used to having one editor. Now there were about thirty editors, none of whom had any great skill with the language.

Representatives from different agencies and offices within the White House would try to get their perspectives included.

That problem was especially pronounced during the drafting of a State of the Union address. The writers struggled to achieve a coherent, thematic address whereas cabinet heads insisted that the president mention all of their major issues.

Tony Snow joined the Bush White House in March 1991 as the head of the speechwriting division. Unlike in the first two years, under Snow the division head also was a speechwriter. With that exception, and some changes in personnel, the process remained the same.

McGroarty and Furgeson both described the speechwriting process as a place where the major policy squabbles within the administration converged.

McGroarty: Sometimes differences in policy positions in the administration can co-exist, until they come together in speeches. Then a choice has to be made. . . . In the speechwriters' office you have a good vantage from which to view the policy differences.

Furgeson: The speechwriter . . . gets to see the various perspectives within the administration close up and in all of their intensity. All the conflict over policy in an administration comes together when the president speaks. All of those conflicts had to be resolved by the time that the president opened his mouth— and they often weren't. It was a great viewpoint of the various tensions within the administration—ideological, personal, and so forth.

Furgeson added that "given that importance, you would think that more care would have been given" to the process of writing and editing speeches. He, Snow, and some others argued that the White House did not attach sufficient importance to speechwriting, much to the detriment of Bush's image. "And in all candor," Furgeson added, "I don't think that the president did." Snow described Bush's relations with the speechwriting division as "distant."

Because "there were a thousand chefs" involved in the process, the speechwriting division became a place in which cabinet secretaries and presidential assistants promoted their agendas. McGroarty noted that some were more effective than others. Housing and Urban Development secretary Jack Kemp, for example, got to know the speechwriters and quickly moved his issues on the presidential agenda by skillfully influencing Bush's pronouncements. Kemp realized that working the issues through the bureaucracy would take years, whereas a presidential pronouncement would resolve a debate within the government in a day.

Ultimately the speechwriters believed that the process did not facilitate the creation of coherent, thematic speeches. Bush cared enough about speeches to edit them and to ensure that the process was not hurried so as to avoid misstatements. He wanted completed speeches two days before his presentation to allow practice and preparation for delivery. Yet his administration did not expend as many resources as his predecessor's in staffing and supporting the speechwriting division.

PERSPECTIVES OF BUSH'S PRESS RELATIONS AND IMAGE

Bush's communications advisers evaluated the administration's press relations and strategies. Their comments help to explain the nature of the difficulties that the Bush White House experienced in creating a positive presidential image.

Timing

George Bush's rise to the presidency as the heir to the Reagan legacy profoundly shaped his press relations and strategy. Indeed, Bush ran for president in 1988 pledging continuity with the policies of his predecessor. But those who evaluated Bush's performance as president also expected him to demonstrate that he was his own man—not a Reagan carbon copy. At the same time, they constantly compared Bush to Reagan. As David Demarest said, "we were in a kind of conundrum early on, because whatever we did was compared to Reagan. The press wouldn't just let us be ourselves. And by just trying to be ourselves, the media portrayed that as our making an implicit criticism of Reagan."

Several press officers and speechwriters recalled the frustrations of that dilemma. As vice president, Bush could not escape the press portrayal of him as loyal to a fault to President Reagan. When Bush tried to define himself as president, many said that he had chosen to denigrate Reagan.

To be sure, some of the speechwriters said that certain Bush White House staff thought that they could best help their president by denigrating Reagan. Such efforts fueled news stories of Bush trying to establish himself by implicitly criticizing Reagan.

Journalists perhaps had good reason to suspect that stylistically Bush would follow in Reagan's footsteps. Not only did Bush loyally follow the Reagan game plan for eight years, his 1988 presidential campaign was carefully scripted and packaged, Reagan-style. Bush's approach only changed after the election. He went out of his way to open the White House to former political foes and to speak graciously toward Democratic leaders. Journalists interpreted many of these efforts to heal the wounds of a hard-fought campaign as conscious efforts to show that the president would not emulate the high partisanship of the Reagan era. They portrayed Bush as thereby making an implicit criticism of his predecessor's leadership.

Some conservative Reaganites in the Bush White House agreed that the president had gone too far to differentiate himself from his predecessors. Tony Snow joined the Bush White House in March 1991 to direct the speechwriting operation. A conservative editorial writer, Snow was convinced when he joined the White House that Bush had erred by misreading the mandate of 1988 and trying too hard not to be Reagan.

There was a deliberate decision right from the beginning to differentiate Bush politically from Reagan. The whole "kinder, gentler" rhetoric was in part a response to the press portrayal of the 1980s as the "decade of greed." Bush did not want to appear greedy, cold-hearted, or, whatever.

Much of the impetus for this criticism of Bush was his inaugural address, which many took as a direct criticism of Reagan's policies and the so-called "decade of greed." Bush asked, "are we enthralled with material things, less appreciative of the nobility of work and sacrifice?" Many felt that Bush's two-sentence inaugural tribute to Reagan was conspicuously brief and inadequate. Conservatives protested when Reagan's portrait was removed from the White House while portraits of Gerald Ford and Jimmy Carter remained. Some suggested that Bush had gone too far to show that he was not Reagan.

Former Reagan and Bush speechwriter Peggy Noonan, who had crafted the "kinder, gentler" language, wrote after the 1992 election that Bush had made the mistake of believing that "the American people voted for *him* in 1988. They didn't. They voted for the continuation of basic Reaganesque policies." She attributed Bush's loss to the disconnect between what people expected him to be—Reagan-like—and who he actually was.[4]

Demarest maintained that the Bush White House communications strategy reflected the fact that the 1988 election was a referendum for continuity over change. Reagan's administration established elaborate procedures for communicating its message, such as generating a "line of the day" and constantly feeding it to the media. Because Reagan's 1980 election was about change, his administration needed to adopt such procedures to alter the dialogue coming out of Washington. For Bush, Demarest argued, no need existed for such media manipulation because the context had changed and the president had sought to achieve continuity—with marginal revisions—with the Reagan years.

During the Bush years, critics often charged that the president purposefully escaped complex domestic issues to focus on his real priority—foreign policy. Many in the Bush White House acknowledged this criticism and retorted that the nature of the times had the most to do with Bush's emphasis on world affairs. The deputy director of speechwriting, Dan McGroarty, said that "the circumstances of the times" dictated Bush's priorities. "Put yourself back to the events of 1989. With everything going on in the world, we put our emphasis where it belonged."

By the time of the 1992 election, much of the political context had changed significantly. The 1988 election may have been about continuity, but in 1992 the leading theme in election discourse was "change." What many found incredible was that Bush, in response to this context, tried to position himself as the agent of change. But as Snow and others pointed out, by 1992, "the White House simply had not responded to the changing mood of the electorate" in any substantive way.

Snow went so far as to suggest that the Bush White House, in response to the public's preference for change, put forth a number of domestic policy initiatives in 1992 merely to politically rebut the charge that Bush lacked an agenda.

In part, the Bush White House was insincere. They went through the motions in 1992 to make it appear that they had an agenda. They put forth a health care plan that they had no intention of promoting. They talked some about Congress, but they never really took on Congress. People saw that Bush could not offer a distinct agenda that they could watch and evaluate over time. As a result, the public said, "forget it. If you don't know what you want to do, we'll take our chances on someone who does. We'll take this Clinton guy. We may not completely trust him, but at least he has given us an idea of what he wants to do."

Others iterated Snow's point, albeit without such a critical edge. The most common assessment was that by 1992 the context had changed, but Bush remained the same. What he had to offer for nearly the first three years and had then suited much of the public, according to polling data, did not fit the electoral mood of 1992.

Almost every person interviewed for this study said that in 1992 the media were "a part of the agenda for change," as Demarest put it. He speculated that reporters "had become bored covering the Republican White House for twelve years. They wanted a new story, new personalities." Bush White House staff agreed that media coverage of the 1992 campaign tilted heavily to Clinton and made exceedingly difficult Bush's task of conveying a positive leadership image. Bush's counsel, C. Boyden Gray, said that the media had felt strongly the effects of the 1991–1992 recession, making them more inclined to accept Democratic attacks on Republican policies. Yet Gray acknowledged that the White House had failed to adequately rebut media criticism. "In that sense, perhaps we deserved to lose."[5]

In sum, the interviewees assessed that evaluations of Bush's actions must account for the leadership context. The Reagan legacy, dramatic world events, an economic downturn, and a reelection campaign were the central factors that established the context for the evaluations of the Bush presidency.

Symbolism/Rhetoric

In February 1989, President Bush held a luncheon meeting with the White House speechwriters to explain his rhetorical approach.[6] What he told the speechwriters is very revealing of how he perceived himself and of how he wanted others to understand him.

The president asked the writers to avoid "rhetorical overkill." Bush said that he didn't want to sound as if he was promising too much; he did not like lofty language ("Churchill's o.k., but not the really lofty stuff"); he wanted to avoid broad thematic addresses and preferred to detail the administration's accomplishments; furthermore, he said that he didn't want to sound too "Rambo-like" or "macho."

Bush emphasized that speeches and quotations used in speeches "must fit me comfortably." That meant avoid the use of "I" in favor of "we"; use self-deprecating humor and not humor at someone else's expense; keep speeches short; use sports and historical analogies that people will understand. He asked the writers not to dwell on his war experience in speeches.

Foreshadowing the leadership approach that he would adopt as president, Bush told the writers to emphasize that foreign policy was "where the action is" whereas domestic programs "are constrained by resources." Regarding Congress, he said that he did not want to publicly attack the institution and the Democratic leadership but preferred instead to emphasize that the administration "must approach them and work with them." Bush said that he would "take [his] shots at Congress" when necessary through the use of the veto or when he thought that the legislature was encroaching on presidential power.

Bush's rhetorical style and modest use of the bully pulpit reflected these preferences. According to the speechwriters, Bush understood himself well and consequently knew that he could never live up to the Reagan standard when it came to public speaking. As Mary Kate Cary stated, "[Bush] knew that he wasn't that good with the public speeches, that he wasn't Reagan." She recalled what Bush had once told the speechwriters, "You're all good writers and are all capable of giving me a speech that's a 10. But don't give me a 10 because I can't give a 10 speech. Give me an 8 and maybe I'll make it come out a 5."

Cary also recalled how Bush had conveyed to the speechwriters his limitations. Bush told how he had traveled with Reagan in 1988 to a campaign event. An aide handed Reagan a speech that the president had not yet seen. Reagan leafed through the text once in the car and then later delivered the speech as though he had done so ten times before. Bush told his writers, "don't ever think that I can do that. I am not Ronald Reagan." Bush established the rule that he needed his speeches early enough to make changes, practice, and commit passages to memory.

Curt Smith explained that Bush cared much more about other, more substantive presidential tasks, than rhetoric and presentational style.

I think that he saw the rhetorical aspect of the presidency as just one investment of his job. . . . He did not consider it as ubiquitous and all-encompassing as Reagan did. . . . [Bush] did not feel as comfortable as Reagan at giving the tour-de-force, stemwinding speech. But then again, who could compare to Reagan?
Bush once said, "I'm not Ronald Reagan. I couldn't be if I wanted to." So he understood himself very well.

Snow agreed that "Bush didn't try to be Reagan. Bush was not a naturally gifted speaker." The president would agree to speech coaching from Roger Ailes maybe once or twice a year. The president "would be on 'good behavior' for a while and then he inevitably would lapse into 'Bush speak.' "

Andrew Furgeson added that "Bush was very conscious that he was following Reagan. He would say, 'now Reagan would do that, but I can't.'" Bush didn't have the same flair as Reagan for telling good stories, illustrating broad themes with attention-grabbing anecdotes. "[Bush] was very suspect of any kind of sentimentality, high-flown rhetoric, big words, any kind of ideologically florid expressions. He was very uncomfortable with any kind of rhetorical extravagance."

Several speechwriters identified as problematic Bush's penchant for muddled syntax and disuse of pronouns. These habits made a usually colorless president excellent fodder for comedic imitators. Speechwriter Peggy Noonan explained how she worked with Bush's speaking style. "I became adept at pronoun-less sentences. Instead of, 'I moved to Texas and soon we joined the Republican Party.' it was, 'moved to Texas, joined the Republican Party, raised a family.' "[7]

None of this suggests that Bush was incapable of giving a good speech. Rather, Bush suffered from the inevitable comparison with his predecessor and had trouble downplaying expectations that better suited Reagan. Bush indeed gave a number of strong speeches. His speechwriters identified those pertaining to the Persian Gulf War and a December 7, 1991, fiftieth anniversary remembrance at Pearl Harbor.

Smith made the convincing point that the president delivered very good speeches on subjects about which he felt strongly. In the case of the Persian Gulf War, for example, Bush had a clear sense of purpose about the use of the military, and his convictions were undoubtable. "The essence and moral fiber of George Bush really came out at that time." Bush didn't need "high-flown" rhetoric and speech coaching to make these speeches work. The president wrote a good many of those speeches about which he felt so strongly.

Reagan had the gift of the actor. He understood role playing. He therefore could make a convincing, emotional presentation on a topic about which he did not feel strongly, if he needed to do so. Bush lacked that ability, but his speechwriters maintained that when he did feel real emotion about an issue, he could give a strong presentation, even if not Reaganesque. According to Fitzwater, Bush's Operation Desert Storm press briefings were "just spectacular. Everybody came away very impressed." "During the war," he said, "his press briefings were incredible. They showed his ability to educate the people as to the purpose of the war and his knowledge of military issues at hand."

Fitzwater said that "Bush wanted to do it his way." Critics charged that Bush thereby denigrated Reagan by trying to be different. Fitzwater replied that "drawing a distinction is not to denigrate. He was never trying to denigrate Reagan. The fact is, he knew he wasn't as good as Reagan at prime-time news conferences and major addresses." Bush therefore avoided the prime-time press conference format because he knew that it showcased his weakness as a speaker.

Bush developed a press relationship that suited his own style. Whereas Reagan kept reporters at a distance and reached out directly to the public, Bush preferred being accessible to the press. Bush also liked informal, usually small gatherings with reporters better than the prime-time events. This approach reflected Bush's own view of his strengths. He perceived himself as an experienced, "hands-on" leader who understood issues and how the government works. Consequently, he saw no need to keep reporters at a distance.

Demarest: He was very comfortable meeting with reporters. It was one of his best forums. He had no problems with access. . . . Whereas one of Reagan's weak suits was the press conference, that was one of Bush's strong suits.

Cary: Bush didn't care for the big, high stakes speech. He was turned off the idea after the speech in 1989 in which he waved a bag of crack. He concluded that those events were overly scrutinized and just caused him problems. He much preferred short remarks and press conferences.

McGroarty: President Reagan was carefully scripted. He was comfortable with doing that and he was good at it. Some who had come from the Reagan White House

wanted to do that with Bush. . . . The Bush White House preferred instead the
press conference strategy.

Although Bush did not warm up to television very well, he liked the
town meeting format in which he could field questions from citizens.
Fitzwater thought that this means of communication displayed Bush's
strength as a knowledgeable statesman. "He was terrific at it. It also bred
the impression —which was true—that he knew his stuff." Fitzwater added
that if the event were staged for television, the president "would tense up
and not do well." Fitzwater said that Bush "felt guilty about" doing contrived, stage-managed events of any type.

Indeed, everyone interviewed for this study pointed out that Bush,
unlike his predecessor, did not enjoy the public relations presidency and
many of its requirements. According to Fitzwater, "he did not like it or come
to it naturally. He resisted the public relations [presidency]."

It represented a kind of phoniness to him, or fakery, that repelled them. There was
the basic old–New England, Yankee honesty of spirit about George Bush that made
him distrustful of anything that was staged. He used to say to me, "don't tell me
what to do Marlin, I'm not a piece of meat."

Curt Smith made a similar point.

Bush really didn't like the grandstanding, the glad-handing, the flesh-pressing, the
phony-baloney rituals of politics. He doesn't like it. Doesn't think he's good at it.
It's a stunning contrast with Clinton who likes nothing better.
    In four years, I was never asked to revamp substance for style, to politicize a
policy.

That is not to suggest that Bush ignored public relations. As Demarest
noted, the president understood, for example, the need to schedule events
to meet media deadlines and the importance of cultivating positive relations with reporters. "What Bush didn't like was anything that appeared to
go overboard in trying to manage the news." Several of the speechwriters
explained that when they would reach for some grandiose rhetoric or catch
phrase, Bush would edit that portion out of the speech and send back a note
that stated "that's not me."

Kolb argued that by downplaying public relations, Bush undermined his
own effectiveness. "He inexplicably downplayed and virtually ignored two
factors that had contributed mightily to Reagan's success: the importance
of presidential rhetoric and the creation of a well-oiled propaganda ma-
chine for swaying public opinion."[8]

A good many of the speechwriters also believed that downplaying public
relations hurt the Bush presidency. Smith said that he admired Bush for
emphasizing substance over image. But he lamented that by 1992, too few

Americans appreciated Bush's admirable qualities. People around the president saw "the fidelity to country, the decency, the honor, the integrity— the embodiment of the kind of person you want to have as your com- mander-in-chief," but the White House did not do enough to project those qualities. According to Smith,

[Bush] was reticent to put himself forward. Bush believes that deeds—not words— speak for themselves. But unfortunately, in politics that's not always the case. In retrospect, we should have done more to try to push him to show the country who he was and what he had accomplished.

He gave extraordinarily little attention to the public relations presidency. George Bush, to his credit as president but to his detriment politically, tried to divorce politics from policy.

Furgeson made a similar point when he argued that the Bush White House gave insufficient attention to presidential speeches as substantive occasions to communicate the president's worldview or policy priorities. This failure harmed the president's image and ability to lead. Yet it also reflected Bush's own sense of priorities. Bush "didn't like giving speeches. He didn't think he was very good at it."

Generally, [Bush] was a very pragmatic and practical man who was of the opinion, "watch what we do, not what we say." He thought of speeches as superficial P.R. events. . . . Bush was not a verbal man. His approach to politics was pragmatic, not rhetorical.

Snow agreed when he stated that "Bush did not spend too much time worrying about how to polish his public image." The president also "did not spend a lot of time worrying about how to best schmooze with the media." Snow believed—and some of the other speechwriters agreed—that Bush would have helped himself had he done more to focus on the public relations presidency.

The Bush administration did not do enough to develop its message or, like Reagan, a theme of the day. . . . Bush might deliver several messages in various speeches . . . and the press could choose whatever it wanted to focus on.

Reagan understood the importance of having a central message of the day and he was not afraid to deliver the same message day-after-day, week-after-week, until it became fixed in the public's mind.

Bush's people were sometimes so smug about how smart they were they figured, "we'll get five or six messages a day. . . . " Well, what they did was create chaos.

Snow and others pointed out that this failure to focus the message was especially troublesome during the 1992 campaign. They said that it rein- forced the image of Bush as lacking a vision for directing the country for another four years. The White House lacked a central message and the campaign floundered from one theme to another. Snow argued that Bush's "old style" campaign—one that preferred political rallies over talk shows—"never geared up to give the quick response and control the message the way the Clinton campaign did. And that just strengthened the public's perception that Bush was out of touch and did not care."

Fitzwater acknowledged that the Clinton campaign benefited from making better use of "the new communications technology." Bush was reluctant to embrace some of the new campaign formats.

It caused the president to resist MTV, to resist the talk shows that are entertainment. He saw them as a denigration of the presidency. If you suggested Donahue, Arsenio Hall, or even Larry King, the president saw their programs as entertainment, not something that a president should be involved with. It wasn't beneath his dignity. It was beneath the dignity of the office. We suffered for that.

Although Bush was reluctant "to put himself forward," to develop a theme of the day, and to embrace new communications technologies, several interviewees said that he was highly cognizant of the impact of a presidential statement and was very disciplined about what he said. According to Fitzwater, "unlike President Clinton, [Bush] did not say things about foreign policy that he didn't mean or that he had to take back later." During Operation Desert Storm, for example, "Bush was always aware that the twenty-six-member coalition was listening." The president thereby crafted his statements very carefully, fully aware that his words reverberated both domestically and abroad. Nonetheless, almost all agreed with Kolb's assessment that "George Bush's presidency was an antirhetorical operation."[9]

Policy Development/Agenda

According to the speechwriters, Bush's pragmatic nature influenced how he chose to identify policy priorities and build support for them. Several pointed out that Bush preferred bipartisanship over battling his political opponents. Bush accepted the reality of Democratic control of Congress and tried to work around that situation. The great problem, they said, was that the Democratic Congress had a different view. According to Smith,

[Bush] oftentimes said that his model for the presidency was Dwight Eisenhower. He tried to govern as Ike had—to be above the fray, to be bipartisan and nonpartisan, both abroad and at home.

George Bush would have loved to govern like Eisenhower and could have done it if the 1990s were like the 1950s—they're not. The other side was not like Sam Rayburn and Lyndon Johnson, who, like Ike, wished to be nonpartisan. The other side wished for Bush's surrender. They wanted the destruction of the Bush presidency.

Dan McGroarty contrasted Bush's relationship with Congress to that of Reagan. For six of eight years in office, Reagan's party controlled the Senate. Reagan also had temporary working majorities in the House on certain issues. Bush lacked those advantages. Consequently, Bush found that many of his domestic policy initiatives stood no chance of passing the Democratic Congress. McGroarty maintained that in contrast to the press portrayals, Bush cared about domestic issues, "but everything we did was DOA in Congress."

How long do you think that an operation will continue doing that over and over and over and over again when everything is declared DOA? As opposed to going to the constitutional side of the equation—the latitude the president has in foreign policy, the interest and expertise George Bush has in foreign policy, the events of the world in 1989? Given all of those factors, where do you spend your time? This is not rocket science.

Structurally speaking, if you knew you were going to get nowhere on the Hill, then why would you run up a string of DOA's? People in the White House were acutely aware of that reality. Once you get the two-by-four in the head enough times, you get the picture.

Some suggested nonetheless that if the president had better used the bully pulpit, he could have had more success at setting the agenda. Snow said that "Bush didn't seem to have an agenda." By 1992,

There was no sense of what Bush was going to do. No sense of the two or three basic issues that would enable people to grasp the essence of the man and also his future administration. . . . I remember people from the campaign complaining, "they didn't cover our message, they didn't cover our message." Well, I was in the White House and *I* didn't know what the message was.

Fitzwater made a similar assessment.

The president used to complain, "we're not getting our message out." Well, the fact was, there wasn't a strong message on the economy to get out.

A president can get out any message he wants. There is no such thing as a president not getting his message out. Everything that he does is covered. The fact is, he may be getting the wrong message out. Or, he may not have a message. But something is being communicated. In our case, it was that President Bush was out of touch with the economy.

Several of the speechwriters maintained that Bush paid relatively little heed to the political impact of his policy priorities. They said that he genuinely cared most about what was "best for the country." Smith said that the president's desire to be bipartisan and do what was right, not in the administration's political interest, "governed the Bush agenda at home."

It's evident in the Americans with Disabilities Act, the Clean Air Act, the Budget Agreement of 1990, the Civil Rights Act of 1991.

One could argue whether those policies were good or bad for the country. You cannot say that they were good for him politically.

Mistakes that were made resulted from good impulses. George Bush wanted what was good for the country. He did try to sever politics from policy. The contrast with Clinton could not be more severe.

Demarest said that "what undid the Bush presidency ultimately, was policy. It was throwing away the tax pledge in 1990 and it was not launching some kind of domestic Desert Storm after the troops came home from the Persian Gulf." Demarest and several of the speechwriters agreed with the press criticism of Bush for not moving aggressively on the domestic front and not being an "activist" president with a bold agenda.

Staff

A number of speechwriters commented that their operation did not have sufficient staffing and support. They cited a telling contrast: President Reagan gave about 180 speeches per year and had nine speechwriters, each one with his or her own researcher. President Bush delivered from 360 to 400 speeches per year with five speechwriters. In addition to the smaller-sized staff, the Bush White House gave the speechwriting office a relatively small budget and the writers a mediocre salary. One speechwriter said that—unlike the Reagan White House—the Bush White House, under John Sununu's leadership, revoked dining privileges for the writers and did not always hire the best people for the speechwriting office. Furgeson said that all of these slights—which another speechwriter, John Podhoretz, bitterly detailed in a book[10]—had sent "a strong signal."

This wasn't going to be like Reagan. We weren't going to be trying to sell the big speeches, we weren't going to be having the prime time speeches or going on TV all of the time. This president doesn't need to sell himself that way. He's more hands-on. We don't have to coddle him. We can let him out in front of the press on his own.

Although several of the speechwriters said that they felt the White House had somewhat denigrated their operation, for the most part they had little else critical to say of Sununu's leadership. They leveled their strongest criticisms at White House staff who openly denigrated Reagan's legacy and bragged that someday historians would judge the Reagan years as merely having set the stage for "the Bush era." Many criticized the leadership of Sununu's replacement, Sam Skinner, and attributed to him much of the negative image of the Bush White House in 1992 as disorganized and lacking a coherent strategy to move forward an agenda. According to Demarest, "we suffered chaotic paralysis the six months that he was chief-of-staff. Nothing got done."

The speechwriters maintained that during the 1992 campaign, there was little coordination of White House activities with the speechwriting operation. A part of the difficulty was the fact that during the campaign months, Bush generally gave the same speech everywhere he went. The White House consequently paid little heed to the speechwriting office.

CONCLUSION

According to Bush's communications advisers, the president suffered a number of disadvantages in press relations. First, there were the inevitable comparisons to Reagan. Bush could not live up to Reagan's public relations presidency and did not aspire to be like the "great communicator." Second, the partisan composition of Congress made it almost impossible that Bush could become a successful activist domestic policy president. Third, the White House downplayed public and press relations, placing its priorities elsewhere.

Nonetheless they acknowledged that Bush hurt his image and his administration's ability to promote policies by downplaying public and press relations. The president did not ignore those areas altogether, but his White House rejected the use of Reagan-era tactics to focus the message, generate a line of the day, and control, to the extent possible, the outflow of news from the administration. Although some of the communications advisers defended Bush's approach as praiseworthy, others said that it ultimately caused the president to be rejected by a public that had no idea of the administration's goals, priorities, or vision for the future. By the spring of 1992, Fitzwater recalled, "we still had no message, no campaign plan . . . and no answer to the basic question: Why should George Bush be reelected president?"[11]

These conclusions are reinforced by scholarly interpretations. Mary Stuckey and Frederick Antczak write that Bush's failure to define himself and his presidency in an appealing fashion for the public was disastrous for his presidency. By 1992, the void was filled by Bush's opponents, who defined him instead in an unappealing fashion.[12] Ronald Wendt and Gail Fairhurst add that "Because of this lack of definition, Bush left it open for the news media . . . to define his presidency."[13] Ryan J. Barilleaux writes that the context was not well suited to domestic policy achievement in the Bush years. Following a president who had achieved much in domestic policy, Bush was not well positioned to promote an aggressive policy agenda.[14] And as Bert Rockman reports, philosophically Bush was not inclined to promote that kind of far-reaching domestic program advocated by many who called for "visionary leadership."[15]

NOTES

1. John Anthony Maltese, *Spin Control: The White House Office of Communications and the Management of Presidential News*, 2d ed. (Chapel Hill: University of North Carolina Press, 1994), p. 217.

2. David Ignatius, "Press Corps to Bush: Manipulate Us," *Washington Post*, May 7, 1989, pp. B1, B4.

3. Charles Kolb, *White House Daze: The Unmaking of Domestic Policy in the Bush Years* (New York: Free Press, 1994), p. 5.

4. Peggy Noonan, "Why Bush Failed," *New York Times*, November 5, 1992, p. A35.

5. Quoted in "Gray Blames Recession and the Media for Bush Defeat," *Miller Center Report*, vol. 10, no. 1 (Spring 1994), pp. 2–3.

6. I am grateful to Mary Kate Cary for sharing with me her notes from that meeting.

7. Peggy Noonan, *What I Saw at the Revolution: A Political Life in the Reagan Era* (New York: Random House, 1990), p. 301.

8. Kolb, *White House Daze*, p. 3.

9. Ibid.

10. John Podhoretz, *Hell of a Ride: Backstage at the White House Follies, 1989–1993* (New York: Simon and Schuster, 1993). See also Kolb, *White House Daze*, p. 4.

11. Marlin Fitzwater, *Call the Briefing!* (New York: Times Books, 1995), p. 323.

12. Mary Stuckey and Frederick Antczak, "The Battle of Issues and Images: Establishing Interpretive Dominance," *Communication Quarterly*, vol. 42, no. 2 (Spring 1994), p. 130.

13. Ronald F. Wendt and Gail T. Fairhurst, "Looking for 'The Vision Thing': The Rhetoric of Leadership in the 1992 Presidential Election," *Communication Quarterly*, vol. 42, no. 2 (Spring 1994), pp. 186–187.

14. Ryan J. Barilleaux, "George Bush and the Changing Context of Presidential Leadership," in Ryan J. Barilleaux and Mary Stuckey, eds., *Leadership and the Bush Presidency: Prudence or Drift in an Era of Change?* (New York: Praeger, 1992), p. 21.

15. Bert A. Rockman, "The Leadership Style of George Bush," in Colin Campbell, S. J., and Bert A. Rockman, eds., *The Bush Presidency: First Appraisals* (Chatham, N.J.: Chatham House, 1991), p. 21.

8

Presidential–Press Relations in the Post-Watergate Era

Marlin Fitzwater described the advantages that the president has in communicating the administration point of view: the president can command public attention almost anytime that he wants to; the media cover almost everything that he does on a daily basis; he has the staff and communications technology needed to reach the public. The president can communicate any message that he wants to. "There is no such thing as a president not getting his message out." Fitzwater lamented that in Bush's case, the White House ultimately communicated the wrong message: that the president lacked a credible plan to revive the ailing economy.[1]

Bush nonetheless did try to communicate his concern about the economy and that his administration had a plan. But his method of presentation failed to help him. When campaigning in New Hampshire in early 1992, the president, in response to the advice of his aides, awkwardly stated, "message: I care." His action plan to restore the economy, announced in that year's State of the Union address, was a themeless series of initiatives that appeared to tinker at the margins of the nation's economic problems.

Bush's efforts merely appeared to confirm what his critics had said about him all along: that he was unwilling, even unable, to define and promote a large-scale domestic action agenda. He lacked a vision of how his leadership could improve the nation's future.

Although it is true that the president has enormous tools at his disposal to communicate any message, he has a limited ability to influence the media interpretations of his actions. And those interpretations profoundly influence how the public perceives the president's actions and leadership. For most Americans, understanding the presidency is a mediated experience. People learn about their president—his goals, strategies, leadership style, as well as his successes and failures—from media accounts. Scholarly studies portray the media as capable of setting the agenda of political discourse and presidents therefore concerned with the nature of their coverage.[2]

Communicating a positive message was especially problematic for Bush in 1992 for these two reasons: (1) it is very difficult, almost impossible, to fundamentally change a presidential image once it is established in media coverage. Evaluations of a president's leadership early in the administration provide the touchstone to which journalists return throughout the term. Bush's image, as framed by the media, was that of a president lacking a domestic agenda, but very capable of strong foreign policy leadership. (2) During that reelection year, as Walter Dean Burnham reported, "foreign policy issues and public concerns about them played the smallest role in any American presidential election since 1936."[3] Bush could not play to his strong suit in 1992 because the public had become fixated on the nation's economy. A statistical content analysis of 1992 campaign coverage showed that Bush received consistently negative coverage, in large part because of the economy and public perceptions of the president's leadership on economic policy.[4]

For the modern presidents, Bush certainly has ample company in which to commiserate about press coverage. In the post-Watergate era, press coverage of presidents generally has been critical, often very harshly so. Earlier studies of the presidential press relationship suggest that Gerald Ford and Jimmy Carter suffered very negative coverage, whereas Ronald Reagan fared better during critical stages of his two terms.[5] Bill Clinton's negative press coverage has been unrelenting from the start of his term.[6]

We can better understand Bush's press coverage by analyzing it in the broader context of modern presidential press relations. Comparisons with other presidencies will illuminate the standards of modern presidential journalism and what presidents can do to improve their coverage. We can then critique the role of the press in educating the public about presidential leadership and performance.

POST-WATERGATE ERA VERSUS POST-REAGAN ERA

The post-Watergate cynicism that especially pervaded the press corps in the mid-late 1970s has not altogether subsided. In the late 1970s Richard M. Pious wrote that "the legacy of Watergate is wolfpack journalism."[7] Thomas Patterson more recently has confirmed the continuing existence of this press cynicism. "The poisonous effect of Vietnam and Watergate on the relationship between journalists and politicians has not dissipated. The antipolitics bias of the press that came out of the closet two decades ago has stayed out."[8] Numerous other scholars and journalists alike confirm that the Watergate scandal on the heels of the Vietnam War debacle resulted in a press corps highly critical in its coverage of the presidency.[9]

Gerald Ford and Jimmy Carter felt this cynicism most strongly. In retrospect, probably neither of these presidents deserved to be treated so severely by a press corps that had overreacted to its own earlier failure to cover the Nixon administration critically enough. *New York Times* columnist James Reston wrote in his memoirs that "the newspapers didn't appreciate the good qualities of Presidents Ford and Carter until they left the White House. The press was, I thought, too hard on President Ford, who held things together after the disaster of Nixon."[10] Interviews with press officers and speechwriters from the Ford and Carter administrations revealed the strong impact of press cynicism on presidential leadership.

Ford's first press secretary, Jerald F. terHorst, said that "the press after Nixon had become a group that no longer would take the presidency at face value."[11] Because of Watergate and Vietnam, Assistant Press Secretary Louis M. Thompson, Jr., said, journalists always doubted "the veracity of official statements. . . . We were really caught in the aftermath of that."[12] Deputy Press Secretary William Greener lamented the "thin veneer of trust that existed" after Watergate. Journalists "were always ready to jump on you."[13] And President Ford added that "We inherited a very bad rapport between the press corps and the presidency as a result of Watergate and the Vietnam war."[14]

Carter's people had similar reactions. One press officer described the press as "traumatized by Watergate." Others also suggested that journalists too easily assumed that official statements were suspect and public leaders could not be trusted.[15] Chief of Staff Hamilton Jordan wrote that "Watergate and Vietnam pushed the American media from wholesome skepticism and doubt into out-and-out cynicism about the American political process generally and the presidency specifically."[16]

The Reagan era represented a period of declining press hostility to the presidency. The post-Watergate cynicism identified by Reagan's White House predecessors had somewhat dissipated. Michael Deaver and other Reagan media advisers said that the president actually had a built-in advantage because he succeeded presidents who had been treated unfavorably by the press.[17] According to the director of communications, David Gergen,

there was a feeling on the part of the press corps when Reagan came in that somehow they had been a participant in a lot of presidential hangings and that they wanted to stand back from the rope this time. . . . There is no question in my mind there was more willingness to give Reagan the benefit of the doubt than there was [for] Carter or Ford.[18]

For Bush, the context had altogether changed again. Unlike Ford and Carter, Bush did not have to entirely live down the Nixon legacy. But Bush's communications advisers said that he had the unenviable task of serving in the shadow of Ronald Reagan. Observers frequently compared Bush's actions to those of his predecessor. For the Bush White House, the problem was how to delicately convey that Bush was not Reagan, while not appearing to denigrate Reagan. Consequently, although Bush's communications advisers lamented the state of press cynicism toward the presidency, they spoke even more about the difficulties posed by the Reagan legacy.

Although following the "great communicator" was no easy task, as Fitzwater and others suggested, Bush did not have to contend with reporting that had a personally "bitter edge" to it—at least not until the 1992 campaign. To be sure, the Reagan–Bush years did not represent a return to the pre-Watergate era of press deference. But Reagan had shown that by mastering the tools of communications, exploiting them fully, and integrating a public policy agenda with a press relations strategy, a president can have substantial success at leading public opinion and enacting a legislative program.[19] Through the Legislative Strategy Group, the Reagan White House coordinated its political and press strategies. That approach clearly paid off during crucial stages of Reagan's presidency.

In part because he was not a great communicator, and also because Reagan's style of leadership did not suit him, Bush did not make full use of the public presidency. The Bush White House failed to control the agenda, and the president largely eschewed many of the public leadership techniques that his predecessor so effectively used. Tony Snow made the key point: "What a White House does or doesn't do drives what goes on in the press. Bush's inability to make use of the bully pulpit meant that the press covered what it wanted to cover."[20]

There is no doubt that Bush could never achieve Reagan-like status as a communicator, and personal interviews with White House staff made it abundantly clear that Bush was ever cognizant of that fact. But it appears that Bush made the mistake of rejecting a good many of the valuable lessons of the Reagan years—in particular, the needs to focus the message and to integrate a policy agenda with a press relations strategy—merely because he knew that he could never achieve Reagan's standard of media mastery.

To distance himself from the Reagan approach, Bush generally avoided prime-time press conferences and addresses. In their place he offered frequent informal press conferences in which reporters could ask their questions in a setting that lacked the theatrical and adversarial nature of the evening press conferences. Bush allowed television to record the sessions. Most networks did not consider the sessions that newsworthy. Only the Cable News Network (CNN) broadcast a significant number of these informal gatherings. Even many White House correspondents missed the events.

The result was that Bush failed to adequately communicate a message about his goals and priorities to the public. The too-frequent press conferences limited substantially the public relations value of each one, whereas a prime-time address can capture a substantial portion of the public's attention at one time. The president tried to control the message by limiting the informal press conferences to discussions of specific issues, but this format did not help him to set the agenda of public discourse. Bush therefore did not adequately use his position to force a discussion through the media of the issues about which he most cared.

Excepting periods of international conflict or crisis, during the Bush years the president's voice was just one of many in the political arena competing for media and public attention. During such events as the invasion of Panama and the Persian Gulf War, Bush increased the frequency of his informal press conferences and kept the focus on his leadership during a perceived or real crisis. During normal times, his approach failed to command attention.

President Clinton suffers the dual problem of a negative press that also has a bitter edge. Although Clinton has a greater gift for eloquence than his predecessor, his early press coverage suffered from a series of strategic blunders and miniscandals. The White House then made the critical error of reacting angrily toward the media and taking steps to cut off access to the president. Clinton later took some steps to bring comity to the presidential press relationship, much at the insistence of David Gergen, who had joined the White House to help manage its image problem. But these efforts failed to turn around an already-deteriorated relationship between reporters and the White House, and Gergen quietly exited the administration. By June 1995, a Cabinet member told the *Washington Post*, "the White House is in such chaos about who's handling which message that no one knows what's going on."[21]

THE OPEN PRESIDENCIES MEET THE PRESS

It is no coincidence that in the post-Watergate era, those presidencies which professed a policy of openness toward the media had the most difficulty controlling the agenda of public debate on issues. Reagan's strategy of limited, or managed, access seemed to best facilitate the effort to focus the message and set the terms of national debate.

In the aftermath of Watergate, Presidents Ford and Carter both went to great lengths to prove that they were not Nixon-like. Both adopted a number of symbolic innovations to try to humanize the presidency. In contrast to Nixon, both professed a policy of openness toward the media.

Because every White House has secrecy needs, their promises of openness and accessibility were difficult to sustain. Furthermore, these promises created unrealistic standards by which to be judged. Journalists judged especially harshly those presidential actions that appeared to fall short of the high standards that Ford and Carter had established for themselves. Ford's pardon of Richard Nixon and Carter's Iran hostage rescue mission are two good examples of times when the media felt betrayed by major presidential decisions made secretly.

Also in reaction to Nixon-era abuses, both Ford and Carter promised to conduct ethical administrations devoid of even the slightest hint of wrongdoing. Once again, though well-intentioned, these presidents established almost impossibly high standards of evaluation. When Ford pardoned Nixon and then–press secretary terHorst resigned in protest, the event took on the aura of an administration scandal. Ford's press coverage never recovered from the pounding journalists had given him over the pardon. When accusations of wrongdoing surrounded Carter's Office of Management and Budget director, Bert Lance, in 1977, journalists lambasted the president for initially defending his appointee. The press accused Carter of not keeping his own promise to run an ethically pure administration. The allegations of illegal financial practices ultimately lacked substance, but Carter, critics charged, had violated his promise to avoid even the appearance of wrongdoing.

Perhaps taking lessons from his predecessors, President Reagan did not conduct an open presidency and never pledged to avoid even the hint of scandal in his administration. In these areas, Reagan kept the standards of evaluation very low. Reagan blunted the severity of press criticism for allowing relatively limited access to the administration because he never promised to be completely open and accessible to the press corps. Limited access also gave the White House a great deal of control over its ability to focus the president's message. Reagan's critics often marveled that he weathered so many administration scandals. Because the president had kept the ethical standards of evaluation so low, critics could not accuse him of breaking a commitment when White House aides and cabinet officers faced accusations of wrongdoing.

Again, Bush failed to benefit from the lessons of his predecessors. In what appeared to many a thinly veiled slap at Reagan, Bush promised that he would conduct an open presidency with the highest standards of ethical conduct.

Bush kept his promise of openness by generally avoiding the highly controlled and staged prime-time events, preferring instead the frequent informal press conferences. This approach had two downsides for him: (1) the press could cover whatever it wanted to, a situation that limited the White House's ability to control the public dialogue; (2)when the president exhibited a penchant for secrecy in foreign affairs, journalists questioned the sincerity of his commitment to openness. At one point of his administration, Bush, feeling that journalists had been unfair to him, threatened retaliation by limiting the number of informal press conferences. The president had begun to realize that his strategy ultimately had harmed his press coverage.

Bush's press coverage actually fared best in those unusual circumstances in which his administration restricted press access. During the Persian Gulf War, the administration enacted far-reaching restrictions on how the media could cover the war. For a period of time, the administration indeed controlled the message and set the terms for national debate.

The president's promise to conduct a highly ethical administration caused him serious problems from the beginning of his term. A number of White House officials early on had to respond to accusations of past wrongdoing, and journalists wondered whether Bush was serious about his own promise. But nothing compared to the firestorm that erupted when critics of former Senator John Tower, Bush's nominee for defense secretary, accused him of personal and professional improprieties. Regardless of whether the accusations had merit, the press judged Bush to have fallen short of his own standards when he strongly defended Tower; he was in the position of President Carter in the Lance affair.

President Clinton too professed a high standard of conduct for his administration. During the 1992 campaign he spoke frequently about the need to end the era of Republican "sleaze." He has had to devote a great deal of time to defending himself against allegations of past financial misdeeds, and some White House nominees and appointees have also been mired in ethical and legal controversies.

Presidents are not responsible for all of the standards by which reporters judge their performance. Thomas Patterson has written that "Journalistic values and political values are at odds with each other."[22] Indeed, for the modern presidency there are common standards of evaluation that journalists apply to each administration, regardless of changes in context and personalities.

STANDARDS OF EVALUATION

A review of press coverage in the post-Watergate years reveals that journalists are enamored of presidents who articulate a bold leadership vision and pursue an activist policy agenda. Journalists define as successful a president who effectively uses the White House bully pulpit to sell his agenda to the public and ultimately Congress.

Frequently, journalists refer to the legislative savvy of such former presidents as Franklin D. Roosevelt and Lyndon B. Johnson as a basis of evaluating the incumbent's leadership of Congress. Ever since FDR's early massive legislative output, journalists compare every incumbent's legislative agenda at the 100-days stage of the term to Roosevelt's extraordinary accomplishments. Nostalgic recollections of past "great" presidents therefore provide a framework for journalistic evaluations of presidential performance. A *Washington Post* reporter wrote that "it is only against the accomplishments of the few giants who have held the office that we can measure the deeds of others."[23]

The trouble is that these standards are highly unrealistic, and they assume that one leadership approach is superior, regardless of any changes in the political context. For example, journalists derided Gerald Ford for lacking a leadership vision and for not promoting a far-reaching legislative agenda. The activist–visionary standard of leadership appears most ill-suited to a president such as Ford who, as Charles O. Jones wrote, came to the presidency "very weak by all of the standard Neustadtian measures of presidential powers."[24] An unelected president serving during a period of strong Democratic congressional majorities, the best that Ford could do for most of his brief time in the White House was to stop the opposition party from setting the nation's agenda and enacting its own programs. Although Ford's extensive use of the veto may not have appeared to be visionary leadership, under the unusual circumstances in which he served he made full use of his power to obstruct the opposition party's initiatives. Consequently, evaluating Ford on the basis of the activist–visionary ideal doesn't make sense.

On the surface, the standard model of evaluation may have appeared more applicable to Jimmy Carter. A popularly elected Democrat with strong partisan majorities in Congress, journalists saw in him the potential for Rooseveltian-style activist leadership. In reality, the standard model made little sense when applied to Jimmy Carter as well.

The notion of presidential leadership as entailing Rooseveltian activism did not suit Carter's conception of governance, which called for a consolidation rather than an expansion of the welfare state. Carter appealed to his party to recognize the limits on government's ability to solve problems, and he put forth a politically difficult agenda that did not lend itself to easy public approval and congressional enactment. That Carter ultimately succeeded with many of his most difficult initiatives—Panama Canal treaties, Middle East arms package, civil service reform, and the energy program— may be testimony to some innovative strategies that the standard model of presidential leadership failed to recognize or appreciate.[25]

Of the post-Watergate presidents, Ronald Reagan comes closest to the activist–visionary model of leadership. Reagan projected an aura of commanding leadership that many observers compared to that of FDR. His simple, ideological approach to governance made him appear to have the leadership vision that his immediate predecessors lacked. He used the bully pulpit effectively at crucial stages of his presidency to promote a policy agenda with far-reaching implications. Yet for all of the talk about Reagan's legislative mastery and his "strong" and "successful" leadership, his record was not as impressive as reputed. Indeed, as Paul Brace and Barbara

Hinckley report, Carter had a slightly stronger average annual success rate with legislative initiatives than Reagan.[26]

However, while Carter built a bad first-year reputation for legislative relations, Reagan built a good one, primarily because of his initial budget victory. Carter grew stronger and Reagan weaker as their terms went on, but the first impressions stuck. To many people, not only was Reagan more successful than Jimmy Carter, but also a "Reagan Revolution" and a "Reagan legacy" were underway.[27]

The comparisons of Carter to Reagan in that regard make it clear that presidential first impressions have a lasting impact on reputation. Carter started poorly, and his press coverage throughout the four years reflected the initial negative impressions of his leadership acumen. Reagan had a number of high-profile policy victories in his first year in office. Despite a subsequently mediocre legislative record, journalists still lauded his legislative acumen.

George Bush never tried to achieve the activist–visionary leadership ideal and even made light of his trouble with "the vision thing." As scholar Mary Stuckey wrote during Bush's term, "Bush consciously tries to reduce the profile of the presidency where Reagan sought the limelight."[28] Bush's modest style did not win him press plaudits. As president during a period of divided government control, he chose to devote much of his energy to those foreign policy areas in which a chief executive has the latitude to act without congressional approval.

Rather than try to change the political environment in his favor, or vigorously challenge the opposition party in Congress, Bush chose a strategy of pragmatic accommodation. Bush also achieved a good deal more domestically than his press coverage acknowledged. His legislative achievements in such areas as clean air and civil rights for the disabled went largely unheralded. It is no small testimony to the importance of press and public relations that Bush received little credit for these accomplishments, and that his reputation for foreign policy acumen was untarnished despite some major setbacks in U.S. policy in Eastern Europe, the Middle East, and Africa.[29]

As a presidential candidate in 1992, Bill Clinton clearly encouraged the expectation that he would exert Rooseveltian-style activism and break legislative gridlock. He even promised a dramatic first 100 days of major legislative initiatives. But during his transition, Clinton tried to lower expectations somewhat and said that he didn't consider the first hundred days a realistic time frame for initiating his programs. Journalists held Clinton to the more ambitious standard of accomplishment.

From the outset, Clinton found himself under a barrage of press criticism for inadequate leadership. Political scientists Timothy E. Cook and Lyn Ragsdale asked appropriately, "whatever happened to the honeymoon?" They answered that "Bill Clinton never had a honeymoon with the press."[30]

Eleven days after his inauguration, the *Washington Post* featured a story entitled "Coverage Quickly Turns Sour as Media Highlight Troubles." The article listed various media descriptions of Clinton that had already been used: "incredibly inept," "slowness and vacillation," "stumbling," "common sense of a gnat," among others.[31] At the 100-day juncture, numerous reports and commentaries declared the Clinton presidency in peril.[32]

The major criticisms were that Clinton's agenda lacked focus, that his administration had failed to move much of its policy agenda through the Congress and that, consequently, gridlock still ruled the government. Just four months into Clinton's term, *Time* magazine featured a cover story entitled "THE INCREDIBLE SHRINKING PRESIDENT" (with a picture of a miniaturized Clinton) and *Newsweek*'s cover screamed "WHAT'S WRONG?"[33]

For Bush and Clinton alike, the problem of the activist–visionary model of leadership was especially pronounced by the post–cold war shrinking of the institution of the presidency. Even as the office of the presidency itself became somewhat miniaturized by events beyond any president's control, journalists still appeared enamored of a leadership model better suited to an earlier time, if ever.

CONCLUSION

Presidents have enormous resources of their own to communicate with the public. But not every president is willing to expend the time and effort necessary to make full use of those resources. And not every president is a gifted communicator. George Bush did not place a very high priority on those aspects of the public presidency that could have helped him to lead. His priorities were elsewhere, although it is unarguable that he could have better promoted his goals by integrating his political and public relations strategies.

Bush instead was the consummate political insider. He had moved up the scale of the government ladder primarily through comfortably politicking among leadership elites. In a political era characterized by the demands of mass persuasion, Bush seemed like a throwback to an earlier time in which elites cut deals away from public scrutiny. It is no wonder that Bush appeared more comfortable engaging in private diplomacy with world leaders than he did reaching out to the American public to support some legislative proposal against Democratic congressional opposition.

To lead effectively, modern presidents need to be effective at both elite and mass persuasion. It is through the media that presidents can most effectively reach the public.

Constitutionally there is no requirement or even expectation that the president try to lead public opinion. The framers worried about the potentially harmful consequences of public appeals by presidents and devised a constitutional scheme that guarded against popular leadership.

Indeed, throughout the nation's first century, it was Congress—not the presidency—that generally set the nation's agenda. Presidents were not expected to "lead," in the modern sense of the word. That is, they were not expected to establish and publicly promote a broad-based national policy agenda. Presidents did not need the press the way that they do today because they did not rely on mass support to promote their more modest goals.

Today, no president can adequately lead without "going public." By reaching out to the public, through the media, presidents seek to overcome the stalemate engendered by the constitutional scheme of separation of powers. Rather than defer to Congress, modern presidents set national priorities, promote their goals before the public, and try to entice the Congress to follow their lead. Yet George Bush, like all modern presidents, found out that journalists are not willing allies in the cause of promoting an agenda. Journalistic reporting of the presidency can often become a hindrance in the quest to promote an agenda.

For one thing, journalists are quick to judge the effectiveness of any new president's leadership. Leading journalists try to grasp the essence of a new administration—its style, tactics, potential for success—as soon as possible; even during the transition period and then the first 100 days in office. They form early impressions and make their judgments, often harshly, as a new administration team is at the stage of learning its way around the government. Early White House mishaps can be especially damaging because these initial impressions are mostly resistant to change.

Furthermore, journalists have notions of good leadership that color their evaluations of a president's actions. They are most favorably inclined toward a chief executive who loves the political presidency, someone who is eager to make a major mark on history and do it fast through bold public gestures and pressuring of Congress to enact an action agenda. The historical ideal is the Rooseveltian activist of the first 100 days of the 63rd Congress—the man with a vision and a plan to enact the agenda.

In some respects, although generally accurate, the press characterizations of Bush as not a visionary domestic leader appear inappropriate to the political context and to the man. The standard model of evaluation that demands that a president be an activist–visionary in the FDR mold is an unrealistic ideal that lacks historical context. It is especially unhelpful to understanding a minority party president who doesn't view government as the best vehicle for solving domestic problems. Bush never envisioned his role as that of embarking on a broad-scale action agenda. He wanted to encourage greater self-reliance and voluntary community activity—his "thousand points of light"—rather than expansive government. The activist–visionary model suited neither the times (divided government, budget deficits) nor the man (a moderate-conservative).

Bush's situation therefore somewhat resembled Ford's. Both men had a similar, limited view of the government's appropriate role in society. Both had to contend with large opposition party majorities in Congress. Both lacked a governing mandate, Ford by lack of electoral consent for him as president and Bush by the issueless nature of his successful 1988 campaign.

Although every president since the New Deal has had to contend with the FDR legacy, Bush also had to contend with the legacy of Ronald Reagan. Neither presidential exemplar was appropriate for Bush. He was neither the activist leader nor the eloquent, bold visionary.

The more appropriate standard by which to judge Bush is the one that he did articulate for himself: that of a competent, "hands-on" leader who believed in bipartisan governing and subscribed to a philosophy of a compassionate, inclusive conservatism. But by that standard as well, journalists found the Bush presidency generally a disappointment, and there is some credibility to their conclusion. To be sure, Bush deserved credit for administrative competence that reflected his long-standing work in and knowledge of the government. Yet presidents rarely benefit in press coverage from administrative acumen. Bush tried at times to promote bipartisanship—such as on clean air legislation—although on such issues as civil rights he could equally engage in divisive leadership. Generally there was little that he could do to promote an active domestic policy agenda short of supporting Democratic initiatives.

Press criticism of the president's failure to articulate a philosophy of governance appears most on target. Because the president eschewed some of the most important persuasion powers at his disposal, he was unable to convey to the public the central thrust of his administration. He may have had trouble with "the vision thing," and his rejection of the activist model of leadership won him few press plaudits, but he still needed to convey a positive, clear message of what he hoped to achieve as president. To this day, few could adequately explain the points-of-light concept and how it fit into a broader conception of governance. The program had a justification grounded in the Tocquevillean theory of governance that an overbearing public sector stifles community spirit and discourages local action to solve public problems. Bush never connected his points-of-light, environmental, educational, and other policies into a coherent message of what should be government's central role in society. Because of that failure, to a large extent one of communication, by 1992 he appeared crassly indifferent to society's economic dislocations. Bush had ultimately failed to connect a theory of governance with a program, and he never integrated his policy agenda with a press relations strategy. Those shortcomings were devastating to his presidency and his quest for a second term.

NOTES

1. Author interview with Marlin Fitzwater, July 9, 1994.

2. See, for example, Maxwell E. McCombs and Donald L. Shaw, "The Agenda-setting Function of the Mass Media," *Public Opinion Quarterly*, vol. 36, no. 3 (Summer 1972), pp. 176–187; Jarol B. Manheim, *All of the People All of the Time: Strategic Communication and American Politics* (Armonk, N.Y.: M. E. Sharpe, 1991).

3. Walter Dean Burnham, "The Legacy of George Bush: Travails of an Understudy," in *The Elections of 1992: Reports and Interpretations*, ed. Gerald M. Pomper et al. (Chatham, N.J.: Chatham House, 1993), p. 21.

4. Ann N. Crigler, Marion R. Just, and Timothy Cook, "Constructing the Campaign Discourse: News Coverage and Citizen Perspectives in the 1992 Presidential Election." Paper presented at the annual meeting of the International Communication Association, Washington, D.C., 1993. See also Dean Alger, *The Media, the Public and the Development of Candidates' Images in the 1992 Presidential Election* (Cambridge, Mass.: Joan Shorenstein Center at Harvard University Research Paper R-14, October 1994), pp. 8–11; James W. Ceaser and Andrew Busch, *Upside Down and Inside Out: The 1992 Elections and American Politics* (Lanham, MD: Rowman & Littlefield, 1993), pp. 21–22.

5. Mark J. Rozell, *The Press and the Carter Presidency* (Boulder, Colo.: Westview Press: 1989); and *The Press and the Ford Presidency* (Ann Arbor: University of Michigan Press, 1992); Mark Hertsgaard, *On Bended Knee: The Press and the Reagan Presidency* (New York: Farrar, Straus Giroux, 1988).

6. According to S. Robert Lichter, during the first 100 days of Clinton's term, broadcast coverage of the president's leadership was "negative" 64 percent of the time. See his "Clinton and the Press: The First Hundred Days." Presented at the annual meeting of the International Communication Association, Washington, D.C., May 29, 1993.

7. Richard M. Pious, *The American Presidency* (New York: Basic Books, 1979), p. 417.

8. Thomas E. Patterson, *Out of Order* (New York: Alfred A. Knopf, 1993), p. 19.

9. See Gladys Engel Lang and Kurt Lang, *The Battle for Public Opinion: The President, the Press, and the Polls during Watergate* (New York: Columbia University Press, 1983), pp. 258–261; William L. Rivers, *The Other Government: Power and the Washington Media* (New York: Universe Books, 1982), p. 19; Robert M. Entman, "The Imperial Media," in *Analyzing the Presidency*, 2d ed., ed. Robert E. DiClerico (Guilford, Conn.: Dushkin Pub., 1990), p. 156; Michael Baruch Grossman and Martha Joynt Kumar, *Portraying the President: The White House and the News Media* (Baltimore: The Johns Hopkins University Press, 1981), pp. 299–301; David Broder, *Behind the Front Page: A Candid Look at How the News Is Made* (New York: Simon & Schuster, 1987), p. 167; James Deakin, *Straight Stuff: The Reporters, the White House, the Truth* (New York: William Morrow, 1984), p. 295; Sam Donaldson, *Hold On, Mr. President* (New York: Ballantine Books, 1987), pp. 68–69; Haynes Johnson, *In the Absence of Power* (New York: Viking Press, 1980), p. 170; Tom Wicker, *On Press* (New York: Viking Press, 1978), p. 61.

10. James Reston, *Deadline: A Memoir* (New York: Random House, 1991), p. 264.

11. Author interview with Jerald F. terHorst, June 27, 1990.

12. Author interview with Louis M. Thompson, Jr., November 20, 1990.

13. Author interview with William Greener, January 23, 1990.

14. Author interview with President Gerald R. Ford, December 13, 1989.

15. See interview data in White Burkett Miller Center of Public Affairs, University of Virginia, Charlottesville, Virginia. Project on the Carter Presidency, vol. 10, pp. 16–18 and passim.

16. Hamilton Jordan, *Crisis: The Last Year of the Carter Presidency* (New York: Berkley Books, 1982), p. 359.

17. Hertsgaard, *Bended Knee*, p. 44.

18. Ibid., p. 101.

19. See Robert E. Denton, Jr., *The Primetime Presidency of Ronald Reagan: The Era of the Television Presidency* (New York: Praeger, 1989).

20. Author interview with Tony Snow, April 24, 1995.

21. Quoted in Al Kamen, "Frozen in Their Tracks?" *Washington Post*, June 23, 1995, p. A21.

22. Patterson, *Out of Order*, p. 36.

23. Edward Walsh, "A Flawed Presidency of Good Intention," *Washington Post*, January 18, 1977, p. C4.

24. Charles O. Jones, "Presidents and Agendas: Who Defines What for Whom?" in *The Managerial Presidency*, ed. James P. Pfiffner (Pacific Grove, Ca.: Brooks/Cole, 1991), p. 204.

25. See Erwin Hargrove, *Jimmy Carter as President: Leadership and the Politics of the Public Good* (Baton Rouge: Louisiana State University Press, 1989).

26. Paul Brace and Barbara Hinckley, *Follow the Leader: Opinion Polls and the Modern Presidents* (New York: Basic Books, 1992), appendix B.

27. Ibid., pp. 86–87.

28. Mary Stuckey, *The President as Interpreter-in-Chief* (Chatham, N.J.: Chatham House, 1991), p. 127.

29. Patterson (p. 13) also contends that Bush had a good record of keeping his campaign pledges as president. Of course, everyone remembers Bush breaking the "no new taxes" pledge, but that was just one of many commitments made by him as a candidate.

30. Timothy E. Cook and Lyn Ragsdale, "The President and the Press: Negotiating Newsworthiness at the White House," in *The Presidency and the Political System*, 4th ed., ed. Michael Nelson (Washington, D.C.: Congressional Quarterly, 1995), p. 298.

31. Howard Kurtz, "Coverage Quickly Turns Sour as Media Highlight Troubles," *Washington Post*, January 31, 1993, p. A1.

32. See, for example, Jeffrey H. Birnbaum and Michael K. Frisby, "Clinton's Zigzags between Politics and Policy Explain Some Problems of His First 100 Days," *Wall Street Journal*, April 29, 1993, p. A16; Richard Cohen, "Mr. Clinton Goes to Washington," *Washington Post*, May 6, 1993, p. A23; Matthew Cooper, "The Next 100 Days: Stress Test," *U.S. News and World Report*, May 10, 1993, pp. 26–32; Thomas B. Edsall, "Clinton Loses Focus—And Time," *Washington Post*, May 2, 1993, pp. C1, C5; David Gergen, "After 100 days, a President in Distress," *U.S. News and World Report*, May 3, 1993, p. 51; Kenneth T. Walsh and Matthew Cooper, "Great Expectations Meet Bleak House," *U.S. News and World Report*, May 3, 1993, p. 11.

33. Both issues were June 7, 1993.

Bibliography

Alger, Dean. *The Media, the Public and the Development of Candidates' Images in the 1992 Presidential Election.* Cambridge, Mass.: Joan Shorenstein Center at Harvard University Research Paper R–14, October 1994.

Barrilleaux, Ryan, and Mary Stuckey, eds. *Leadership and the Bush Presidency: Prudence or Drift in an Era of Change?* New York: Praeger, 1992.

Brace, Paul, and Barbara Hinckley. *Follow the Leader: Opinion Polls and the Modern Presidents.* New York: Basic Books, 1992.

Broder, David S. *Behind the Front Page: A Candid Look at How the News Is Made.* New York: Simon and Schuster, 1987.

Campbell, Colin, S. J., and Bert Rockman, eds. *The Bush Presidency: First Appraisals.* Chatham, N.J.: Chatham House, 1991.

Cater, Douglass. *The Fourth Branch of Government.* Boston: Houghton Mifflin, 1959.

Ceaser, James W., and Andrew Busch. *Upside Down and Inside Out: The 1992 Elections and American Politics.* Lanham, Md.: Rowman & Littlefield, 1993.

Cohen, Bernard. *The Press and Foreign Policy.* Princeton, N.J.: Princeton University Press, 1963.

Crigler, Ann N., Marion R. Just, and Timothy Cook. "Constructing the Campaign Discourse: News Coverage and Citizen Perspectives in the 1992 Presidential Election." Paper presented at the annual meeting of the International Communication Association, Washington, D.C., 1993.

Deakin, James. *Straight Stuff: The Reporters, the White House, the Truth.* New York: William Morrow, 1984.

Denton, Robert E., Jr. *The Primetime Presidency of Ronald Reagan: The Era of the Television Presidency.* New York: Praeger, 1989.

Denton, Robert E., Jr., and Gary Woodward. *Political Communication in America.* 2d ed. New York: Praeger, 1990.

Diclerico, Robert E., ed. *Analyzing the Presidency*. 2d ed. Guilford, Conn.: Dushkin, 1990.

Donaldson, Sam. *Hold On, Mr. President*. New York: Ballantine Books, 1987.

Duffy, Michael, and Dan Goodgame. *Marching in Place: The Status Quo Presidency of George Bush*. New York: Simon and Schuster, 1992.

Edwards, George C. *The Public Presidency: The Pursuit of Popular Support*. New York: St. Martin's Press, 1983.

Fitzwater, Marlin. *Call the Briefing!* New York: Times Books, 1995.

Graber, Doris A. *Mass Media and American Politics*. 4th ed. Washington, D.C.: Congressional Quarterly, 1993.

_____ , ed. *Media Power in Politics*. Washington, D.C.: Congressional Quarterly Press, 1984.

Grossman, Michael Baruch, and Martha Joynt Kumar. *Portraying the President: The White House and the News Media*. Baltimore, Md.: The Johns Hopkins University Press, 1981.

Hargrove, Erwin. *Jimmy Carter as President: Leadership and the Politics of the Public Good*. Baton Rouge: Louisiana State University Press, 1989.

Hertsgaard, Mark. *On Bended Knee: The Press and the Reagan Presidency*. New York: Farrar, Straus Giroux, 1988.

Hess, Stephen. *The Washington Reporters*. Washington, D.C.: Brookings Institution, 1981.

Johnson, Haynes. *In the Absence of Power*. New York: Viking Press, 1978.

Jones, Charles O. *The Presidency in a Separated System*. Washington, D.C.: Brookings Institution, 1994.

Jordan, Hamilton. *Crisis: The Last Year of the Carter Presidency*. New York: Berkley Books, 1982.

Kernell, Samuel. *Going Public: New Strategies of Presidential Leadership*. 2d ed. Washington, D.C.: Congressional Quarterly Press, 1993.

Kolb, Charles. *White House Daze: The Unmaking of Domestic Policy in the Bush Years*. New York: Free Press, 1994.

Lang, Gladys Engel, and Kurt Lang. *The Battle for Public Opinion: The President, the Press, and the Polls during Watergate*. New York: Columbia University Press, 1983.

Lichter, S. Robert. "Clinton and the Press: The First Hundred Days." Presented at the annual meeting of the International Communication Association, Washington, D.C., 1993.

McCombs, Maxwell E., and Donald L. Shaw, "The Agenda-setting Function of the Mass Media," *Public Opinion Quarterly*, vol. 36, no. 3 (Summer 1972).

Maltese, John Anthony. *Spin Control: The White House Office of Communications and the Management of Presidential News*. 2d ed. Chapel Hill: University of North Carolina Press, 1994.

Manheim, Jarol B. *All of the People All of the Time: Strategic Communication and American Politics*. Armonk, N.Y.: M. E. Sharpe, 1991.

Mann, Thomas, and Norman Ornstein, eds. *Congress, the Press and the Public*. Washington, D.C.: American Enterprise Institute/Brookings, 1994.

Nelson, Michael, ed. *The Presidency and the Political System*, 4th ed. Washington, D.C.: Congressional Quarterly Press, 1995.

Neustadt, Richard. *Presidential Power and the Modern Presidents: The Politics of Leadership from Roosevelt to Reagan*. New York: Free Press, 1990.

Noonan, Peggy. *What I Saw at the Revolution: A Political Life in the Reagan Era*. New York: Random House, 1990.

Patterson, Thomas E. *Out of Order*. New York: Alfred A. Knopf, 1993.

Pfiffner, James. *The Modern Presidency*. New York: St. Martin's Press, 1994.

_____, ed. *The Managerial Presidency*. Pacific Grove, Calif.: Brooks/Cole, 1991.

Pious, Richard. *The American Presidency*. New York: Basic Books, 1979.

Podhoretz, John. *Hell of a Ride: Backstage at the White House Follies, 1989–1993*. New York: Simon and Schuster, 1993.

Pomper, Gerald M., et al., eds. *The Elections of 1992: Reports and Interpretations*. Chatham, N.J.: Chatham House, 1993.

Renshon, Stanley A., ed. *The Clinton Presidency: Campaigning, Governing, and the Psychology of Leadership*. Boulder, Colo.: Westview Press, 1995.

Reston, James. *Deadline: A Memoir*. New York: Random House, 1991.

Rivers, William L. *The Other Government: Power and the Washington Media*. New York: Universe Books, 1982.

Rozell, Mark J. *The Press and the Carter Presidency*. Boulder, Colo.: Westview Press, 1989.

_____. *The Press and the Ford Presidency*. Ann Arbor: University of Michigan Press, 1992.

Stuckey, Mary. *The President as Interpreter-in-Chief*. Chatham, N.J.: Chatham House, 1991.

Stuckey, Mary, and Fred Antczak. "The Battle of Issues and Images: Establishing Interpretive Dominance," *Communication Quarterly*, vol. 42, no. 2 (Spring 1994).

Wendt, Ronald F., and Gail Fairhurst. "Looking for 'The Vision Thing': The Rhetoric of Leadership in the 1992 Presidential Election," *Communication Quarterly*, vol. 42, no. 2 (Spring 1994).

Wicker, Tom. *On Press*. New York: Viking Press, 1978.

Index

About the Author

MARK J. ROZELL is a lecturer in the Catholic University graduate program in congressional studies. He is the author of six books, including *In Contempt of Congress* (Praeger, 1996).

ISBN 0-275-95653-9

9 0 0 0 0>

EAN

9 780275 956530

HARDCOVER BAR CODE